LightFoot Guide
to the
Via Francigena
Edition 6

Canterbury to Besançon

910 kilometres

The authors have done their best to ensure the accuracy and currency of the information in this LightFoot Guide to the Via Francigena, however they can accept no responsibility for any loss, injury or inconvenience sustained by any traveller as a result of information contained in the guide. Changes will inevitably occur within the lifespan of this edition and the authors welcome notification of such changes and any other feedback that will enable them to enhance the quality of the guide.

The Lightfoot Guide to the Via Francigena, written by Paul Chinn and Babette Gallard presents, in great detail, the official routes for cyclists, walkers and horse riders.

The European Association of Via Francigena (EAVF), founded in 2001, is the custodian of the Cultural Route Via Francigena. In 2006 it became the official body recognised by the Council of Europe for supporting, promoting and developing the route.

In France, the Association Via Francigena France (associated to the EAVF) manages the co-ordination of regional walking groups and liaison with other national organisations.

For more information and for downloading the Italian route see : www.viefrancigene.org"

Massimo Tedeschi
President
European Association of Francigena Ways

About the Authors

We are two very ordinary people who quit the world of business and stumbled on the St James Way during our search for a more viable, rewarding alternative to our previous lifestyle. Since then we have completed four pilgrimages, one of which was particularly tough and finally prompted us to create Pilgrimage Publications and the LightFoot guide series. We have no religious beliefs, but share a 'wanderlust' and need to know about and contribute to the world we occupy.

Pilgrimage Publications is a not-for-profit organisation dedicated to the identification and mapping of pilgrim routes all over the world, regardless of religion or belief. Any revenue derived from the sale of guides or related activities is used to further enhance the service and support provided to pilgrims.

The ethos of Pilgrimage Publications has 4 very basic aims:
To enable walkers, cyclists and riders to follow pilgrim routes all over the world.
To ensure LightFoot guides are as current and accurate as possible, using pilgrim feedback as a major source of information.
To use eco-friendly materials and methods for the publication of LightFoot guides and Travel Books.
To promote eco-friendly travel.

Also by LightFoot Guides
Riding the Milky Way
Riding the Roman Way
LightFoot Guide to the via Francigena - Besançon to Vercelli
LightFoot Guide to the via Francigena - Vercelli to Rome
LightFoot Companion to the via Francigena
LightFoot Guide to the Three Saints Way - Winchester to Mont St Michel
LightFoot Guide to the Three Saints Way - Mont St Michel to St Jean d'Angely
LightFoot Guide to Foraging - a guide to over 130 of the most common edible and medicinal plants in Western Europe
LightFoot Companion to the via Domitia- Arles to Rome
Your Camino - information, maps for Camino routes in France and Spain
Camino Lingo - 'cheats' guide to speaking Spanish on the Camino
Slackpacking the Camino Frances - provides all the information and advice you'll need to plan your perfect Camino.

LightFoot Guides are designed to enable everyone to meet their personal goals and enjoy the best, whilst avoiding the worst, of following ancient pilgrimage routes. Written for Walkers, Cyclists (mountain bikes) and Horse Riders, every section of this LightFoot guide provides specific information for each group.

The authors would like to emphasise that they have made great efforts to use only public footpaths and to respect private property. Historically, pilgrims may not have been so severely restricted by ownership rights and the pressures of expanding populations, but unfortunately this is no longer the case. Today, even the most free- spirited traveller must adhere to commonly accepted routes. Failure to do so will only antagonise local residents, encourage the closure of routes and inhibit pilgrims following on behind.

Please let us know about any changes to the route or inaccuracies within this guide book. mail@pilgrimagepublications.com

Our special thanks go to:
We would like to thank François Louviot and all the members of the Association Via Francigena France for their commitment to sign posting.
Adelaide Trezzini for her contribution to the development and mapping of the via Francigena route. http://www.francigena-international.org/

Openstreetmap: The maps in this book are derived from data (c) Openstreetmap (http://www.openstreetmap.org) and its contributors and are made available under the Creative Commons agreement http://creativecommons.org/licenses/by-sa/2.0/

Maperitive for the creation of an indispensable tool used in the drawing of our maps. http://igorbrejc.net/about

Contents

909 Km

129
250.2
170
169
200
161

AVE 24.75 Km/d   *909*

6 d

Your LightFoot Guide to the via Francigena

This book traces the Via Francigena from Canterbury to Besançon. You will find an introductory section followed by 40 chapters, each of which covers a segment of the route.

Each chapter contains:
- A Route Summary
- Detailed instructions
- Map
- Altitude profile
- Addresses and contact information for accommodation and other facilities

Layout
The entire distance has been divided into manageable sections of approximately 22 kilometres, but accommodation (where it exists) is listed for the entire length of the section so that is up to you and your body where you decide to stop.

Instructions
The entire route has been GPS traced and logged using way point co-ordinates. On this basis, it should be possible to navigate the route using only the written instructions, though a map is provided for additional support and general orientation. Use of a compass is recommended.

Each instruction sheet provides
- Detailed directions corresponding to GPS way point numbers on the map - GPS waypoint data can be downloaded from www.pilgrimagepublications.com
- Cross Reference to GPS and Compass direction to next waypoint
- Verification Point - additional verification of current position
- Distance (in metres) between each way point

Each map provides:
- A north/south visual representation of the route with way point numbers
- Altitude Profile for the section
- Icons indicating facilities en route (see Map symbols)
- A map scale bar. The scale differs from map to map.

Accommodation Listings:
The price banding is based on the least expensive option for two people in each establishment - accurate at the time of entry, but subject to change. For simplicity, the listing is divided into 3 price bands:

A = (€/£) 70+   **B** = (€/£) 35 - 70   **C** = (€/£) 0 - 35   **D** = Donation

There are no listings above 80£/€ per night, unless nothing else is available in the area. Accommodation is listed in ascending order (i.e. cheapest first). Prices may or may not include breakfast and some establishments charge a tariff for dogs. In general, dogs are not welcome in Youth or Religious Hostels. Similarly, the general rule for accommodation in Religious Houses is that reservations must be made 24 hours ahead of arrival. Note: **Donation** means just that, you are expected to give what you can and think the accommodations warrants.

Accommodation is classified as follows:

Pilgrim Hostel
Hostel that specifically offers accommodation to via Francigena pilgrims. Usually with dormitory accommodation, kitchen facilities and shared bathrooms. The hostels may be run by commercial, municipal or religious authorities.

Religious Hostel
A facility with accommodation managed by a religious group which may have space for via Francigena pilgrims. Usually with dormitory accommodation, kitchen facilities or the possibility of prepared meals and shared bathrooms.

Church or Religious Organisation
Places where limited, basic accommodation or assistance may be offered.

Commercial Hostel
Commercial or municipal hostel including gîte d'etape in France. Usually with dormitory accommodation, kitchen facilities and shared bathrooms.

Hotel and Bed and Breakfast
More expensive commercial accommodation including chambres d'hôtes in France and Agriturismos in Italy. Usually double or family sized rooms with the possibility of a private bathroom. Hotels normally are priced by room while bed and breakfast and chambres d'hôtes may charge by room or by person. Bed and Breakfasts and Agriturismos may be isolated from shops and restaurants. Often dinner can be provided if requested in advance. Kitchen access may be possible. Where there is a choice of room types the price band is given for the room type with the lowest price. In some situations there may be seasonal premiums.

Following the route :

In England the route follows the established and well sign posted North Downs Way. In Canterbury you will also find a small number of via Francigena signs.

France is administered on a hierarchical basis of nation, region, department and commune. Work is in hand to have the via Francigena adopted as a national facility in the form of a route Grand Randonée – the GR145. The process requires a negotiation between all levels of the hierarchy and with implementation e.g. signposting taking place at a regional level.

In France the route passes through 4 regions Nord-Pas-de-Calais, Picardie, Champagne-

Ardenne and Franche-Comté. The implementation of the GR145 and its signposting have been completed in Nord-Pas-de-Calais and Chapagne-Ardenne, but has not been started in Picardie and has been undertaken without national agreement and therefore without GR status in Franch-Comté. In Nord-Pas-de-Calais the route has been constructed by largely following the pre-exiting GR128 while in Champagne-Ardenne an existing chemin de St Jacques GR654 has been adopted. This approach has led to better route maintenance, but at the expense of a loss of some of the historical context e.g. many of the Sigeric sub-mansions are bypassed and a substantial increase in distance.

The GR signposting comprises red and white painted or adhesive signs sometimes also showing the number of the GR. Beware of confusion where 2 GR routes intersect it is often unclear to which route the signs refer. On the GR145 the red and white signs have been supplemented with bi-directional via Francigena signs on metal poles. These are normally located at main intersections where access is possible for the installation crews and are typically between 1 and 3 kilometres apart.

In populated areas both types of sign are subject to vandalism. In agricultural areas free standing signs have been damaged by farm machinery. Unfortunately it is not possible to rely on every junction being signposted.

In Picardie signs only exist where a local group have adopted the route or where the route happens to overlap with existing local or national routes.

In Franche-Comté the stencilled yellow and white pilgrim is extensively used. While there is also some GR signs where the route overlaps with the existing GR595 and GR5.

The books primarily follow the GR145 where it exists. This we call the « Official Route » but we also propose a large number of Alternative Routes that either reduce distance or have greater historic relevance.

The Basics in Britain

The British currency
The pound sterling. A few of the big shops will accept Euros, but they are rarely used in Britain. Standard Banking Hours Monday-Friday 09:30 - 15.30. Some branches stay open until 17.30, and a few are open Saturday morning. Most banks will have an ATM (Automated Teller Machine) outside the bank where you can draw out money with a credit or debit card. Many of these are available to use 24 hours a day, but some do still close for a few hours during the night.

Emergencies
999 is the historic emergency number for the United Kingdom, but calls are also accepted on the European Union emergency number, 112, and from mobile phones, the United States emergency number, 911. All calls are answered by 999 operators. Calls are always free.

Post Offices
Standard Opening Hours 09.00 - 17.30 Monday - Friday. Few open on Saturday morning and are increasingly found as counters within other shops. Post Offices are shut on Sundays and Bank Holidays.

POSTE RESTANTE addresses - Your name, Post Office name, Full address of the Post Office Postcode of the Post Office, Country (if applicable). Your Poste Restante address will be active straight away but don't forget to tell them they'll need to include a return address on the back of the envelope. Pick up your post.

TELEPHONES - There are public telephones in many places. Some of them also give internet access. Illustrations and instructions demonstrate how to use the phone. 999 is the emergency number, but European 112 will also connect you with the Emergency Services. Calls are always free.

Basic Business Hours

Mondays - Saturdays 09.00 - 17.30, though some shopping centres stay open until 8 pm or later. Sunday - 10.00 - 16.00, though Sunday shopping has become popular in recent years and most large shops in towns are open for 6 hours on Sundays. On public holidays some shops open and some shops do not. Nearly all shops are closed on Christmas and New Year's Day. Most shopping centres are closed on Easter Sunday with reduced shopping hours on Easter Monday. In villages, some rural shops still follow the tradition of an early closing day (usually a Wednesday) when they close at 13.00pm.

Health Care

All EU citizens are eligible for free health care if they have the correct documentation. Non EU Citizens must arrange personal health insurance.

Food

British food has traditionally been based on beef, lamb, pork, chicken and fish and generally served with potatoes and one other vegetable, but now you can eat any meal from just about every culture - the Indian curry probably being the most popular. You will find that food is served at just about every hour of the day, but rarely cheaply.

Accommodation

English hotels are graded from zero to five stars and the price more or less corresponds to the number of stars.

Bed and Breakfast (B&B). Guests have accommodation in private houses and are served breakfast by the owner, who often has useful local knowledge.

Youth Hostels provide accommodation where guests can rent a bed (sometimes a bunk bed) in a dormitory and share a common bathroom, kitchen, and lounge. You will need to be a member of the International Youth Hostel Federation (www.ehic.org.uk).

As the birthplace of camping, England has a large number of places to stay of every kind – from small, quiet spots to big lively parks offering a wide range of facilities and entertainment. Camping and caravan parks are excellent for families -they offer great value for money in a friendly environment. They are located both near the coast and in the heart of the countryside.

The Basics in France

Currency:
Euro. Standard banking Hours: Monday-Friday 09.30-12.00 and 14.00-16.00. Closed on Sundays and usually Monday, with half day opening on Saturday morning Post Offices (La Poste): Standard opening hours Mon - Fri - 09.30-12.00 and 14.00-17.00. Half day opening on Saturday morning.

Emergencies
112 will give you access to the following services: Fire, Police, Ambulance, Coastguard, Mountain Rescue or Cave Rescue. This is free and can be dialled from any telephone (including mobile phones).

Basic Business Hours
08.00-12.00 and 14.00-18.00. Almost everything in France - shops, museums, tourist offices etc. - closes for two hours at midday. Food shops often don't reopen until half way through the afternoon, but close at 19.30 or 20.00. The standard closing days are Sunday and Monday in small towns, but you will find that many large supermarkets are now staying open throughout the day.

Post Offices (La Poste):
Standard opening hours Mon - Fri - 09.30-12.00 and 14.00-17.00. Half day opening on Saturday morning. You can make domestic and international phone calls from any public telephone box and can receive calls where there is a new logo of a ringing bell. Poste Restante. You can receive mail at the central post offices of most towns. It should be addressed (preferably with the surname first and in capitals) "Poste Restante, Poste Centrale", followed by the name of the town and its postal code. To collect your mail you will need a passport or other convincing ID, and there may be a charge of around a euro or less. You should ask for all your names to be checked, as filing systems are not brilliant.

Health Care
All EU citizens are eligible for free health care if they have the correct documentation.

Food
In France, the best way of eating breakfast is in a bar or café, at a fraction of the cost charged by most hotels. Expect a croissant or some bread with coffee or hot chocolate. At lunchtime and sometimes in the evenings you'll find most cafés and restaurants offering a plat du jour, which is by far the cheapest alternative if you don't fancy cooking yourself.

Accommodation
In country areas, in addition to standard hotels, you will come across chambre d'hôtes and ferme auberge, bed and breakfast accommodation in someone's house or farm. These are rarely an especially cheap option, usually costing the equivalent of a two star hotel.
Youth hostels (auberges de jeunesse) are great for travellers on a budget. They are often beautifully sited and they allow you to cut costs by preparing your own food in their kitchens or eating in cheap canteens. The majority will require that you are a member of the International Youth Hostel Federation.
Gites d'étape are basic but do not require membership and provide bunk beds with primitive kitchen and washing facilities at a reasonable price.
Campsites in France are nearly always clean and have plenty of hot water. On the coast there are superior categories of campsite where you will pay prices similar to those of a hotel for the facilities -bars, restaurants and usually elaborate swimming pools too. For horses, it is useful to know that campsite owners often allow horses to be tethered at the edge of the site.

Useful Links

www.Pilgrimstales.com
PILGRIM TALES publishing is passionate about inspiring others with the possibility of discovery, understanding and peace through travel.

www.pilgrimstorome.org.uk
Practical information for the pilgrimage to Rome.

http://avff.fr/ – French language site containing: news of the Via Francigena in France

http://www.tourisme-champagne-ardenne.com/balades/voyageurs/via-francigena.

aspx – multilingual site containing: information on the route in the Champagne-Ardenne region of France

http://www.tourisme-langres.com/ – French language site withy information on the route in the south of Champagne-Ardennes

www.theexpeditioner.com
THE EXPEDITIONER popular travel-themed webzine featuring articles about travel, music and film.

http://pilgrim.peterrobins.co.uk/ – English language site with information on pilgrim routes throughout Europe

www.eurovia.tv/
EUROVIA serves as a platform made by pilgrims, for pilgrims. Everybody is welcome to share their experiences withothers, and to contribute their views and opinions. Other pilgrims are always grateful to receive useful tips.

www.camminideuropageie.com
An Italian, Spanish, French collaboration.

http://www.urcamino.com/ – English language site with accommodation information

www.groups.yahoo.com/group/viafrancigena/
VIA FRANCIGENA YAHOO DISCUSSION GROUP A lively discussion group with a large amount of useful information.

www.csj.org.uk
CONFRATERNITY OF ST JAMES providing a wealth of information about the many pilgrim routes to Santiago de Compostela in Spain as well as general guidance and advice to pilgrims. It is well worth visiting if this is your first pilgrimage.

www.francigena-international.org
INTERNATIONAL ASSOCIATION OF VIA FRANCIGENA publishes maps of the route in walking stages as well as route instructions and accommodation lists.

British Tourist Authority, Thames Tower, Black's Road, London W6 9EL Tel: 0044 (0) 20 846 9000 www.uktouristinfo.com

Youth Hostel Association, 0870 770 8868 (UK)   0044 1629 592700 (Outside UK) customerservices@yha.org.uk www.yha.org.uk

French Tourist Board, 300 High Holborn, London WC1V 7JH Tel: 0044 (0)9068 244 123 info.uk@franceguide.com http://uk.franceguide.com

French Youth Hostelling Association, FUAJ - National Centre Office, 27 rue Pajol, 75018 Paris Tel: 0033 (0)1 44 89 87 27

IGN Maps http://ign.fr

Facebook groups:
Via Francigena – multilingual group for all with a valid interest in the route
Via Francigena España – Spanish language group

Recommended Reading

The Art of Pilgrimage	Phil Cousineau
Have Saddle Will Travel	Don West
The Essential Walker's Journal	Leslie Sansone
The Pilgrim's France - A Travel Guide to the Saints	Jonathan Sumption
Along the Templar Trail	Brandon Wilson
Rome: a pilgrim's companion	David Baldwin
The Age of Pilgrimage: The Medieval Journey to God	Jonathan Sumption
In Search of a Way: two journeys of spiritual discovery	Gerard Hughes
The Via Francigena Canterbury to Rome	Alison Raju
Traveling Souls: Contemporary Pilgrimage Stories	Brian Bouldrey (Editor)

 Pilgrim Hostel			Sigeric Route
Religious Hostel			Submansion
Church or Religious Organisation			Main Route
Pilgrim Hosts			Alternate Route
Commercial Hostel			Motorway
B&B, Hotel, Gîte d'Etape			Main Road
Camp Site			Minor Road
Equestrian Centre			Track
Town Hall or Tourist Information			Railway Track
Bank or ATM			Restaurant
Public Transport Location			Supermarket
Hospital			Public House
Doctor			Café
Veterinary			Site of Historic Interest
Hiking Equipment Store			Church
Bicycle Store			View-point
Farrier			
Railway Station			

Canterbury to Besançon
909 kilometres

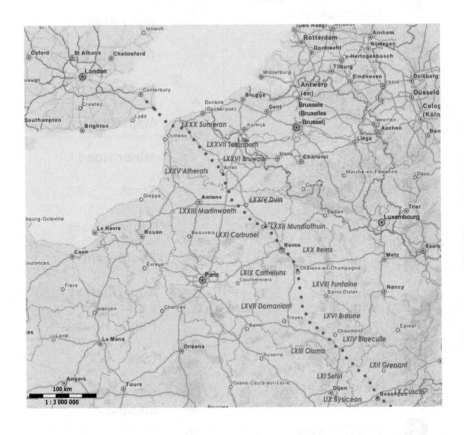

Traveller, there is no path, paths are made by walking.

Antonio Machado

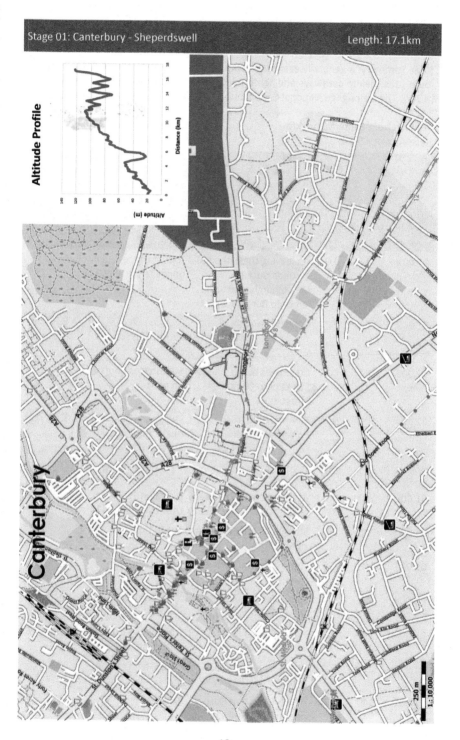

Stage Summary: a generally easy stage, with gentle hills. After leaving Canterbury the route uses mainly pathways and some minor roads following the North Downs Way (NDW). The well signed National Cycle Route n° 16 also connects Canterbury to Dover.

482 ~~3000~~ mi.

Distance from Canterbury: 0km

Distance to Besançon: 910km

Stage Ascent: 289m

Stage Descent: 185m

Waypoint	Distance between waypoints	Total km	Directions	Verification Point	Compass	Altitude m
01.001	0	0.0	On leaving the cathedral grounds through Christchurch gate turn left onto Burgate Street	Tourist Office opposite the gate	SE	18
01.002	170	0.2	Continue straight ahead	Pass church of St Thomas on your right	E	18
01.003	130	0.3	Cross over Lower Bridge Street onto Church Street	Magistrates Court on right	E	17
01.004	100	0.4	Turn right and then immediately left onto Longport	The grounds of St Augustine's Abbey are behind the buildings on your left	E	16
01.005	160	0.6	At the roundabout, bear left	Direction Littlebourne, A257	E	16
01.006	300	0.9	Straight ahead on North Holmes Rd	St Martins Church on left	E	22
01.007	110	1.0	Turn right onto Spring Lane	Stone NDW sign	S	26
01.008	80	1.1	Turn right to follow NDW	VF sign on signpost	SW	21
01.009	140	1.2	Turn left onto footpath	Iron railings on left and VF sticker	SE	22
01.010	220	1.4	At the T-junction, turn left onto Pilgrim's Way	Sports field on the left	SE	25
01.011	140	1.6	At the T-junction, turn right to cross railway bridge	NDW sign	SE	27

11

Waypoint	Distance between waypoints	Total km	Directions	Verification Point	Compass	Altitude m
01.012	500	2.1	Continue straight ahead on small tarmac road	NDW sign, VF sign	SE	31
01.013	500	2.6	At the crossroads, continue straight ahead on the track	Towards a line of trees ahead	SE	35
01.014	600	3.1	Fork left	NDW sign, VF sign	SE	41
01.015	400	3.5	Straight ahead	NDW sign, VF sign	SE	47
01.016	1400	4.8	At the T-junction, bear left	Cycle Route n° 16	SE	31
01.017	90	4.9	At mini roundabout, bear right direction Patrixbourne	NDW sign	SE	28
01.018	400	5.3	Turn right onto Patrixbourne Road, towards St Mary's church	Cycle Route N)16 leaves to the left	SW	22
01.019	190	5.5	Immediately after the last house on the left, turn left onto the path and diagonally cross the field	NDW sign	S	25
01.020	140	5.6	Turn right, keep the woods close on the left	NDW sign	S	29
01.021	900	6.5	At the end of the field, bear left through the trees	Highway parallel on the right, NDW sign	S	65
01.022	500	7.0	Cross over small road	Road bridge on right, NDW sign	S	72
01.023	120	7.1	Bear left and cross field towards trees	NDW sign	SE	70
01.024	110	7.2	Bear right	Keep edge of wood on left	SE	72
01.025	190	7.4	Continue along the edge of the field, trees to left	Telephone mast ahead, NDW sign	SE	78
01.026	180	7.6	Cross Coldharbour Lane and continue straight ahead down the middle of the field	NDW sign	SE	75

Waypoint	Distance between waypoints	Total km	Directions	Verification Point	Compass	Altitude m
01.027	1200	8.8	Go through small wicket gate and continue straight ahead	Telephone mast on left	SE	88
01.028	600	9.3	Cross the small road and continue straight ahead into the field	NDW sign	SE	89
01.029	500	9.8	At the junction in the tracks bear right	Towards the farmhouse on the ridge, NDW sign	SE	96
01.030	800	10.6	Continue straight ahead	Upper Digges farmhouse on left	SE	105
01.031	50	10.7	Turn left onto a track between a line of trees and fence and go through the metal gate	NDW sign	NE	105
01.032	80	10.7	Turn right onto gravel track	NDW sign	SE	104
01.033	300	11.0	Bear left across the field, towards the road	NDW sign	E	106
01.034	300	11.4	Cross the road and continue straight ahead on the track	Electricity post to the left, NDW sign	SE	108
01.035	500	11.9	Fork left	NDW Sign	SE	101
01.036	150	12.0	At the junction in Womenswold centre, turn left and then immediately right onto a gravelled track	Brick wall and house on left, NDW sign	E	101
01.037	100	12.1	Continue straight ahead along edge of field	Line of trees directly on right	SE	97
01.038	600	12.7	Cross the road and continue into the wood	NDW sign	SE	103
01.039	50	12.8	At the next road, turn right	Towards Woolage, NDW Sign	SW	104
01.040	70	12.9	Turn left just before entering village and follow edge of field	Pass playground on right, NDW sign.	E	105

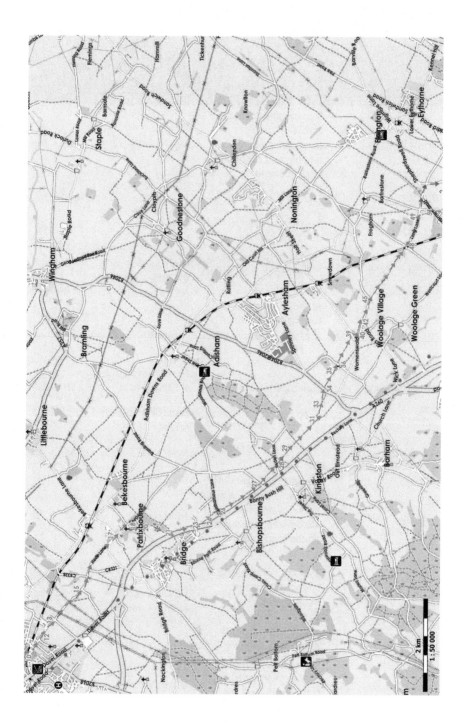

14

Waypoint	Distance between waypoints	Total km	Directions	Verification Point	Compass	Altitude m
01.041	250	13.1	Sign indicates cutting across children's playground, but we recommend continuing straight ahead	Around edge of field	E	93
01.042	40	13.1	Turn right	Towards the road	SW	92
01.043	50	13.2	Turn left just before reaching the road	Keep hedge to your right	E	90
01.044	500	13.6	Turn right through a gap in the hedge and turn left on the road	Farm buildings on the ridge to the right	E	72
01.045	130	13.8	At the bend in the road, turn right to continue on the track between trees on left and hedge on the right	NDW sign	SE	71
01.046	1400	15.1	Turn right towards road	NDW sign	SE	87
01.047	50	15.2	Turn left onto road	Cross over railway bridge	E	89
01.048	50	15.2	Turn right along Long Lane	NDW sign	SE	91
01.049	700	15.9	Walkers turn right onto the track. Note:- to avoid a stile, cyclists and riders are advised to remain on the road and take the Alternate Route	NDW sign	SE	75
01.050	400	16.3	Turn right on the road and then right again in the direction of Shepherdswell. Note:- Shepherdswell is also known as Sibertswold	NDW sign and Meadow Bank cottage on left	SW	86
01.051	60	16.3	Immediately after the railway level crossing, turn left through the kissing gate	NDW sign	S	86

Waypoint	Distance between waypoints	Total km	Directions	Verification Point	Compass	Altitude m
01.052	80	16.4	Pass through the small gate and turn left on the gravel road and then right	NDW sign	S	88
01.053	100	16.5	Continue straight ahead over stile	NDW sign	S	92
01.054	190	16.7	Cross over stile and continue across the field in the direction of houses	NDW sign	S	102
01.055	120	16.8	Bear right after going through 5-bar gate	NDW sign	S	113
01.056	90	16.9	Continue straight ahead between two fences	Equestrian Centre on right, NDW sign	S	120
01.057	80	17.0	Continue ahead on narrow path	Wooden fence on right, high hedge on left, NDW sign	S	122
01.058	110	17.1	At the T-junction with the road, turn right on Mill Lane	Towards the village green	SW	123
01.059	50	17.1	Arrive at Sheperdswell village green with the Bell public house ahead	Church on the left		122

Accommodation & Facilities .... Canterbury - Sheperdswell

Franciscan Study Centre,Giles Lane,CT2 7NA Canterbury,Kent,United Kingdom; Tel:+44(0)1227 769349; Email:info@franciscans.ac.uk *Religious*

Kipps Hostel,40 Nunnery Fields,CT1 3JT Canterbury,Kent,United Kingdom; Tel:+44(0)1227 786121; Email:info@kipps-hostel.com; Web-site:www.kipps-hostel.com; Price:B *Commercial*

YHA,54 New Dover Road,CT1 3DT Canterbury,Kent,United Kingdom; Tel:+44(0)8453 719010; Email:canterbury@yha.org.uk; Web-site:www.yha.org.uk; Price:B *Commercial*

Pilgrims Hotel,18 The Friars,CT1 2AS Canterbury,Kent,United Kingdom; Tel:+44(0)1227 464531; Email:pilgrimshotel@aol.com; Web-site:www.pilgrimshotel.com; Price:A *B & B Hotel*

Canterbury Cathedral Lodge,The Precincts,CT1 2EH Canterbury ,Kent,United Kingdom; Tel:+44(0)1227 865350; Email:stay@canterbury-cathedral.org; Web-site:canterburycathedrallodge.org; Price:A *B & B Hotel*

Castle Court - Guest House,8 Castle Street,CT1 2QF Canterbury,Kent,United Kingdom; Tel:+44(0)1227 463441; Price:B

Wincheap Guest House,94 Wincheap,CT1 3RS Canterbury,Kent,United Kingdom; Tel:+44(0)1227 762309; Web-site:wincheapguesthouse.org; Price:A

Woodlands Farm B&B,154 The Street,CT3 3LA Adisham,Kent,United Kingdom; Tel:+44(0)1304 840401; Email:Woodlands.farm@btinternet.com; Price:B

Hornbeams B&B,Jesse's Hill,CT4 6JD Canterbury,Kent,United Kingdom; Tel:+44(0)1227 830119; Email:hornbeamsbandb@btinternet.com; Web-site:www.hornbeams.co.uk; Price:A

Keswick House B & B,Barfrestone Road,CT15 4AH Eythorne,Kent,United Kingdom; Tel:+44(0)1304 831011; Email:keswickhousekent@gmail.com; Web-site:www.keswickhousekent.co.uk; Price:A

Sunshine Cottage,The Green,CT15 7LQ Shepherdswell,Kent,United Kingdom; Tel:+44(0)1304 831359; Price:B

Oast Cottage B&B,Cox Hill,CT15 7NQ Shepherdswell,Kent,United Kingdom; Tel:+44(0)1304 831532; Email:elliottnicky@btinternet.com; Web-site:www.oastcottage.com; Price:A

Molehills B&B,Bladbean,CT4 6LU Canterbury,Kent,United Kingdom; Tel:+44(0)1303 840051; Email:molehills84@hotmail.com; Web-site:www.molehillsbedbreakfast.co.uk; Price:B

Colret House - Bed and Breakfast,(Jackie & Darryl),The Green,CT15 5AP Coldred,Kent,United Kingdom; Tel:+44(0)1304 830388; Email:jackiecolret@aol.com; Web-site:www.colrethouse.co.uk; Price:A; Note:North Downs Way warden. Will transport luggage, ; PR

Neals place Farm Campsite,(Ken Jordan),Neals place Farm, Neal's-place-Road,CT2 8HX Canterbury,Kent,United Kingdom; Tel:+44(0)1227 765632; Email:kenjordan@orbitalnetwork.net; Web-site:www.nealsplacefarmcampsite.co.uk; Price:C

Canterbury Camping and Caravanning Club Site,Bekesbourne Lane,CT3 4AB Canterbury,Kent,United Kingdom; Tel:+44(0)1227 463216; Web-site:www. campingandcaravanningclub.co.uk/campsites/uk/kent/canterbury/ canterbury; Price:C

Mount Pleasant Livery Stables,Hoath Road,CT3 4LN Canterbury,Kent,United Kingdom; Tel:+44(0)7980 646087

Sparrow Court Farm,London Rd,ME13 9LF Faversham,Kent,United Kingdom; Tel:+44(0)1227 752585

Britton Farm,Ickham,CT3 1SN Canterbury,Kent,United Kingdom; Tel:+44(0)1227 728207

Iffin Equestrian,Iffin Lane,CT4 7BE Canterbury,Kent,United Kingdom; Tel:+44(0)7906 923904

The Paddocks,76 New House Lane,CT4 7BJ Canterbury,Kent,United Kingdom; Tel:+44(0)1227 451721

Bursted Manor Riding Centre,Petts Bottom,CT4 6EH Canterbury,Kent,United Kingdom; Tel:+44(0)1227 830568

Tourist Information Centre,12/13 Sun Street,CT1 2HX Canterbury,Kent,United Kingdom; Tel:+44(0)1227 378100

Nationwide,4/5 High Street,CT1 2JH Canterbury,Kent,United Kingdom; Tel:+44(0)8452 660287

Lloyds TSB,High Saint,CT1 2SE Canterbury,Kent,United Kingdom; Tel:+44(0)8453 000000

HSBC,Whitefriars Shopping Centre, 9 Rose Lane,CT1 2JP Canterbury,Kent,United Kingdom; Tel:+44(0)8457 404404

Barclays Bank,9 Saint.Georges Street,CT1 2JX Canterbury,Kent,United Kingdom; Tel:+44(0)8457 555555

The Royal Bank of Scotland,14 Rose Lane,CT1 2ST Canterbury,Kent,United Kingdom; Tel:+44(0)1227 763345

The Royal Bank of Scotland (Safeway's),Ten Perch Road,CT1 3TQ Canterbury,Kent,United Kingdom; Tel:+44(0)1227 763345

Canterbury West Railway Station,39 Palace Street,CT1 2DZ Canterbury,Kent,United Kingdom; Tel:+44(0)8457 484950; Web-site:www.nationalrail.co.uk

Canterbury East Railway Station,Station Road East,CT1 2RB Canterbury,Kent,United Kingdom; Tel:+44(0)8457 484950; Web-site:www.nationalrail.co.uk

Kent and Canterbury Hospital,Ethelbert Road,CT1 3NG Canterbury,Kent,United Kingdom; Tel:+44(0)1227 766877

London Road Surgery,49 London Road,CT2 8SG Canterbury,Kent,United Kingdom; Tel:+44(0)1227 463128

Companion Care Vets,Riverside Retail Park, 10 Perch Rd,CT1 3TQ Wincheap,Kent,United Kingdom; Tel:+44(0)1227 812884

Millets,47 Burgate,CT1 2HW Canterbury,Kent,United Kingdom; Tel:+44(0)1227 479698

Blacks,44 Burgate,CT1 2HW Canterbury,Kent,United Kingdom; Tel:+44(0)1227 764385

Ridgeway Forge Farriers,5-19 Ridgeway Rd,CT6 7 Canterbury,Kent,United Kingdom; Tel:+44(0)1227 283714

Fabcab Taxis,14 Chestnut Close,CT4 7TD Canterbury,Kent,United Kingdom; Tel:+44(0)1227 731100

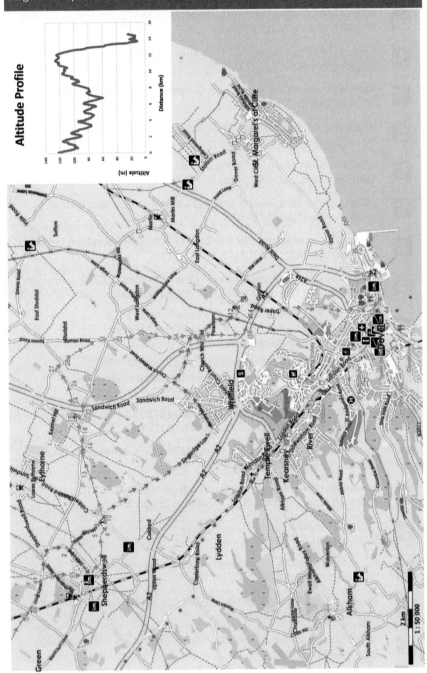

Stage Summary: the walking route continues on the paths of the North Downs Way before following minor roads into Dover. The Alternate Route enables cyclists and riders to bypass many barriers by following National Cycle Route n° 16 before rejoining the "Official Route" for the entry into Dover.

Distance from Canterbury: 17km   Distance to Besançon: 893km
Stage Ascent: 221m   Stage Descent: 320m

Waypoint	Distance between waypoints	Total km	Directions	Verification Point	Compass	Altitude m
02.001	0	0.0	From the village green in Sheperdswell, return along Mill Lane	Public House directly behind	NE	122
02.002	20	0.0	From Mill Lane turn right and pass through the kissing gate onto the North Downs Way. Note:- to avoid more obstacles, cyclists and riders should continue on Mill Lane and follow the Alternate Route	NDW sign	E	122
02.003	160	0.2	Straight ahead into large open field	Keep hedgerow close on the right	SE	115
02.004	220	0.4	Cross second open field after passing through a line of trees	NDW sign	E	104
02.005	600	1.0	Proceed through narrow gap in fence between two posts	NDW sign	SE	99
02.006	40	1.0	Straight ahead across the next field after crossing fence	Towards stile	SE	101
02.007	120	1.1	Turn left after crossing stile into the grounds of Coldred Court Farm	Fence on left, large white house on the right	E	107
02.008	220	1.4	Cross over stile and continue through a small wood and turn right onto road	NDW sign	SE	112

Waypoint	Distance between waypoints	Total km	Directions	Verification Point	Compass	Altitude m
02.009	50	1.4	At the crossroads continue straight ahead onto Singledge Lane	NDW sign, Coldred village on right	SE	114
02.010	40	1.4	Immediately turn left onto track	NDW sign	NE	115
02.011	40	1.5	Cross stile into a field		E	114
02.012	210	1.7	After 3rd stile cross field towards the corner of an area of woodland - Waldershare Park	Tower on the right	E	108
02.013	800	2.5	From the corner of the woods, cross the field diagonally		E	103
02.014	400	2.9	Cross over stile and continue straight ahead towards the road junction with the driveway	Waldershare House on the right	E	94
02.015	200	3.1	On reaching the road turn right		SE	83
02.016	80	3.2	Fork left	Just after passing the Waldershare House	NE	81
02.017	100	3.3	Pass through white gates marked private access only	Home Farm on the left and NDW sign	E	77
02.018	260	3.5	At the fork, take the track between the two roads. Cross diagonally across the field and skirt the copse of trees on your left	NDW sign on gate	E	78
02.019	290	3.8	Cross over a stile and go through churchyard		E	92
02.020	80	3.9	Turn right after passing through the churchyard gateway	Wooden covered gate	SE	94

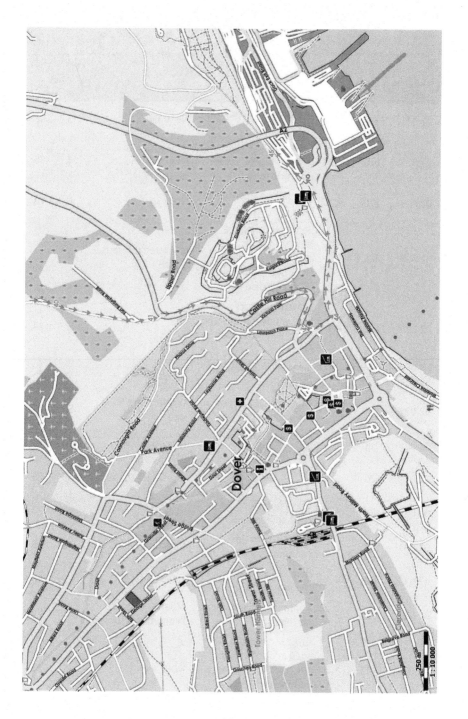

Waypoint	Distance between waypoints	Total km	Directions	Verification Point	Compass	Altitude m
02.021	80	4.0	Turn right on Sandwich Road	NDW sign	S	88
02.022	120	4.1	Turn left in the direction of East Studdle, cross road bridge	NDW sign	E	85
02.023	170	4.3	Turn left on a concreted road	NDW sign	N	78
02.024	300	4.6	Before entering the farm turn right. The road leads to a track, cross over a stile and through a field	Minacre farmhouse on left	E	73
02.025	160	4.7	Leave main track and turn left over a stile and diagonally cross the field		E	74
02.026	230	5.0	Cross stile and turn left on the road	NDW sign	NE	85
02.027	400	5.4	Turn right at junction in the village of Ashley	Waldershare Road sign	SE	79
02.028	180	5.5	Turn right into North Downs Close	NDW sign	S	75
02.029	20	5.6	Turn left down narrow track	Houses on the right	SE	75
02.030	900	6.5	Leave field and turn right on Roman Road	NDW sign	S	70
02.031	260	6.7	At the crossroads continue straight ahead	Direction Whitfield	S	59
02.032	140	6.9	Bear left on the track at the top of the hill	NDW sign	S	65
02.033	800	7.7	Continue straight ahead on the track	Milestone "5 kilometres to Dover"	S	79
02.034	600	8.2	Cross straight over the road and continue on the track ahead. Note:- continuing to follow ancient Roman road	NDW sign	S	91

Waypoint	Distance between waypoints	Total km	Directions	Verification Point	Compass	Altitude m
02.035	500	8.7	At the road junction, turn left and then immediately right	Pass through the hamlet of Pineham	SW	95
02.036	130	8.8	Bear left on the road	NDW sign	S	94
02.037	150	9.0	Turn right onto track - Roman Road	NDW sign	S	96
02.038	900	9.9	Turn left and continue following track	Parallel to the main road on the right	SE	114
02.039	700	10.6	At the T-junction with Dover Road, turn right and cross the bridge over the A2. Note:- Alternate Route joins from the left	Village of Guston to the left	S	111
02.040	1600	12.2	Continue straight ahead on Dover Road	Connaught Barracks to the left	S	120
02.041	500	12.7	At the T-junction turn right onto the A258, direction Dover	Castle directly ahead	S	97
02.042	900	13.6	Turn left and left again into St. James Street	Pass the ruins of St James the Apostle church on the left	S	17
02.043	80	13.7	At the crossroads, turn left	Woolcomber St.	SE	11
02.044	90	13.7	At the traffic lights, turn left on the A20, Townwall Street	Direction Ferries	E	12
02.045	800	14.5	Arrive at Dover Eastern Docks ferry terminal	Ticket office to the right		23

Alternate Route #02.A1			Length: 9.8km			
Stage Summary: cyclists and riders route to Guston						
Stage Ascent: 221m			Stage Descent: 320m			
02A1.001	0	0.0	Continue straight ahead on Mill Lane		NE	122
02A1.002	800	0.8	Turn right	Follow Cycle Route n°16	SE	110

Waypoint	Distance between waypoints	Total km	Directions	Verification Point	Compass	Altitude m
02A1.003	1000	1.8	At the crossroads, continue straight ahead onto Singledge Lane	Cycle Route n° 16, Coldred to the right	SE	114
02A1.004	3300	5.1	Turn left onto Nursery Lane	Cycle Route n° 16	NE	127
02A1.005	700	5.8	At the crossroads in the centre of Whitfield, continue straight ahead onto Napchester Road	Cycle Route n° 16	NE	114
02A1.006	800	6.5	At the crossroads, turn right in the direction of Dover	Cycle Route n° 16	SE	95
02A1.007	900	7.4	Turn left towards West and East Langdon	Cycle Route n° 16, cross road bridge	NE	102
02A1.008	90	7.5	Immediately after crossing the bridge, turn right	Direction Pineham	SE	98
02A1.009	260	7.7	Turn right rejoining North Downs Way	Pass through the hamlet of Pineham	SW	95
02A1.010	130	7.9	Bear left remaining on the North Downs Way	Cycle Route n° 16	SE	94
02A1.011	150	8.0	Bear left remaining on the road and leaving the NDW		SE	96
02A1.012	1200	9.2	Turn right on The Street	Cycle Route n° 16, direction Dover	SE	110
02A1.013	250	9.5	At the T-junction in Guston, turn right on Dover Road	Cycle Route n° 16, towards the public house	SW	102
02A1.014	400	9.8	Rejoin NDW and the "Official Route"	Bridge over highway ahead		111

Hostel Alma & Cafe Express,37 Folkestone Road,CT17 9RZ Dover,Kent,United Kingdom; Tel:+44(0)1304 241762; Email:info@almadover.com; Web-site:www.almadover.com; Price:B

The Castle - Dover Backpackers,Russell Street,CT16 1PY Dover,Kent,United Kingdom; Tel:+44(0)7776 127592; Email:thecastleinndover@gmail.com ; Web-site:doverbackpackers.wordpress.com; Price:C

Maison Dieu Guest House,89 Maison Dieu Road,CT16 1RE Dover,Kent,United Kingdom; Tel:+44(0)1304 204033; Email:maisondieu@brguest.co.uk; Web-site:www.brguest.co.uk; Price:B; PR

Bellrose Hotel,East Cliff,CT16 1LU Dover,Kent,United Kingdom; Tel:+44(0)1304 213009; Web-site:www.bellrose.co.uk; Price:B

East Cliff Hotel,28 East Cliff,CT16 1LU Dover,Kent,United Kingdom; Tel:+44(0)1304 202299; Price:B; PR

Dover's Restover Bed & Breakfast,69 Folkestone Road,CT17 9RZ Dover,Kent,United Kingdom; Tel:+44(0)1304 206031; Email:enquiries@ doversrestover.co.uk; Web-site:www.doversrestover.co.uk; Price:A

Saint Albans B&B,71 Folkestone Road,CT17 9RZ Dover,Kent,United Kingdom; Tel:+44(0)1304 206308; Price:B

Perfect Ponies,19 Thistledown,CT14 7XE Walmer,Kent,United Kingdom; Tel:+44(0)7807 306663

Cornilo Riding - Sutton Court Farm,Church Hill,CT15 5DF Sutton,Kent,United Kingdom; Tel:+44(0)7768 172777

Owl House Stables,Station Rd,CT15 6HN Saint-Margarets-at-Cliffe,Kent,United Kingdom; Tel:+44(0)1304 852035

Braeside Riding Stables,Nelson Park Road,CT15 6HL Saint-Margarets-at-Cliffe,Kent,United Kingdom; Tel:+44(0)1304 852959

Minnismoor Riding Stables,Abbey Rd,CT15 7DJ Hougham,Kent,United Kingdom; Tel:+44(0)7816 664529

Limes Farm Equestrian Centre,Pay Street,CT18 7DZ Hawkinge,Kent,United Kingdom; Tel:+44(0)1303 891222

Visitor Information Centre,The Old Town Gaol,CT16 1DL Dover,Kent,United Kingdom; Tel:+44(0)1304 205108

Abbey National (Tesco),Honeywood Parkway,CT16 3PT Whitfield,Kent,United Kingdom; Tel:+44(0)8457 654321

HSBC,26 Biggin Street,CT16 1BJ Dover,Kent,United Kingdom; Tel:+44(0)8457 404404

Abbey National,24 Cannon Saint,CT16 1ST Dover,Kent,United Kingdom; Tel:+44(0)8457 654321

Lloyds TSB,4-6 Market Square,CT16 1ND Dover,Kent,United Kingdom; Tel:+44(0)8453 000000

$ Natwest,25 Market Square,CT16 1NG Dover,Kent,United Kingdom; Tel:+44(0)8456 002803

$ Barclays Bank,21 Market Square,CT16 1NH Dover,Kent,United Kingdom; Tel:+44(0)8457 555555

⚓ P&O Ferries,Eastern Docks,CT161JA Dover,Kent,United Kingdom; Tel:+44(0)1304 863000; Web-site:www.poferries.com

⚓ Myferrylink,Eastern Docks,CT161JA Dover,Kent,United Kingdom; Tel:+44(0)8442 482100; Email:clientservices@myferrylink.com; Web-site:www.myferrylink.com

⚓ Port of Dover,Harbour House, Waterloo-Crescent,CT17 9BU Dover,Kent,United Kingdom; Tel:+44(0)8457 484950; Web-site:www.doverport.co.uk

⚓ Dover Priory Railway Station,Folkestone Road,CT17 9SB Dover,Kent,United Kingdom; Tel:+44(0)8457 484950; Web-site:www.nationalrail.co.uk

H Buckland Hospital,Coombe Valley Road,CT17 0HD Dover,Kent,United Kingdom; Tel:+44(0)1304 201624; Web-site:www.nhs.uk/Services/hospitals/Overview/DefaultView.aspx?id=RVV02

+ Dover Medical Practice,Maison Dieu Road,CT16 1RH Dover,Kent,United Kingdom; Tel:+44(0)1304 865555

🐕 Mobi Vet,Roosevelt Road,CT16 2BT Dover,Kent,United Kingdom; Tel:+44(0)1843 598641

🚲 Halfords,2 Granville Street,CT16 2LG Dover,Kent,United Kingdom; Tel:+44(0)1304 212515

🚲 Grizzlys Custom Bikes,Highfield Industrial Estate,CT19 6DD Folkestone,Kent,United Kingdom; Tel:+44(0)1303 240440

☎ Dover White Cliff Taxi,Albert Road,CT16 1RD Dover,Kent,United Kingdom; Tel:+44(0)1304 202070

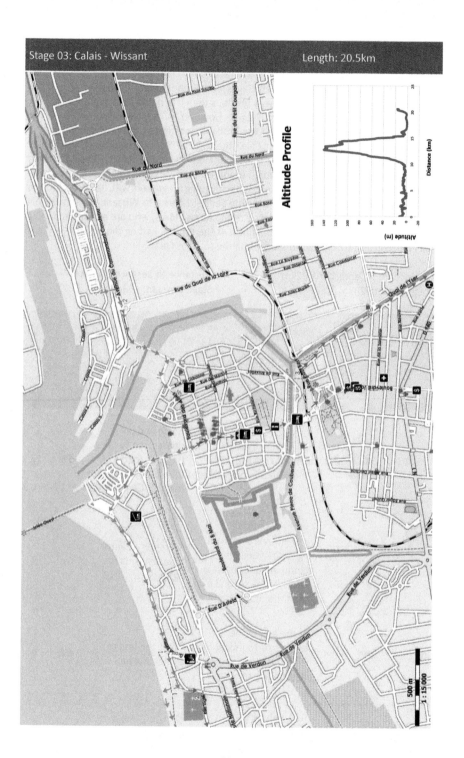

Stage Summary: the route between Calais and Guînes offers a number of choices depending on your priorities. If time is precious then it is possible to avoid the dog-leg via Wissant and proceed directly to Guînes. However, Wissant was formerly a part of the commune of Sombre (LXXX) and the probable location of the final submansion in the chronicle of Sigeric. After leaving Calais the "Official Route" leads along the coast by the beach, then follows sandy paths through the dunes before climbing Mont d'Hubert and then returning to the beach for the approach to Wissant where there is ample accommodation. The sand will make for difficult going for walkers with heavy packs. The route also known as the GR145 follows the Sentier Litorral to Wissant. Unfortunately the Sentier Littoral is prohibited to cyclists and horse-riders, who are advised to follow the road or take the direct route to Guînes. At the time of writing there were very few Via Francigena or Grand Randonée signs in the town of Calais.

Distance from Canterbury: 32km   Distance to Besançon: 878km
Stage Ascent: 263m   Stage Descent: 258m

Waypoint	Distance between waypoints	Total km	Directions	Verification Point	Compass	Altitude m
03.001	0	0.0	On leaving the Ferry control area turn right and take the foot bridge	Horse and bike riders need to take the feed road and then turn sharp right towards Centre Ville	SW	12
03.002	180	0.2	At the foot of the pedestrian ramp, turn right on Avenue du Commandant Cousteau and take the second exit from the roundabout	Direction - Centre Ville, towards the lighthouse	SW	6
03.003	400	0.6	At the end of the fencing surrounding the ferry terminal, continue straight ahead	Cross the bridge beside the lock	SW	4
03.004	170	0.7	Turn right, direction Plage	Pass lighthouse on your left	W	6

Waypoint	Distance between waypoints	Total km	Directions	Verification Point	Compass	Altitude m
03.005	700	1.4	After passing under the apartment building that spans the road, turn right towards the Pont Automatique. Note: to dramatically reduce the distance to Guînes by bypassing Wissant, take the Alternate Route to the left	Direction la Plage and Fort Risban	N	7
03.006	400	1.8	Continue straight ahead at the roundabout on avenue Raymond Poincaré	Direction la Plage and Centre Européen de Séjour	NW	7
03.007	400	2.2	At the roundabout take the second exit	Beach and Poste de Secours on the right, red and white GR sign on lamp-post	SW	6
03.008	1000	3.2	As the road turns inland, turn right into the car park and take the paved footpath beside the beach	House n° 1167 on the left, weathered wooden VF GR145 sign	W	7
03.009	230	3.4	At the circle at the end of the paved footpath, turn right towards the beach. Note:- the "Official Route" crosses stretches of sand and involves wooden stairways over the dunes. The path is prohibited for cyclists and horse-riders and may be difficult for heavily packed walkers, who should bear left on the tarmac to take the Alternate Route by road to Wissant	Yellow VF GR145 sign	N	4

Waypoint	Distance between waypoints	Total km	Directions	Verification Point	Compass	Altitude m
03.010	90	3.5	After passing the beach huts turn left and proceed parallel to the sea		W	1
03.011	1000	4.5	Approximately 50m after the line of wooden posts following the last bunker on the left, turn left and take the path between wire fences into the dunes	Partially destroyed GR sign	S	0
03.012	190	4.6	At the foot of the flight of wooden steps, before reaching the wooden kissing gate, turn right on the gravel track	Keep dunes to your right, GR sign	W	6
03.013	190	4.8	Take the left fork on the gravel track	Between bushes	SW	4
03.014	110	4.9	Take the right fork on the gravel track		W	2
03.015	600	5.5	Continue straight ahead, avoiding the track to your left. At the foot of a flight of wooden steps, take right fork on the less well defined track	Close beside the fencing on your right and behind the buildings with the triangular features on the roofs	W	4
03.016	800	6.4	Shortly after reaching a concrete section of track, continue straight ahead at the crossroads	Dunes on your right and the main road on the left	W	6
03.017	230	6.6	Take the left fork on the broader track	Remnants concrete bunker right	W	6
03.018	1000	7.5	With the car park on your left, bear right, pass through a kissing gate and then turn right on the broad gravel track to join the sandy path towards the sea	Pass the radar beacon on your left	N	5

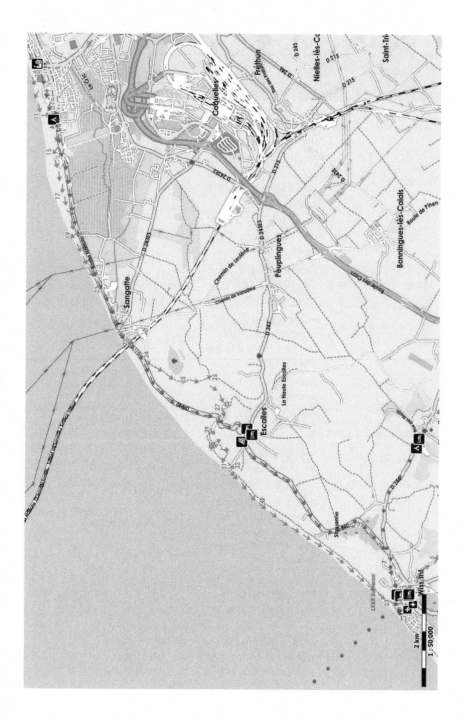

Waypoint	Distance between waypoints	Total km	Directions	Verification Point	Compass	Altitude m
03.019	70	7.6	After descending the steps, turn left on the sea wall	GR145 sign	SW	5
03.020	1400	9.0	Shortly before reaching the end of the concrete path, turn left up the steps	Towards the Mairie in Sangatte, GR145 sign	SE	3
03.021	50	9.0	At the foot of the steps, turn right beside the D940	War memorial ahead	SW	4
03.022	1300	10.3	On the exit from Sangatte, turn left towards the cemetery	Yellow VF sign	S	10
03.023	50	10.4	At the entrance to the cemetery, turn right on the track parallel to the main road	GR145 sign	SW	11
03.024	400	10.7	At the crossroads, with a tarmac road, continue straight ahead on the gravel track uphill. Note:- the road to the left leads leads to the ancient route from the Sangatte, la Leulene	Calvaire to the right at the junction, yellow VF signs	SW	20
03.025	1300	12.0	After passing through the gate, with a view of the lake and Calais on your left, take the right fork	Uphill, towards radio tower	S	86
03.026	500	12.5	At the crossroads in the track, turn right and pass through the gate	Uphill, yellow VF sign	SW	132
03.027	800	13.3	At the junction with the tarmac road, turn right and continue downhill	Radio tower to the left, view of the Dover Patrol monument on the right	W	138

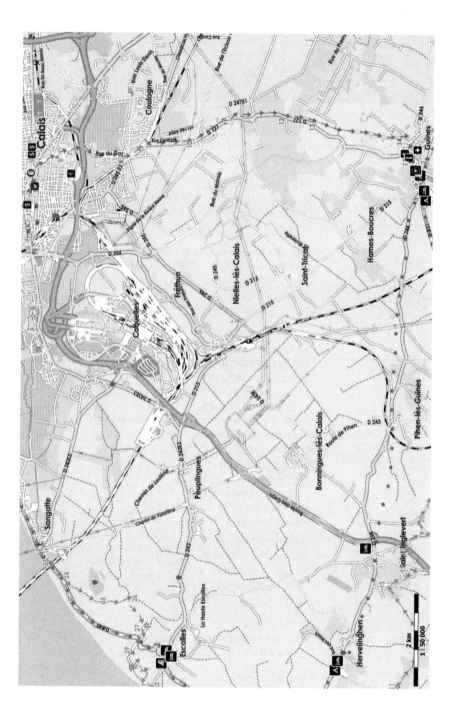

Waypoint	Distance between waypoints	Total km	Directions	Verification Point	Compass	Altitude m
03.028	400	13.7	Carefully cross the main road and follow the tarmac road straight ahead	Towards the Cap Blac Nez car park	NW	111
03.029	290	14.0	At the end of the car park pass through the barrier and continue straight ahead	Towards the monument	NW	110
03.030	30	14.0	Take take the gravel path to the left	Keep the monument on your right	SW	111
03.031	1200	15.2	At the foot of the hill turn left in the car park	Cran d'Escalles	SE	22
03.032	40	15.3	At the end of the car park, turn sharp right and descend the steps to the beach. Turn left and follow the beach to the town of Wissant. Note:- if you wish to avoid the beach, then take the road to the left and then turn right on the D940 in Escalles to follow the remainder of the Alternate Route for cyclists and riders	Pass shrine on your right	SW	23
03.033	4900	20.1	Shortly before reaching the sea wall in Wissant, turn left to leave the beach on the tarmac road	Wooden chalets overlooking the sea on your left, yellow VF sign	S	8
03.034	40	20.2	At the junction, continue straight ahead up the hill	GR sign	SE	11
03.035	160	20.3	At the T-junction, turn right, direction Hôtel de la Plage	House n° 6 directly ahead	SE	16

Waypoint	Distance between waypoints	Total km	Directions	Verification Point	Compass	Altitude m
03.036	50	20.4	At the T-junction turn right	Towards the church	S	15
03.037	140	20.5	Arrive at Wissant centre, place de la Mairie	Tourist Office to your right		17

Alternate Route #03.A1				**Length: 11.9km**		
Stage Summary: direct route from Calais to Guînes beside the canals - "Calais à St. Omer" and "Calais à Guînes"						
Stage Ascent: 60m				**Stage Descent: 57m**		
03A1.001	0	0.0	Turn left on rue de la Mer	Towards Office de Tourisme	S	7
03A1.002	900	0.9	At the roundabout in front of the Hotel de Ville turn left	Pass the tower of the Hotel de Ville on your right	E	7
03A1.003	300	1.2	Just before the bridge over the canal turn right	Keep trees and canal close on the left	SE	4
03A1.004	700	1.9	Continue straight ahead on Quai du Commerce	Pass footbridge and mobile bridge on the left	SE	3
03A1.005	500	2.4	Continue straight ahead on Quai Gustave Lamarle	Pass bridge on the left, keep canal on your left	SE	5
03A1.006	700	3.0	Continue straight ahead on Quai Gustave Lamarle	Pass further footbridge and mobile bridge on the left	S	3
03A1.007	290	3.3	Continue straight ahead on Quai d'Amérique	Pass under railway and motorway bridges	S	1
03A1.008	1300	4.6	Continue straight ahead onto the chemin de Halage	Pass third footbridge and mobile bridge on the left and bar on the right	SE	2

Waypoint	Distance between waypoints	Total km	Directions	Verification Point	Compass	Altitude m
03A1.009	600	5.1	With the railway bridge over the canal on the right, cross the bridge over the joining canal, pass under the railway and turn right	Canal on the right, chemin de Contre Halage	S	4
03A1.010	1100	6.3	Cross the road and continue straight ahead on the chemin de Contre Halage	Moving canal bridge on your right	SE	1
03A1.011	1000	7.3	At the junction with rue de l'Ecluse Carrée cross straight over and continue with canal on the right	Track bears left temporarily leaving the canal and passing 2 farms before retuning to the canal-side	S	1
03A1.012	1300	8.5	Bear left away from the canal	Chemin de Halte, houses on the right	S	2
03A1.013	800	9.3	Continue straight ahead on the track		S	1
03A1.014	2000	11.3	On entering Guînes, at the T-junction with rue Léo Lagrange, turn right		SW	8
03A1.015	220	11.5	At the roundabout turn right	Towards the Office de Tourisme	NW	10
03A1.016	270	11.8	At the T-junction turn left	Rue Massenet	SW	10
03A1.017	120	11.9	Arrive in the centre of Guînes	Beside clock tower and Office de Tourisme		11

Alternate Route #03.A2　　　　　　　　**Length: 16.2km**

Stage Summary: cyclist and horse-riders route to Wissant

Stage Ascent: 214m　　　　　　　　**Stage Descent: 203m**

Waypoint	Distance between waypoints	Total km	Directions	Verification Point	Compass	Altitude m
03A2.001	0	0.0	Turn left on avenue de la Plage	Towards cemetery	S	5
03A2.002	150	0.2	At the crossroads turn right on rue Vigier	Keep cemetery to the right	W	6
03A2.003	1000	1.1	Turn sharp left on rue du Fort Lapin	Path from the beach on the right	S	6
03A2.004	160	1.3	Turn right onto the D940, road runs parallel to the beach	After Sangatte look to the right for the white cliffs of Dover	SW	4
03A2.005	9200	10.4	At the crossroads in Escalles turn right onto rue de la Mer, remain on D940	Keep hotel to the left	SW	39
03A2.006	3700	14.1	Beside the junction to your left, continue straight ahead on the D940	Direction Wissant, the main road bears right	SW	30
03A2.007	1100	15.2	Fork right on rue Paul Crampel	Towards Wissant Centre	W	32
03A2.008	900	16.1	In the place Edouard Houssin turn left	Towards Hôtel de la Plage	SW	16
03A2.009	130	16.2	Arrive in the centre of Wissant	Place de la Mairie		15

Centre Européen de Séjour,116 rue du Marechal de Lattre de Tassigny,62100 Calais,Pas de Calais,France; Tel:+33(0)3 21 34 70 20; Email:adjcalais@ wanadoo.fr; Web-site:www.auberge-jeunesse-calais.com; Price:B

Hôtel Victoria,10 rue Madrid,62100 Calais,Pas de Calais,France; Tel:+33(0)3 21 34 38 32; Price:B

Hotel Folkestone,28 rue Royale,62100 Calais,Pas de Calais,France; Tel:+33(0)3 21 34 63 26; +33(0)3 59 44 08 23; Price:B

Hotel Bonsai,Quai du Danube,62100 Calais,Pas de Calais,France; Tel:+33(0)3 21 96 10 10; Price:B

Chambres d'Hôtes du Cap Blanc Nez,(Mme Arlette Cordonnier),8 route de Peuplingues,62179 Escalles,Pas de Calais,France; Tel:+33(0)3 21 36 21 16; +33(0)6 75 29 81 86; Email:capblancnez@free.fr; Web-site:capblancnez.free.fr; Price:B

Chambres d'Hôtes - Ferme de l'Église,(Boutroy Larue Eric),Rue de l'Eglise,62179 Escalles,Pas de Calais,France; Tel:+33(0)3 21 85 20 19; +33(0)6 07 74 24 16; Email:info@ferme-eglise.com ; Web-site:www.chambres-hotes-blanc-nez.com; Price:B

Hôtel de la Plage,1 place Édouard Houssin,62179 Wissant,Pas de Calais,France; Tel:+33(0)3 21 35 91 87; Web-site:www.hotelplage-wissant.com; Price:A

Le Normandy Hôtel,Place de Verdun,62179 Wissant,Pas de Calais,France; Tel:+33(0)3 21 35 90 11; +33(0)3 21 82 19 08; Email:hnormandy@wanadoo.fr; Web-site:www.lenormandy-wissant.com; Price:A

Chambres d'Hôtes - Chez Edwige,9 rue Gambetta,62179 Wissant,Pas de Calais,France; Tel:+33(0)3 21 35 95 84; Email:chezedwige@wanadoo.fr; Web-site:www.chezedwige.com; Price:B

Hotel - le Vivier,3 rue Gambetta,62179 Wissant,Pas de Calais,France; Tel:+33(0)3 21 35 93 61; Email:le.vivier@wanadoo.fr; Web-site:www.levivier.com; Price:B

Chambres d'Hôtes la Leulène,708 rue Principale,62179 Hervelinghen,Pas de Calais,France; Tel:+33(0)3 21 97 98 70; +33(0)6 20 17 07 11; Email:catherine. louchez@laleulene.com; Web-site:www.laleulene.com; Price:A

Gîtes Ruraux - les Santolines,301 rue de la Vallée,62250 Audembert,Pas de Calais,France; Tel:+33(0)3 21 91 70 01; +33(0)6 70 82 37 94; Email:les.santolines@free.f

Camping du Fort Lapin,Route Nationale,62231 Sangatte,Pas de Calais,France; Tel:+33(0)3 21 97 67 77; Price:C

Camping Côte d'Opale-le Blanc Nez,18 rue Mer,62179 Escalles,Pas de Calais,France; Tel:+33(0)3 21 85 27 38; Email:camping.blancnez@laposte.net; Web-site:camping.blancnez.free.fr; Price:C; Note:Chalets, mobile homes and rooms also available to rent,

Camping de la Vallée,901 rue Principale,62179 Hervelinghen,Pas de Calais,France; Tel:+33(0)3 21 36 73 96; Web-site:www.campingdelavallee.net; Price:C

Centre Equestre de Calais,390 route Gravelines,62100 Calais,Pas de Calais,France; Tel:+33(0)3 21 19 29 38

Centre Equestre de Calais,390 route Gravelines,62100 Calais,Pas de Calais,France; Tel:+33(0)3 21 19 29 38

Cheval Loisir,182 route Gravelines,62100 Calais,Pas de Calais,France; Tel:+33(0)3 21 97 18 18

Les Caleches d Opale,1197 Digue Gaston Berthe,62100 Calais,Pas de Calais,France; +33(0)6 10 28 86 73

Poney-Club Jules Verne,133 rue Jules Verne 62730 Marck,62100 Calais,Pas de Calais,France; Tel:+33(0)3 21 82 90 13

Office du Tourisme,12 Boulevard Clémenceau,62100 Calais,Pas de Calais,France; Tel:+33(0)3 21 96 62 40

Office du Tourisme,Place Mairie,62179 Wissant,Pas de Calais,France; Tel:+33(0)3 21 82 48 00

Crédit Mutuel,36 rue Royale,62100 Calais,Pas de Calais,France; Tel:+33(0)8 20 35 20 52

LCL,2 rue Royale,62100 Calais,Pas de Calais,France; Tel:+33(0)8 20 82 31 06

BNP Paribas,92 Boulevard Jacquard,62100 Calais,Pas de Calais,France; Tel:+33(0)8 20 82 00 01

Société Générale,76 Boulevard Jacquard,62100 Calais,Pas de Calais,France; Tel:+33(0)3 21 46 74 00

Crédit du Nord,75 Boulevard Jacquard,62100 Calais,Pas de Calais,France; Tel:+33(0)3 21 85 94 94

Crédit Mutuel,2 Boulevard Pasteur,62100 Calais,Pas de Calais,France; Tel:+33(0)8 20 35 20 49

BNP Paribas,65 Boulevard de l'Égalité,62100 Calais,Pas de Calais,France; Tel:+33(0)8 20 82 00 01

Crédit Mutuel,117 Boulevard Egalité,62100 Calais,Pas de Calais,France; Tel:+33(0)8 20 35 20 50

Myferrylink,Nouveau Terminal Car Ferry,62100 Calais,Pas de Calais,France; Tel:+33(0)8 11 65 47 65; Email:clientservices@myferrylink.com; Web-site:www.myferrylink.com

Port de Calais,Avenue du Commandant Cousteau,62104 Calais,Pas de Calais,France; Tel:+33(0)3 21 46 00 00; Web-site:www.calais-port.fr

Gare SNCF,46 avenue du Président Wilson,62100 Calais,Pas de Calais,France; Tel:+33(0)8 92 33 53 35; Web-site:www.sncf.fr

P&O Ferries,Car Ferry Terminal,62100 Calais,Pas de Calais,France;
Tel:+33(0)8 25 12 01 56

Centre Hospitalier,11 Quai du Commerce,62100 Calais,Pas de Calais,France;
Tel:+33(0)3 21 46 33 33

Jean-Marie Claudine,13 rue Temple,62100 Calais,Pas de Calais,France;
Tel:+33(0)3 21 97 82 00

Coupin Jean-Pierre,Rue Tennis,62179 Wissant,Pas de Calais,France;
Tel:+33(0)3 21 35 91 56

Lescaillez Dominique,24 rue Louise Ball Demont,62179 Wissant,Pas de
Calais,France; Tel:+33(0)3 21 35 92 28

Delval Gernez Valerie Emmanuelle,11 place Crèvecoeur,62100 Calais,Pas de
Calais,France; Tel:+33(0)3 21 00 71 01

Brame Sports,Rue Gutenberg,62100 Calais,Pas de Calais,France;
Tel:+33(0)3 21 34 55 48

Allo Taxi Calais,35 rue Félix Cadras,62100 Calais,Pas de Calais,France;
Tel:+33(0)3 21 17 36 94

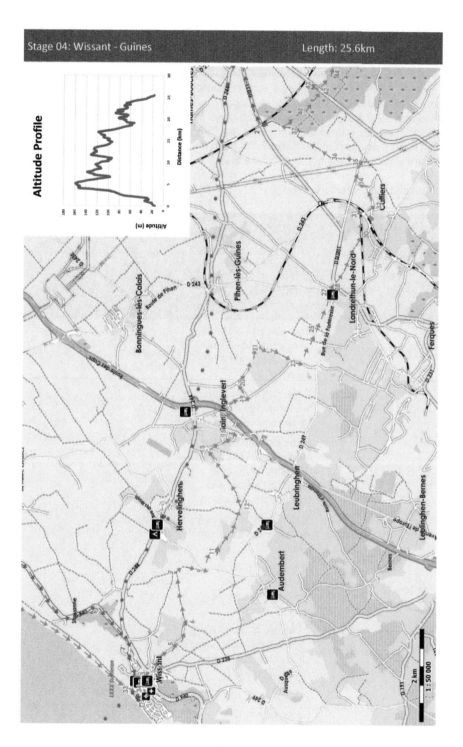

Stage Summary: the route follows the GR145/128 on farm and forest tracks and climbs Mont de Couple, before entering la Forêt Domaniale de Guînes. In common with many of the forest paths, you will encounter muddy conditions in all but the driest periods and with the risk of the GR signs being obscured by new tree growth. It is advisable to follow the guide instructions with care. The "Official Route" bypasses Guînes(LXXVII) but offers a circuitous route "'variante" to reach the facilities of the town. An Alternate Route provides more direct access to the town.

Distance from Canterbury: 52km   Distance to Besançon: 858km
Stage Ascent: 412m   Stage Descent: 412m

Waypoint	Distance between waypoints	Total km	Directions	Verification Point	Compass	Altitude m
04.001	0	0.0	From place de la Mairie (beside the church) take rue du Lieutenant André Baude	Entrance to the Mairie directly behind, GR sign	E	17
04.002	90	0.1	At the foot of the short hill, fork right on rue Ferdinand Buisson	VF sign	SE	15
04.003	150	0.2	At the junction with the main road (D940), beside the traffic lights, take the zebra crossing and continue straight ahead	Towards Herlen, VF sign	SE	18
04.004	230	0.5	At the junction continue straight ahead on chemin d'Herlen	Direction Herlen, no through road, VF sign	SE	19
04.005	700	1.2	At the crossroads with the track, continue straight ahead on the road	Yellow VF sign on your left	SE	32
04.006	600	1.8	Immediately after passing the stone farm buildings on your left, turn left on the gravel track	Yellow VF sign	E	31
04.007	1100	2.9	At the T-junction in the tracks, turn right	Direction Mont de Couple, yellow VF sign	S	80

43

Waypoint	Distance between waypoints	Total km	Directions	Verification Point	Compass	Altitude m
04.008	600	3.5	At the T-junction with a tarmac road, turn right	View of Wissant and the coast on your right, GR sign	S	96
04.009	100	3.6	Turn left, uphill on the track	Yellow VF sign	SE	96
04.010	500	4.0	Continue straight ahead up the steep incline	Concrete bunker on your right	SE	137
04.011	110	4.1	At the T-junction at the top of the hill turn left	Pass the monument on the summit to your right, GR145 sign	SE	152
04.012	1100	5.3	At the crossroads in the track, turn left on the gravel track	The bell tower of the Calais Mairie is visible on the left, yellow VF sign	NE	159
04.013	1500	6.7	At the T-junction at the foot of the hill, turn right on the tarmac road	Yellow VF sign	SE	96
04.014	500	7.3	At the junction in the centre of Hauteville, turn left	Pass a sign for rue du Moulin on your right, GR sign	E	125
04.015	140	7.4	At the T-junction with the main road in Hauteville turn right and continue beside the road	Towards the tabac, GR sign	S	125
04.016	300	7.7	Just before the brow of the hill, turn left onto a gravel track	House n°114 on your right at the junction, yellow VF sign	NE	134
04.017	800	8.5	At the junction, continue straight ahead on the partially tarmaced track	Motorway close on your right	NE	121
04.018	240	8.7	At the T-junction with the tarmac road, turn right and pass under the motorway	Yellow VF sign	S	112

Waypoint	Distance between waypoints	Total km	Directions	Verification Point	Compass	Altitude m
04.019	700	9.4	Shortly after the road bends to the left, turn left onto the gravel track between the fields. Note:- the "Official Route" makes a tour of the fields and woods to your left and returns to this road 1300m ahead. By remaining on the road you can reduce your journey by 1500m	Yellow VF sign	NE	120
04.020	400	9.8	At the T-junction, turn right	Towards wind-generators in the distance, yellow VF sign	SE	118
04.021	1000	10.8	At the T-junction in the tracks, turn right on the broad track	Yellow VF sign	S	96
04.022	900	11.7	At the T-junction, bear left to rejoin the tarmac road	Yellow VF sign	SW	123
04.023	130	11.8	Just before the brow of the hill turn left on the track between the fields	Towards the wind generators and mobile phone tower, yellow VF sign beyond the junction	SE	131
04.024	600	12.4	At the crossroads in the tracks, continue straight ahead	Towards the church steeple, VF sign	SE	124
04.025	280	12.7	At the next crossroads, again continue straight ahead	Towards the church steeple, yellow VF sign	E	121
04.026	700	13.4	At the T-junction with the road, turn left beside the road into Landrethun-le-Nord	Yellow VF sign	E	125

Waypoint	Distance between waypoints	Total km	Directions	Verification Point	Compass	Altitude m
04.027	160	13.5	At the roundabout beside the church, continue straight ahead	Direction Guînes, yellow VF sign	SE	122
04.028	140	13.7	Turn right on the gravel track	Beside the calvaire	SE	119
04.029	90	13.7	At the crossroads with a main road, continue straight ahead on the track between the fields	Towards distant church spire	SE	115
04.030	1300	15.0	At the junction beside the tunnel under the railway, continue straight ahead on the broad track	Keep the railway on your right	E	96
04.031	500	15.5	At the T-junction with the D250, turn right beside the road and cross the railway	Village of Caffiers, yellow VF sign	SE	98
04.032	400	15.8	Beside the bar, turn left	Pass the church on your right, yellow VF sign	E	108
04.033	400	16.2	At the junction immediately after passing the château, bear left towards the large pylons	GR sign	NE	108
04.034	400	16.6	At the T-junction, turn right	Pass under the electricity lines, yellow VF sign	E	113
04.035	500	17.0	Under the electricity lines, turn left onto a gravel track	Yellow VF sign	N	117
04.036	800	17.8	At the junction, continue straight ahead towards the woods. Avoid the farm track on the left	Electricity line parallel to track ahead	NE	87

Waypoint	Distance between waypoints	Total km	Directions	Verification Point	Compass	Altitude m
04.037	1000	18.8	At the T-junction, with the woods directly ahead, turn left	Yellow VF sign	N	60
04.038	400	19.2	As the railway pylons come into view turn sharp right into the woods on the partially hidden track. Note:- the "Official Route" and "variante" to Guînes follow a dog-leg route through the sometimes difficult forest tracks. The distance to Guînes can be reduced by 3km by following the Alternate Route	Yellow VF sign	S	53
04.039	50	19.3	At the T-junction in the woods, bear right and then immediately bear left	Yellow VF sign	SE	58
04.040	600	19.9	At the T-junction in the tracks, turn right	Broad track	SW	67
04.041	80	19.9	Turn left into the woods	VF and Piste Equestre signs	SE	72
04.042	600	20.5	At the T-junction with the very busy road, turn left beside the road	VF sign	NE	79
04.043	200	20.7	Immediately before reaching the crash barriers, turn sharp right into the forest	GR sign	SE	66
04.044	600	21.2	At the crossroads with a broad forest track, continue straight ahead on the narrow track which bears slightly to the left		E	73

Waypoint	Distance between waypoints	Total km	Directions	Verification Point	Compass	Altitude m
04.045	400	21.6	At the crossroads in the track, continue straight ahead	At the time of writing there was a fallen tree partially blocking the way	E	86
04.046	120	21.7	At the T-junction with the broader track, turn right on the stony track	Metal barrier and centre equestre to your left at the junction	SE	81
04.047	80	21.8	At the crossroads in the tracks, continue straight ahead on the small track	Yellow VF sign	SE	80
04.048	600	22.4	At the T-junction with the road, turn left to follow the "Official Route" – "variante" to the centre of Guînes		N	71
04.049	600	22.9	After descending from the railway bridge, turn sharp left on the small tarmac road	Yellow VF sign	S	67
04.050	150	23.1	At the end of the track, facing the fencing beside the railway, turn right on the very narrow track	Yellow VF sign, keep the fencing immediately on your left	NW	67
04.051	600	23.7	Bear right on the broad track between the fields	Towards the white house	NE	67
04.052	500	24.1	Bear left to remain on the broad track	Pass the white house on your right	N	56
04.053	1100	25.2	At the T-junction with the main road, turn right towards the centre of Guînes	Yellow VF sign	NE	25
04.054	400	25.6	Arrive at Guînes (LXXVIII) beside the crossroads	Bar at the junction, Office du Tourisme and other facilities ahead on rue de Guizelin		17

| Alternate Route #04.A1 | | | | Length: 2.5km | | |

Stage Summary: shorter approach to Guînes centre by the D231 avoiding dog leg through the forest

Stage Ascent: 10m   **Stage Descent: 47m**

Waypoint	Distance between waypoints	Total km	Directions	Verification Point	Compass	Altitude m
04A1.001	0	0.0	Continue straight ahead towards the railway track and then bear left	Forest initially on your right	N	52
04A1.002	500	0.4	Descend the embankment towards the main road and then turn right and proceed with care beside the road	Pass under the railway	E	44
04A1.003	1700	2.1	At the roundabout take the second exit towards Guînes centre	Pass la Bien Assise on your right	E	11
04A1.004	400	2.5	Arrive in Guînes (LXXVIII) at the end of the stage beside the crossroads	Bar at the junction, turn left for the Office du Tourisme		15

Accommodation & Facilities .... Wissant - Guines

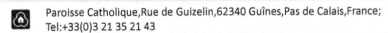

Paroisse Catholique,Rue de Guizelin,62340 Guînes,Pas de Calais,France; Tel:+33(0)3 21 35 21 43

Chambres d 'Hôtes - la Labigeoise,31 rue des Fermettes,62250 Saint-Inglevert,Pas de Calais,France; Tel:+33(0)3 21 82 19 29; +33(0)6 25 71 52 29; Email:lalabigeoise@aol.fr; Web-site:www.lalabigeoise.com; Price:B

La Forge - Chambres d'Hôtes,32 rue de Guizelin,62340 Guînes,Pas de Calais,France; Tel:+33(0)3 21 34 70 14; +33(0)6 61 86 44 50; +33(0)6 62 99 44 50; Email:la_forge_2@hotmail.fr; Web-site:www.chambrehotelaforge.com; Price:B; PR

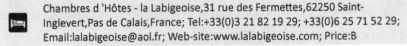

Auberge du Colombier,Bien Assise avenue Verdun,62340 Guînes,Pas de Calais,France; Tel:+33(0)3 21 36 93 00; Web-site:www.aubergeducolombier. com; Price:A; Note:Price Group B in low season,

Chambres d'Hotes – la Ferme du Dizacre,(Chantal & Gérald Leleu),4 la Baronnerie,62250 Leubringhen,Pas de Calais,France; Tel:+33(0)3 21 33 70 76; Price:A

Chambres d'Hôtes - Chantebise,8 rue du 8 Mai 1945,62250 Landrethun-le-Nord,Pas de Calais,France; Tel:+33(0)3 21 33 64 42; +33(0)6 26 10 69 64; Email:chantebise@hotmail.fr; Price:B

Camping la Bien Assise,Rd231, la Bien Assise,62340 Guînes,Pas de Calais,France; Tel:+33(0)3 21 35 20 77; Email:castels@bien-assise.com; Web-site:www.camping-la-bien-assise.comr; Price:C; Note:Can also provide rooms with advanced booking and presentation of credentials,

Lepretre Magali,Route Moulin À Corneilles,62340 Guînes,Pas de Calais,France; Tel:+33(0)3 21 85 78 34

Office du Tourisme,14 rue Clemenceau,62340 Guînes,Pas de Calais,France; Tel:+33(0)3 21 35 73 73

Crédit Agricole,29 rue Georges Clemenceau,62340 Guînes,Pas de Calais,France; Tel:+33(0)3 21 35 20 61

Hillebrante Gérard,39 Boulevard Blanchard,62340 Guînes,Pas de Calais,France; Tel:+33(0)3 21 35 23 60

Cadet Jean Paul,1 place d Angerville,62340 Guînes,Pas de Calais,France; Tel:+33(0)3 21 36 89 39

Cadet Jean Paul,1 place d Angerville,62340 Guînes,Pas de Calais,France; Tel:+33(0)3 21 36 89 39

Taxis des Trois Pays,34 rue Georges Clemenceau,62340 Guines,Pas de Calais,France; Tel:+33(0)3 21 19 60 06

Taxi de la Leulene,178 route de Bonningues,62231 Peuplingues,Pas de Calais,France; Tel:+33(0)3 21 85 21 60

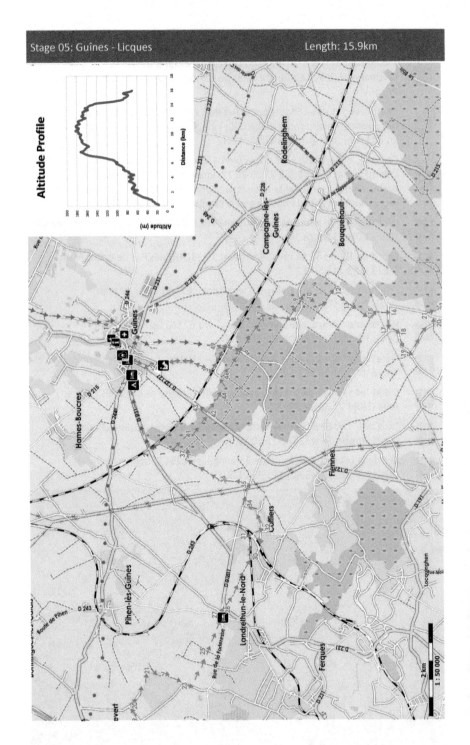

Altitude Profile

Stage Summary: the route retraces its path towards the TGV track and re-enters the Forêt Dominiale de Guînes and then continues generally on broad farm tracks following the GR145/128 to the small town of Licques

Distance from Canterbury: 78km
Distance to Besançon: 832km
Stage Ascent: 271m
Stage Descent: 219m

Waypoint	Distance between waypoints	Total km	Directions	Verification Point	Compass	Altitude m
05.001	0	0.0	From the crossroads of Boulevard Delannoy and Avenue de Verdun, take the D127. Note:- to avoid the very narrow track beside the TGV line cyclists should take the Alternate Route using the tarmac chemin di Bois de Guînes	Direction Hardinghen	SW	17
05.002	400	0.4	Bear left on chemin du Moulin aux Corneilles	Calvaire and wooden footpath sign	S	25
05.003	1500	1.9	On reaching the TGV track, turn left	Proceed close by the railway	SE	67
05.004	600	2.5	Turn left on the track	Keep road parallel on the right	N	67
05.005	170	2.7	Turn sharp right and join the road. Note:- Alternate Route for cyclists joins from the left	Cross railway bridge	S	66
05.006	500	3.2	Beside the picnic ahead, turn left onto the track, follow long straight track through the woods	Pass red and white metal barrier, yellow VF sign	SE	70
05.007	1000	4.2	At the T-junction at the end of the long straight track, turn right on the broad track	Pas de Calais GR sign	S	67

Waypoint	Distance between waypoints	Total km	Directions	Verification Point	Compass	Altitude m
05.008	600	4.8	At the T-junction, turn left, slightly uphill on the gravel track		SE	81
05.009	600	5.4	At the crossroads with a tarmac road, continue straight ahead	Yellow VF sign	SE	89
05.010	110	5.5	At the bottom of the short descent, turn right on the narrow path into the woods. Note:- caution this path is easily missed	Sentier de l'Epinette, cycle route n° 11	S	90
05.011	500	6.0	At the junction with a broad stony track, turn left up the hill on the stony track	Yellow VF sign	SE	100
05.012	400	6.3	Shortly before the top of the rise, following the dip, turn right on a smaller forest track	Yellow VF sign	SW	108
05.013	600	6.9	At the crossroads with a broad grass track, continue straight ahead on the clear, but narrower track		SW	148
05.014	500	7.4	At the crossroads in the track, turn left	Parallel to the edge of the forest, yellow VF sign	SE	169
05.015	200	7.6	Exit from the forest under power lines and beside a metal barrier. Continue on the broad farm track between the fields	Pas de Calais GR sign	S	169
05.016	270	7.9	At the T-junction, turn right onto a minor road towards the farmhouse	GR sign	W	163

Waypoint	Distance between waypoints	Total km	Directions	Verification Point	Compass	Altitude m
05.017	400	8.2	At the T-junction, after the farm buildings - Puits de Sars, turn left, slightly uphill	Wind generators to the right, GR sign	S	156
05.018	200	8.5	Bear right on road	Modern house on left	SW	161
05.019	600	9.0	Immediately after passing Gîte du Mât take the first turning to the left	Yellow VF sign	SE	169
05.020	900	9.9	Turn left onto a deeply rutted track and continue along the edge of woods	VF sign	NE	172
05.021	190	10.1	At the T-junction, turn left beside the D248	Yellow VF sign	NE	176
05.022	80	10.2	Just before the road bends to the left, turn sharp right onto track	GR sign	S	176
05.023	500	10.7	At the T-junction at the foot of the slope, turn right and then immediately left	Towards the houses	S	176
05.024	250	10.9	Just after passing house n° 467, turn left on the broad gravel track	Pass a conifer hedge on your right, yellow VF sign	SE	181
05.025	400	11.4	At the junction, continue straight ahead, avoid sentier du Vontus on the left	GR sign on the tree ahead	SE	174
05.026	400	11.7	At the T-junction, turn left beside the broader tarmac road	Leave chemin d'Eserie, yellow VF signs	SE	177
05.027	400	12.1	Continue straight ahead on the broad stony track	Pass house n° 765	SE	165
05.028	80	12.2	Bear left on the broad gravel track	Yellow VF sign	E	163

Waypoint	Distance between waypoints	Total km	Directions	Verification Point	Compass	Altitude m
05.029	400	12.6	At the junction, continue straight ahead direction Vallée Madame	Ignore the misplaced yellow VF sign	E	167
05.030	400	13.0	Fork right on the track	Remain on the ridge	E	168
05.031	1700	14.7	At the foot of the hill, turn left. Note:- at the time of writing the yellow VF sign had been uprooted	View of Abbaye Notre-Dame de Licques ahead, GR sign	NE	88
05.032	190	14.9	At the junction with the tarmac road, bear left	Keep the Abbaye to your right, faint GR sign	E	86
05.033	300	15.2	At the junction with the main road, just after passing the déchetterie, turn right beside the road	Yellow VF sign	S	79
05.034	400	15.6	At the crossroads beside the Abbaye, turn left beside the D191	Towards Licques centre	E	87
05.035	400	15.9	Arrive at Licques centre	Ivy clad building ahead		69

Alternate Route #05.A1   Length: 2.5km

Stage Summary: shorter approach to Guînes centre by the D231 avoiding dog leg through the forest

Stage Ascent: 10m   Stage Descent: 47m

Waypoint	Distance between waypoints	Total km	Directions	Verification Point	Compass	Altitude m
05A1.001	0	0.0	From the crossroads of Boulevard Delannoy and Avenue de Verdun, take the D231	Towards St Omer	E	17
05A1.002	400	0.4	Shortly after the junction towards the Auberge de Trois Pays, turn right on the small road	Industrial buildings on the right, embankment on your left	S	15

Waypoint	Distance between waypoints	Total km	Directions	Verification Point	Compass	Altitude m
05A1.003	270	0.7	Keep left on the road		S	19
05A1.004	1600	2.3	Continue straight ahead to rejoin the "Official Route"	Towards bridge over the TGV line		65

Accommodation & Facilities .... Guînes - Licques

Gîte Sainte Thérese,54 rue d'Audenfort,62890 Clerques,Pas de Calais,France; Tel:+33(0)3 21 85 07 23; Web-site:www.ardres-tourisme.fr

Auberge du Moulin d'Audenfort,16 Impasse du Gué,62890 Clerques,Pas de Calais,France; Tel:+33(0)3 21 00 13 16; Price:B

Chambres d'Hôtes des Caps et Marais d'Opale,621 rue Haute,62850 Alembon,Pas de Calais,France; Tel:+33(0)3 21 19 99 13; Email:contact@gites-alembon.com; Web-site:www.gites-alembon.com; Price:B

Camping le Canchy,830 rue du Canchy,62850 Licques,Pas de Calais,France; Tel:+33(0)3 21 82 63 41; Web-site:www.camping-lecanchy.com; Price:C; Note:Caravans may also be rented,

Camping les Pommiers des Trois Pays,253 rue du Breuil,62850 Licques,Pas de Calais,France; Tel:+33(0)3 21 35 02 02; Web-site:www.pommiers-3pays.com; Note:Also offers accommodation in chalets,

Rozé Vincent,Rue Courtebourne,62850 Licques,Pas de Calais,France; Tel:+33(0)3 21 35 07 59

Mairie,30 rue Bourg,62850 Licques,Pas de Calais,France; Tel:+33(0)3 21 96 12 20

La Poste,101 rue au Bourg,62850 Licques,Pas de Calais,France; Tel:+33(0)8 00 00 90 42

Clinique Veterinaire Camp Drap d'Or,15 rue A.et G.Parmentier,62850 Licques,Pas de Calais,France; Tel:+33(0)3 21 00 23 09

Denis Jean-Francois Marechal Ferrant,1906 rue Neufchatel,62830 Samer,Pas de Calais,France; Tel:+33(0)3 21 33 55 89

Baron Franck,127 rue A.et G.Parmentier,62850 Licques,Pas de Calais,France; Tel:+33(0)6 03 28 91 31

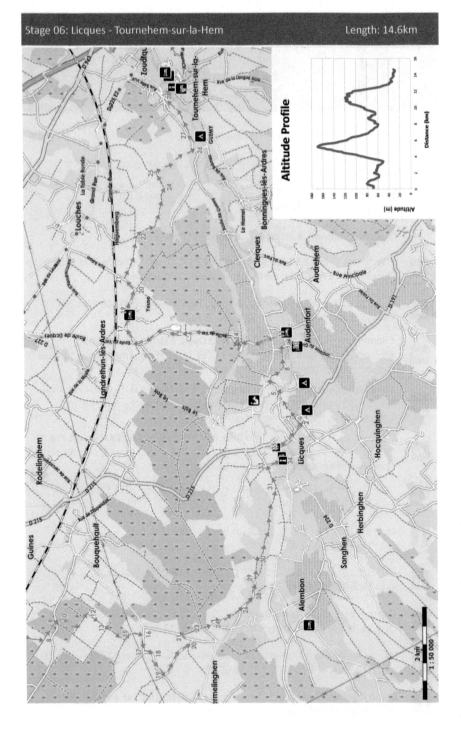

Altitude Profile

Stage Summary: the "Official Route" makes a wide loop to Tournehem-sur-le-Hem crossing and recrossing the ridge on the north side of the Hem valley. The section generally continues to follow the established route of the GR128 on quiet country roads and farm tracks which should offer pleasant travelling for walkers, cyclists and riders.

Distance from Canterbury: 94km   Distance to Besançon: 832km
Stage Ascent: 250m   Stage Descent: 289m

Waypoint	Distance between waypoints	Total km	Directions	Verification Point	Compass	Altitude m
06.001	0	0.0	At the T-junction beside the ivy covered building take the D191	Direction St Omer	SE	69
06.002	700	0.7	At the crossroads, shortly after the top of the hill, turn left on rue de la Commune	Keep Calvaire on the right and sports ground on the left, yellow VF sign	NE	79
06.003	210	0.9	With the children's playground on your left, take the right fork on the track	Impasse des Noisetiers, yellow VF sign	NE	76
06.004	600	1.5	At the T-junction with the tarmac road, turn right beside the road	House n° 561 ahead, GR sign	E	58
06.005	50	1.6	At the junction, continue straight ahead beside the road	Avoid rue de Canchy on the right	NE	58
06.006	400	1.9	Where the road, bends to the left, turn right onto a broad stony track	Pass farm building on the left, yellow VF sign	E	67
06.007	130	2.1	Take the right fork		SE	63
06.008	300	2.4	Continue straight ahead avoiding the track on the right	GR sign	E	63

Waypoint	Distance between waypoints	Total km	Directions	Verification Point	Compass	Altitude m
06.009	500	2.8	At the T-junction with road, turn right down the hill towards the hamlet of Audenfort. Note:- at the time of writing a section of track ahead was overgrown and impassable. To avoid this risk, turn left up the hill and then right at the T-junction and rejoin the "Official Route" by turning left at the next junction on route du Val	Yellow VF sign	S	61
06.010	210	3.0	At the T-junction at the foot of the hill, turn left	Towards the Gîte St. Thérèse	E	54
06.011	260	3.3	With house n° 49 on your left, fork left on rue du Calvaire	Yellow VF sign	N	50
06.012	160	3.5	On the crown of the bend to the right, leave the road and take the track directly ahead uphill. Note:- at the time of writing the track was totally overgrown. It is possible to bypass the track by remaining on the road to the T-junction and then turn left to reach the next waypoint at the end of the track where you should turn right on route du Val		N	55
06.013	240	3.7	At the crossroads with the main road, continue straight ahead on route du Val, and climb the hill	GR sign	N	73
06.014	1400	5.1	At the top of the hill, continue straight ahead beside the road. Note:- the GR128 leaves to the left and rejoins the road at the next waypoint	Ferme du Mont on your right, yellow VF sign	N	169
06.015	1100	6.2	In le Val continue straight ahead on the road	GR sign	N	109

Waypoint	Distance between waypoints	Total km	Directions	Verification Point	Compass	Altitude m
06.016	1200	7.4	At the junction in West Yeuse, turn right on rue de la Chapelle	House n° 642 on your left, yellow VF sign	NE	66
06.017	400	7.8	At the junction at the entry to Yeuse bear right into the centre of the village	Rue de la Chapelle	E	59
06.018	250	8.1	In the centre of Yeuse fork left, pass the chapel on your right	Ferme Auberge au Flot de Yeuse to the right	E	65
06.019	160	8.2	At the road junction, bear left	Keep house n° 790 on your right, GR sign	E	64
06.020	500	8.7	Turn left remaining on the road and avoid the 2 tracks to the right	Broken yellow VF sign	NE	77
06.021	400	9.1	Shortly before reaching the bridge over the TGV track, turn right on the broad stony track	Towards the woods, yellow VF sign	E	67
06.022	1000	10.1	Bear right on the broad gravel track, avoid the turning to the left	Keep the large woods close on the right, yellow VF sign	SE	90
06.023	500	10.5	Turn left on the broad track, avoid the tracks into the woods	Yellow VF sign	E	111
06.024	900	11.4	Continue straight ahead on the track	Pass la Chapelle St Louis on your right	NE	113
06.025	400	11.8	At the foot of the hill, bear left and then turn right on to the road	D225 downhill towards Guémy, yellow VF sign	SE	106
06.026	1100	12.9	In Guémy take first road to the left	Route de Guémy, yellow VF sign	E	37

Waypoint	Distance between waypoints	Total km	Directions	Verification Point	Compass	Altitude m
06.027	400	13.3	After passing the attractive farm buildings on your right, leave the road and take the track to the right	Beside a line of mature trees, yellow VF sign	NE	34
06.028	1100	14.3	At the T-junction at the end of rue des Prés du Roi in Tournehem-sur-la-Hem turn right	Towards the bridge, yellow VF sign	SE	30
06.029	260	14.6	At the T-junction, after crossing the river Hem, turn left	Direction St Omer, GR sign	E	29
06.030	70	14.6	Arrive at Tournehem-sur-la-Hem centre in place de la Comtesse Mahaut d'Artois	Café and Mairie beside the place		30

Accommodation & Facilities .... Licques - Tournehem-sur-la-Hem

Auberge - au Flot de Yeuse,90 rue des Jonquilles,62610 Landrethun-les-Ardres,Pas de Calais,France; Tel:+33(0)3 21 35 07 93; Price:A; Note:Accommodation in a gipsy caravan,

Hotel Bal,500 rue du Vieux Château,62890 Tournehem-sur-la-Hem,Pas de Calais,France; Tel:+33(0)3 21 35 65 90; Email:contact@hotel-bal.com; Website:www.hotel-bal.com; Price:B

Chambres d'Hôtes - Lysensoone,30 rue de Valenciennes,62890 Tournehem-sur-la-Hem,Pas de Calais,France; Tel:+33(0)3 21 35 60 56; Price:B

Bal Parc Camping,291 rue du Vieux Château,62890 Tournehem-sur-la-Hem,Pas de Calais,France; Tel:+33(0)3 21 35 65 90; Price:C; Note:Mobile homes may also be available,

Le Fond d'Ecambre Camping,Guémy,62890 Tournehem-sur-la-Hem,Pas de Calais,France; Tel:+33(0)3 21 85 19 03; Price:C

Lasvignes Olivia,Rue de la Grasse Payelle,62370 Zutkerque,Pas de Calais,France; +33(0)6 70 44 27 98

Mairie,4 place Comtesse Mahaut d'Artois,62890 Tournehem-sur-la-Hem,Pas de Calais,France; Tel:+33(0)3 21 35 61 34

Altitude Profile

Stage Summary: another section on small country roads and farm tracks over rolling countryside which offers easy going for all groups. Th route briefly intersects with la Leulene – the ancient road and pilgrim trail from Sangatte.

Distance from Canterbury: 108km   Distance to Besançon: 801km
Stage Ascent: 371m   Stage Descent: 301m

Waypoint	Distance between waypoints	Total km	Directions	Verification Point	Compass	Altitude m
07.001	0	0.0	From the Mairie in the place turn right and take the second road on the right	Rue de Broukerque	SW	31
07.002	170	0.2	At the T-junction, beside the bus shelter, turn left	Keep the church on your left, Yellow VF sign	SE	33
07.003	100	0.3	As the main road turns to the right, turn left and then immediately right. Note:- the GR128 and GR145 separate at this point, we will continue on the GR145	Direction Nort-Leulinghem, GR 145 and yellow VF signs	E	37
07.004	300	0.6	Take the left fork, chemin de St Omer	Yellow VF sign	E	60
07.005	400	1.0	As the road begins to turn right, turn left on the stony track downhill. Note:- your distance can be reduced by 600m and a stiff climb avoided by remaining on the road and keeping left at the next junction. The "Official Route" will rejoin the road from the left in 800m	Towards the caravan park, yellow VF sign	NE	67

63

Waypoint	Distance between waypoints	Total km	Directions	Verification Point	Compass	Altitude m
07.006	700	1.6	At the T-junction in the tracks, turn right, uphill	GR sign	SE	54
07.007	700	2.3	At the T-junction with the small road turn left	Yellow VF sign	E	96
07.008	400	2.6	Turn right onto a grass track	Towards the woods and the former windmill in the valley	S	93
07.009	300	2.9	Beside the woods bear left	Parallel to the motorway	SE	82
07.010	170	3.1	At the junction with the small tarmac road, continue straight ahead on the stony track	Towards the windmill, yellow VF sign	SE	69
07.011	600	3.7	At the crossroads in the tracks, shortly after passing the windmill, bear slightly right on the minor track between the hedges	Village of Nort-Leulinghem to the left, GR sign	SE	68
07.012	220	3.9	At the crossroads with a tarmac road on the edge of Nort-Leulinghem continue straight ahead on the broad stony track	Yellow VF sign	SE	61
07.013	700	4.6	At the crossroads with D221, cross straight over and continue on the gravel track	Motorway visible on the brow to the left, yellow VF sign	SE	79
07.014	500	5.0	At the T-junction at the top of the hill, turn right		SW	71
07.015	300	5.3	At the T-junction, turn sharp left on the D222, uphill	Yellow VF sign	E	73

Waypoint	Distance between waypoints	Total km	Directions	Verification Point	Compass	Altitude m
07.016	1100	6.4	After crossing the motorway turn right at the first crossroads, downhill	Direction Culem, pass quarry on your left	S	73
07.017	700	7.1	At the bottom of the hill, where the road turns right, take the second track on the left up hill	Woods on your right, yellow VF sign	E	56
07.018	900	8.0	At the junction in the tracks, continue straight ahead downhill on the stony track	Towards the road	SE	85
07.019	500	8.4	At road junction, cross straight over and continue on the stony track uphill	Yellow VF sign	SE	62
07.020	1000	9.5	At the junction in the tracks, continue straight ahead. Note:- there are some confusing GR signs that should be ignored at this point	Up the hill	S	75
07.021	400	9.9	At the crossroads with the D207 turn left beside the road. Note:- 800m may be saved by continuing straight ahead on the road, the "Official Route" will rejoin from the left 300m after the church	Village of Moringhem to the right, yellow VF sign	E	59
07.022	400	10.3	Turn right, downhill on the stony track	La Leulene milestone on your right, yellow VF sign	SE	51
07.023	240	10.5	Continue straight ahead	Uphill	SE	45

Waypoint	Distance between waypoints	Total km	Directions	Verification Point	Compass	Altitude m
07.024	400	10.9	At the T-junction at the top of the hill, turn right		SW	69
07.025	500	11.4	At the T-junction, turn left	Yellow VF sign	SE	85
07.026	80	11.5	At the junction in the tracks, continue straight ahead downhill	Avoid the track leading to the windmill	SE	84
07.027	400	11.9	At the end of the track, turn left		NE	62
07.028	250	12.1	Bear right onto the more defined track, uphill	Woods initially on your left, yellow VF sign	SE	56
07.029	500	12.6	Continue straight ahead, uphill on the tarmac track	Yellow VF sign	SE	72
07.030	700	13.2	At the crossroads with rue de Cormette, continue straight ahead on rue Saint Lambert	Direction Cormette, yellow VF sign	E	78
07.031	240	13.5	With the church on your left, bear left	Yellow VF sign	NE	64
07.032	200	13.7	Bear right on the road downhill, between the trees	Yellow VF sign	SE	61
07.033	400	14.1	Turn right onto the grass track	Yellow VF sign	SW	52
07.034	600	14.7	At the T-junction with the road turn right	Yellow VF sign	SW	84
07.035	300	15.0	Turn left on the D212E2	Direction Leulinghem, yellow VF sign	SE	90

Waypoint	Distance between waypoints	Total km	Directions	Verification Point	Compass	Altitude m
07.036	130	15.1	Turn right on chemin des Marronniers. Note:- approximately 1.5km may be saved by remaining on the D212e2 - route de Leuline, until the "Official Route" rejoins from the right prior to crossing the D942 and entering Wisques	Yellow VF sign	SW	92
07.037	700	15.8	At the crossroads, continue straight ahead	Chambres d'hôtes and boulangerie on your left	SW	102
07.038	120	15.9	With house n° 45 on your left, turn left on the road	Yellow VF sign	SE	103
07.039	500	16.4	At the T-junction, with a radio mast visible ahead, turn right on the road	Yellow VF sign	SW	99
07.040	500	16.9	At the crossroads with a major road, continue straight ahead on the D212	Direction Leulinghem, yellow VF sign	SE	92
07.041	290	17.2	At the crossroads beside the church in Leulinhem, continue straight ahead and climb the hill on the D212	Pass the church close on your right	E	92
07.042	1200	18.4	At the T-junction with the D212e2, turn right. Note:- direct route rejoins from the left	Direction Wisques	SE	99
07.043	500	18.9	At the crossroads, continue straight ahead on the D212	Direction Wisques, GR sign	SE	91
07.044	290	19.2	Arrive at Wisques	Entrance to Abbaye St. Paul on the left		101

Abbaye Saint Paul de Wisques,Rue Ecole,62219 Wisques,Pas de Calais,France; Tel:+33(0)3 21 11 09 21; Web-site:www.abbaye-saint-paul-wisques.com

Abbaye Notre Dame,24 rue Fontaine,62219 Wisques,Pas de Calais,France; Tel:+33(0)3 21 95 57 30; Email:ndwisques@wanadoo.fr; Web-site:arras. catholique.fr; Price:D

Paroisse Catholique,Résidence Marie Curie,62570 Wizernes,Pas de Calais,France; Tel:+33(0)3 21 93 81 41

Chambres d'Hôtes - la Ferme Marcotte,(Thouvenin Béatrice),2 Bis Chemin Lilas,62500 Zudausques,Pas de Calais,France; Tel:+33(0)3 21 88 96 43; +33(0)6 81 10 38 22; Email:be.thouvenin@laposte.net; Web-site:www.ferme-marcotte.fr; Price:B; Note:Will provide meal if request in advance. Pension for horses can be arranged, ; PR

Gîte - Claude Deneuville,49 rue Principale,62380 Acquin-Westbécourt,Pas de Calais,France; Tel:+33(0)3 21 39 62 57

Hotel - la Sapinière,12 route Setques,62219 Wisques,Pas de Calais,France; Tel:+33(0)3 21 38 94 00; Web-site:sapiniere.net; Price:A

Chambre d'Hôtes - Duflot,(Mme Annick Duflos),11 rue du Moulin Leuillieux,62570 Hallines,Pas de Calais,France; Tel:+33(0)7 81 75 53 40; +33(0)0 32 19 59 56 0; Email:annickduflos@voila.fr; Price:B

Mairie,Rue Ecole,62219 Wisques,Pas de Calais,France; Tel:+33(0)3 21 93 45 57

Credit Agricole,1 rue Léon Blum,62570 Wizernes,Pas de Calais,France; Tel:+33(0)3 21 93 85 03

Caisse d'Epargne,8 place Jean Jaurès,62570 Wizernes,Pas de Calais,France; Tel:+33(0)8 20 83 00 80

Lemas Paul,6 Chemin des Berceaux,62219 Longuenesse,Pas de Calais,France; Tel:+33(0)3 21 88 24 62

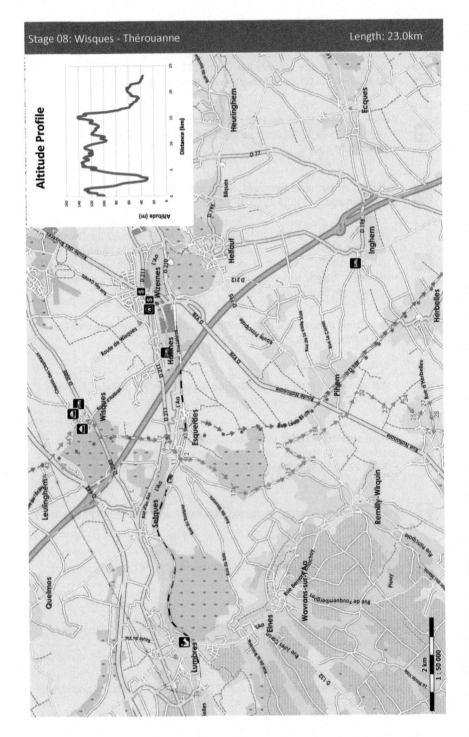

Stage Summary: the "Official Route" makes a large loop on woodland and exposed farm tracks over rolling countryside with few intermediate facilities. An Alternate Route takes a more direct route following the ancient la Leulene, with more wayside facilities. This will save some 10km although sadly the historic route in this stage is generally submerged under modern roadways.

Distance from Canterbury: 128km   Distance to Besançon: 782km
Stage Ascent: 314m   Stage Descent: 379m

Waypoint	Distance between waypoints	Total km	Directions	Verification Point	Compass	Altitude m
08.001	0	0.0	From the gates of the Abbaye de St Paul turn left to follow the D212	Towards the village centre	SE	101
08.002	400	0.4	As road, bends to the left and with a cemetery on your right, continue straight ahead on the pathway	Grounds of the Abbaye de Notre-Dame on your right, yellow VF sign	SE	110
08.003	200	0.6	At the T-junction with the road, turn right uphill	Towards the entrance to the Abbaye, yellow VF sign	SW	113
08.004	90	0.7	Bear left on the road	Entrance to the Abbaye de Notre-Dame on your right	SE	125
08.005	230	0.9	At the crossroads, beside the water tower, turn right and follow the major road with great care	Routes de Setques, yellow VF sign	SW	125
08.006	500	1.4	Shortly after the brow of the hill, turn left on the road into the woods	Direction Esquerdes, yellow VF sign	S	129
08.007	1500	2.9	At the T-junction with a major road in Esquerdes, turn left and then bear right	House n° 765 ahead, yellow VF sign	SE	33

Waypoint	Distance between waypoints	Total km	Directions	Verification Point	Compass	Altitude m
08.008	140	3.1	Immediately after crossing the river bridge, turn right on the riverside path. Note:- to reduce your distance by 10km continue straight ahead on the more direct Alternate Route	GR sign	W	31
08.009	400	3.5	In the place in front of the church, turn left up the hill	Keep the church on your left, yellow VF sign	SW	31
08.010	190	3.6	At the T-junction at the top of the hill, turn right and cross the railway	GR sign	W	41
08.011	170	3.8	Immediately after crossing the railway, turn left on the tarmac	Towards the cemetery, GR sign	E	42
08.012	130	3.9	Immediately after passing the cemetery, turn right uphill on the gravel and tarmac road	Yellow VF sign	SW	45
08.013	1600	5.5	At the T-junction in the heart of the forest, turn left, uphill on the stony track	Yellow VF sign	S	114
08.014	600	6.2	At the crossroads continue straight ahead with the woods on your left and open fields on your right	Towards the wind generator	SE	132
08.015	800	6.9	At the junction with the tarmac road, keep left and continue on the unmade road between the wind-generators	GR sign	SE	124
08.016	400	7.3	At the T-junction, turn left on the gravel track		NE	132
08.017	600	8.0	Follow the track to the right		SE	118

Waypoint	Distance between waypoints	Total km	Directions	Verification Point	Compass	Altitude m
08.018	900	8.9	At the T-junction with the main road, in the village of Crehem, turn right beside the road	Pass a bus shelter on your right, GR sign	SW	124
08.019	100	9.0	With the farmhouse n°1 on your right, turn left between the 2 brick buildings	GR sign	SE	125
08.020	500	9.4	At the junction with the access road towards the wind generators, continue straight ahead	Towards the tree-lined main road, yellow VF sign	SE	129
08.021	220	9.7	At the crossroads with the major road, continue straight ahead on the farm track between the fields	Yellow VF sign	SE	125
08.022	500	10.2	At the junction in the tracks, turn right, downhill on the gravel track	Towards the woods	SW	108
08.023	900	11.1	At the T-junction in the tracks, turn left	Hedgerow on the left of the track, yellow VF sign	SE	105
08.024	300	11.4	At the crossroads in the tracks, turn right	Towards the hamlet, yellow VF sign	SW	98
08.025	600	12.0	At the T-junction in front of the house with the circular window, turn left	Keep the small park on your left, yellow VF sign	SE	119
08.026	190	12.2	At the road junction, continue straight ahead	Rue d'Herbelles, GR sign	SE	117
08.027	200	12.4	As the road bends to the left at the exit from Cléty, turn right on the partially obscured path	Between hedges, yellow VF sign	W	115

Waypoint	Distance between waypoints	Total km	Directions	Verification Point	Compass	Altitude m
08.028	250	12.6	At the junction in the tracks, continue straight ahead on the narrow track	Between hedges, GR sign	W	113
08.029	400	13.0	At the end of the track, turn left beside the road	Between brick buildings	S	113
08.030	600	13.6	At the crossroads with the major road (D341), continue straight ahead on the small road	Towards the radio tower, GR signs	SW	109
08.031	180	13.8	At the crossroads just before the entry to Dohem, turn left on the track	Pass the building with the radio antenna on your right	SE	112
08.032	1300	15.0	At the T-junction at the end of rue de la Froide Orielle, turn right beside the road	Yellow VF sign	W	139
08.033	210	15.2	As the road bends to the right, take the left fork on the small road downhill - la Roullette	Pass the chapel on your left, GR sign	W	141
08.034	210	15.5	At the crossroads, turn left	GR sign	S	133
08.035	400	15.8	Take the right fork steeply downhill between the trees	Yellow sign	S	130
08.036	800	16.7	At the junction in the tracks, continue straight ahead on the grass track continuing downhill towards the wind generators	Hedgerow on your left and open fields on your right	S	71
08.037	400	17.0	At the T-junction in the tracks, turn left	Steep embankments on both side of the track, GR sign	E	58

Waypoint	Distance between waypoints	Total km	Directions	Verification Point	Compass	Altitude m
08.038	1200	18.2	At the T-junction with the main road, turn right	Enter the village of Delettes	SE	46
08.039	130	18.3	At the crossroads with a major road with the bridge on your right, cross the major road and continue straight ahead	GR sign	S	47
08.040	60	18.3	Turn right over the small wooden bridge, follow the cinder track and then turn left. Note:- to avoid this and subsequent bridges, horse riders, should turn left, briefly rejoin the main road, then turn right on the pathway towards the church and follow rue de Centre and rejoin the "Official Route" by turning left at the junction beside the tabac	GR sign	S	46
08.041	150	18.5	Continue straight ahead	Over the metal and concrete bridge	E	46
08.042	100	18.6	At the end of the riverside path, continue straight ahead beside the red and white barriers	Towards the tennis courts, GR sign	E	44
08.043	200	18.8	At the T-junction with the road, turn left	Towards the bar	E	44
08.044	140	18.9	Beside the bar, turn right	Rue Haute, GR sign	SE	44
08.045	230	19.2	At the road junction at the top of the hill, continue straight ahead	Rue de Nielles, GR sign	NE	55
08.046	1500	20.7	At the road junction continue straight ahead	Pumping station on your left	NE	62

74

Waypoint	Distance between waypoints	Total km	Directions	Verification Point	Compass	Altitude m
08.047	1200	21.9	At the road junction in Nielles, continue straight ahead	Pass the church on your left, GR sign	NE	41
08.048	800	22.6	At the T-junction, with house n° 2 directly ahead, turn left	Yellow VF signs	NE	37
08.049	400	23.0	Arrive at Therouanne centre at the T-junction facing the petrol station	Mairie and Tourist Office to the left on the main road		36

Alternate Route #08.A1   **Length: 10.1km**

Stage Summary: this more direct route follows the historic la Leulene and saves 10km. The route follows routes departmentales and small roads prior to joining a major road for the entry into Therouanne

Stage Ascent: 170m   **Stage Descent: 165m**

Waypoint	Distance between waypoints	Total km	Directions	Verification Point	Compass	Altitude m
08A1.001	0	0.0	Continue straight ahead on the road, uphill	Pass small field on your right	S	31
08A1.002	210	0.2	Bear left and then right, uphill on the road	Towards railway crossing	S	37
08A1.003	250	0.5	Bear left remaining on the D192e1	Pass house n° 530 on your right	S	48
08A1.004	3000	3.5	On the outskirts of Crehem, continue straight ahead on the D192, avoid the turning to the right to Lumbres	Direction Therouanne	SE	121
08A1.005	300	3.8	At the crossroads with the major road, continue straight ahead	Rue de Therouanne, café	SE	127
08A1.006	270	4.0	Continue straight ahead on the D192, avoid the turning on the left to Pihem	Direction Therouanne	SE	127

Waypoint	Distance between waypoints	Total km	Directions	Verification Point	Compass	Altitude m
08A1.007	2200	6.2	Take the left fork towards the crossroads and then continue straight ahead on the small road, rue Brocquoise	No Entry sign, pass metal calvaire on the right	SE	81
08A1.008	2000	8.3	At the T-junction with the major road, turn left beside the road. Note:- you are joining the historic Chaussée Brunehaut	Towards the brow of the hill	SE	87
08A1.009	500	8.7	At the roundabout take the second exot	Direction Thèrouanne	SE	80
08A1.010	1000	9.7	At the junction in Thèrouanne, beside the bar and tabac, bear left and then right on Grand Rue	Pass the Mairie on your right	SE	40
08A1.011	300	10.1	Arrive at Thérouanne (LXXVII) centre	Junction beside the petrol station		36

Accommodation & Facilities .... Wisques - Thérouanne

Chambres d'Hôtes - le Clos Mathurin,104 rue Dunkerque,62500 Saint-Omer,Pas de Calais,France; Tel:+33(0)3 21 98 14 70; +33(0)6 77 02 39 90; Price:B

B&B - Nedoncelle,(Josiane Nedoncelle),Rue d'Herbelles,62129 Inghem,Pas de Calais,France; Tel:+33(0)3 21 39 45 90; +33(0)6 14 27 67 31; Price:B

Gîte,3 Bis rue des Fossés,62129 Thérouanne,Pas de Calais,France; Tel:+33(0)3 21 95 33 26; +33(0)6 65 51 38 85; Email:gites1040@aol.com; Price:B

Chambres d'Hôtes - les Dornes,520 rue des Deux Upen,62129 Delettes,Pas de Calais,France; Tel:+33(0)3 21 95 87 09; +33(0)6 88 82 55 96; Email:lesdornes@lesdornes.com; Price:B

Camping du Lac de Rebecques,Chemin Etiais,62120 Rebecques,Pas de Calais,France; Tel:+33(0)3 21 39 58 58; Web-site:www.campingdulac62.fr/ Price:C

Ferme Equestre de Lumbres,21 rue Victor Hugo,62380 Lumbres,Pas de Calais,France; Tel:+33(0)3 21 93 60 69; Web-site:www.cc-paysdelumbres.fr/

i Office du Tourisme,4 rue Lion d'Or,62500 Saint-Omer,Pas de Calais,France;
Tel:+33(0)3 21 98 08 51

i Office du Tourisme,1 place Mairie,62129 Thérouanne,Pas de Calais,France;
Tel:+33(0)3 21 93 81 22

$ LCL,36 rue de Dunkerque,62500 Saint-Omer,Pas de Calais,France;
Tel:+33(0)8 20 82 31 05

$ Société Générale,9 place Mar Foch,62500 Saint-Omer,Pas de Calais,France;
Tel:+33(0)3 21 93 02 25

$ BNP Paribas,5 place Victor Hugo,62500 Saint-Omer,Pas de Calais,France;
Tel:+33(0)8 20 82 00 01

$ CIC,1 route Bruyères,62219 Longuenesse,Pas de Calais,France;
Tel:+33(0)3 21 12 81 50

$ Crédit Mutuel Nord,38 Bis Grand rue,62129 Thérouanne,Pas de Calais,France;
Tel:+33(0)3 21 12 25 90

🚂 Gare SNCF,Place du 8 Mai 1945,62500 Saint-Omer,Pas de Calais,France;
Tel:+33(0)8 92 33 53 35; Web-site:www.sncf.fr

H Centre Hospitalier,4 rue Arsenal,62500 Saint-Omer,Pas de Calais,France;
Tel:+33(0)3 21 12 48 49

+ Bernard Luc,59 rue Marais,62129 Thérouanne,Pas de Calais,France;
Tel:+33(0)3 21 95 51 44

🚶 Sport Evolution,34 rue Calais,62500 Saint-Omer,Pas de Calais,France;
Tel:+33(0)9 64 46 63 27

🐴 Mg Marechalerie,4 Chemin du Boteman,62500 Saint-Omer,Pas de
Calais,France; +33(0)6 60 77 26 52

☎ Hellin Didier,5 Grand'rue,62129 Herbelles,Pas de Calais,France;
Tel:+33(0)3 21 95 23 50

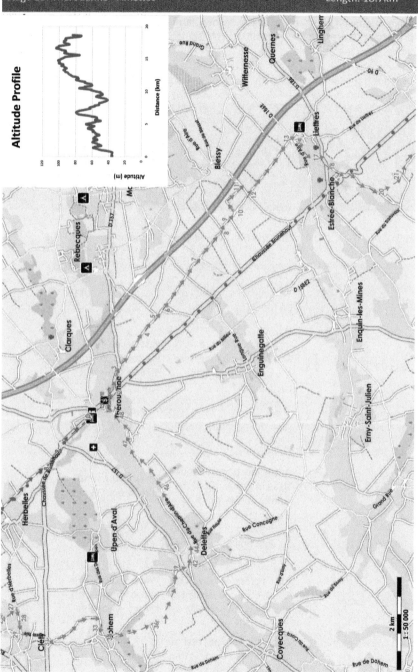

Stage Summary: this section largely follows farm tracks that parallel the Chaussée Brunehaut. There is the opportunity for refreshment and accommodation in Auchy-au-Bois.

Distance from Canterbury: 151km   Distance to Besançon: 759km
Stage Ascent: 261m   Stage Descent: 213m

Waypoint	Distance between waypoints	Total km	Directions	Verification Point	Compass	Altitude m
09.001	0	0.0	Take the D341 Grand Rue	Keep the petrol station and bank on your left, GR sign	SE	36
09.002	270	0.3	At the junction, bear left on the D157	Direction Aire sur la Lys, GR sign	E	36
09.003	600	0.8	Immediately before leaving Therouanne, take the right fork, tarmac road, uphill	Pass house n° 27 on the corner, chemin du Blac Mont, GR sign	SE	39
09.004	900	1.7	Take the right fork, uphill	Towards the wind generators, yellow VF sign	SE	48
09.005	600	2.3	At the junction, continue straight ahead, avoid the turning to the left	Towards the wind generators, GR sign	SE	59
09.006	160	2.4	At the junction, continue straight ahead, avoid the turning to the right	Yellow VF sign	SE	57
09.007	1400	3.9	At the crossroads with the D130, continue straight ahead on the partially made road	Water tower visible above the trees on the left, yellow VF sign	SE	59
09.008	800	4.6	Avoid the turnings first on the right and then on the left and continue straight ahead, uphill	Pass a copse on your right, towards the the wind generators	SE	58

Waypoint	Distance between waypoints	Total km	Directions	Verification Point	Compass	Altitude m
09.009	400	5.0	At the junction, continue straight ahead, downhill	Towards the quarry	SE	67
09.010	170	5.2	At the bottom of the slope, turn left and begin to skirt the quarry	Towards the prominent church on the horizon, GR sign	E	61
09.011	800	6.0	At the T-junction with the D159, turn right, slightly uphill	Pass a conifer hedge on your right, GR sign	SW	53
09.012	220	6.2	Shortly after leaving Blessy, turn left on the track, uphill	Yellow VF sign	SE	60
09.013	1600	7.8	At the crossroads with a main road, turn right	Church visible in the valley, yellow VF sign	SW	56
09.014	80	7.8	Turn left, downhill into the village of Liettres	GR and wooden VF signs	S	57
09.015	110	8.0	Halfway down the hill, with a parking area on your left, turn right	GR sign	SW	51
09.016	300	8.3	Beside the football pitch bear left and take the grassy track downhill	GR sign	S	51
09.017	400	8.7	At the T-junction with the D186 in Longhem, turn right	House n° 21 ahead, yellow VF sign	SW	41
09.018	230	8.9	Turn left onto the small road	Pass large metal barn on your right, yellow VF sign	SW	43
09.019	500	9.4	At the T-junction with the major road – Chaussée Brunehaut, turn left, cross the road with care and immediately turn right beside the stream	Rue du Transvaal, GR sign	SW	52
09.020	900	10.3	Immediately after passing the patterned brick house n° 4, turn left	Yellow VF sign	SE	61

Waypoint	Distance between waypoints	Total km	Directions	Verification Point	Compass	Altitude m
09.021	700	11.0	Shortly before the T-junction with the road, fork left, uphill on the grass track. Note:- there are barriers on the track, which may prove difficult for horse-riders. To avoid these, riders should bear right and then left on the road to the centre of La Tirmande. Then turn left beside the calvaire and then right immediately before the old railway bridge. The "Official Route" will join the road from the left 400m after the bridge	Yellow VF sign	SE	60
09.022	1500	12.4	Emerge from the former railway track onto a small road, bear left, uphill	GR sign	SE	85
09.023	600	13.0	At the crossroads with the D90, continue straight ahead onto the track	Small chapel to the left of the junction, yellow VF sign	SE	91
09.024	1000	14.0	Beside the mobile phone tower, bear left and then right	Skirt the large building and silo on your right	S	96
09.025	200	14.2	At the T-junction with the road, turn left	Towards the water tower, yellow VF sign	SE	94
09.026	170	14.3	At the crossroads beneath the water tower, turn left	D94, GR sign	NE	100
09.027	400	14.7	Shortly after passing under the power lines, turn right and leave the main road, route de Heslan	GR sign	SE	100
09.028	400	15.1	At the T-junction facing house n° 7, turn right	GR sign	SE	95

Waypoint	Distance between waypoints	Total km	Directions	Verification Point	Compass	Altitude m
09.029	110	15.2	In la Place, in the centre of Auchy-au-Bois, continue straight ahead, towards the church spire	Chambres d'hôte to the left, GR sign	SE	93
09.030	190	15.4	Take left fork on rue Louis Part, downhill	Pass church on your right, GR sign	SE	84
09.031	800	16.2	At the crossroads at the foot of the hill, go straight ahead on the stony track	Between open fields, yellow VF sign	SE	92
09.032	1400	17.6	At the crossroads continue straight ahead on the tarmac road	Towards the water tower on the horizon	SE	94
09.033	400	18.0	At the crossroads, continue straight ahead, slightly uphill	Towards the village, yellow VF sign	S	91
09.034	500	18.4	Bear left and at the T-junction with a main road (D69) turn left. Note:- both the GR145 and GR127 pass through Amettes. They join briefly before separating beside the church. Horse and bike riders should turn right at the T-junction and then take the first left, rue de l'Egliset to rejoin the "Official Route" beside the church	Pass the Amettes bus stop on your right, GR127 sign	E	75
09.035	80	18.5	Turn right on the track between houses n°s 19 and 20, pass through the wooden gate and climb the steps towards the church	Pass la maison St Benoit on your right, GR sign	SE	73
09.036	150	18.7	Arrive at Amettes centre, at the top of the steps	Beside the church of St Sulpice		84

Chambres d'Hôtes - les Chambres du Relais,4 rue du Moulin,62145 Liettres,Pas de Calais,France; Tel:+33(0)3 21 38 10 99; +33(0)6 76 35 83 51; Web-site:leschambresdurelais.vpweb.fr; Price:B

Chambre d'Hôtes - la Ferme de la Vallée,13 rue Neuve,62190 Auchy-au-Bois,Pas de Calais,France; Tel:+33(0)3 21 25 80 09; Email:brigitte.de-saint-laurent@wanadoo; Web-site:www.lafermedelavallee.com; Price:B; PR

Chambres d'Hôtes les Cohettes,28 rue de Pernes,62190 Auchy-au-Bois,Pas de Calais,France; +33(0)6 07 06 65 42; Email:ginabulot@gmail.com; Price:B

Chambres d'Hôtes - la Ferme des Deux Tilleuls,(Jean-Baptiste Gevas),2 rue Eglise,62260 Amettes,Pas de Calais,France; Tel:+33(0)3 21 27 15 02; Email:ermedes2tilleuls@wanadoo.fr; Web-site:fermedes2tilleuls.monsite-orange.fr; Price:B

Camping Domaine le Chateau de Mametz,32 rue du Moulin,62120 Mametz,Pas de Calais,France; Tel:+33(0)3 21 12 48 85; +33(0)6 83 45 00 45; Email:jean-pierre.leleux.62@orange.fr; Web-site:www.camping-chateau-mametz.fr; Price:C

Duhautois Sylvain,1 Bis rue Roger Salengro,62260 Ferfay,Pas de Calais,France; Tel:+33(0)6 19 15 73 15

Mairie,Place Mairie,62260 Amettes,Pas de Calais,France; Tel:+33(0)3 21 27 06 60

Mairie,41 Chaussée Brunehaut,62260 Ferfay,Pas de Calais,France; Tel:+33(0)3 21 52 77 10

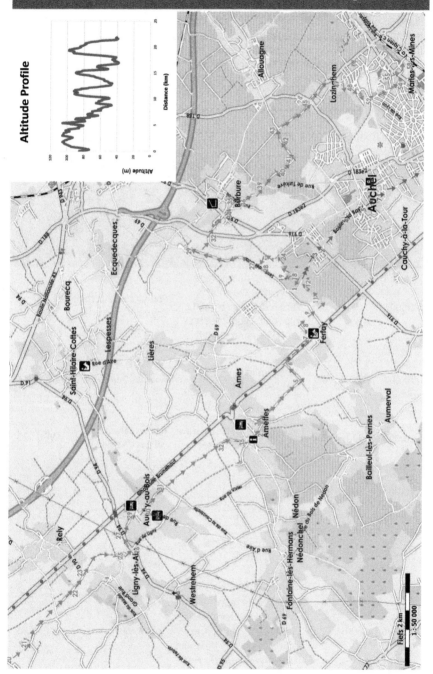

Altitude Profile

Stage Summary: the "Official Route" meanders on country and woodland tracks before finding its way through former mining villages and parkland to reach Bruay-la-Buissière (LXXVI). While Signposting is generally good, but there are some challenges to locate the signs in the woodland and evidence of early some vandalism to the new signs. A more direct Alternate Route is also described. Bruay-la-Buissière offers accommodation and a full range of facilities. The route in Bruay bypasses the town centre and so allow time to locate where you will stay.

Distance from Canterbury: 169km   Distance to Besançon: 741km
Stage Ascent: 338m   Stage Descent: 381m

Waypoint	Distance between waypoints	Total km	Directions	Verification Point	Compass	Altitude m
10.001	0	0.0	At the top of the steps and facing the church, turn left and bear right on the road, avoid the steps and GR sign to the left	Church on your right, downhill	SE	83
10.002	90	0.1	At the road junction, continue straight ahead	Rue des Berceaux	SE	84
10.003	300	0.4	At the foot of the hill, turn left on the tarmac road	Beside calvaire, yellow VF sign	NE	73
10.004	190	0.6	Turn right and leave the road, continue uphill	Yellow VF sign	SE	79
10.005	1400	2.0	Follow the stony track as it turns left	Towards the main road, Chaussée Brunehaut	NE	104
10.006	600	2.5	At the T-junction, turn right beside main road D341 - Chaussée Brunehaut. Note:- the road can be very busy and the grass verges are very narrow	Yellow VF sign	SE	95

Waypoint	Distance between waypoints	Total km	Directions	Verification Point	Compass	Altitude m
10.007	800	3.4	In the village of Ferfay, take the second turning on the left	Pass between the auberge and boulangerie, sentier de Burbure. GR sign	NE	104
10.008	400	3.8	At the T-junction, after passing the cemetery, turn right on the tarmac road	Yellow VF sign	SE	98
10.009	400	4.2	At the crossroads, continue straight ahead. Note:- to avoid the difficult navigation through the woods ahead, turn left at the junction and continue straight ahead at the next crossroads. The "Official Route" will join from the right in 1500m	GR sign	SE	99
10.010	220	4.4	At the road junction, continue straight ahead, downhill	Follow the turn to the left	E	90
10.011	180	4.6	At the end of the concrete road, continue straight ahead on the grass track	GR sign	NE	86
10.012	600	5.1	Take the left fork	GR cross to the right	N	89
10.013	60	5.2	At the crossroads with the main road, continue straight ahead, re-enter the woods and bear right on the broad track. Note:- to reduce the distance to Bruay by 8km, avoid some difficult navigation and possible hunting in the woods ahead, turn right on the road and follow the Alternate Route	Yellow VF sign	NE	92

Waypoint	Distance between waypoints	Total km	Directions	Verification Point	Compass	Altitude m
10.014	110	5.3	At the crossroads in the woods, turn left	Follow sentier de la Scyrendale, mountain bike route	W	96
10.015	50	5.4	Take the right fork	GR cross on the left fork	N	99
10.016	50	5.4	At the T-junction, turn right		E	105
10.017	150	5.6	Take the right and lower fork	GR cross to the left	N	95
10.018	90	5.7	At the T-junction in the tracks, bear left, uphill	GR sign	NW	86
10.019	60	5.7	At the T-junction after a short, but steep climb, turn right on the broad track	Between the pine trees, GR sign	E	85
10.020	150	5.9	At the crossroads in the tracks, turn left on the broader track and then continue straight ahead at the crossroads	Follow the sign for sentier de la Scyrendale, GR sign	NE	83
10.021	120	6.0	Continue straight ahead on the main track, avoid the turnings to the right and left		NE	79
10.022	110	6.1	At the T-junction in the track, turn right on the broad track	Hollow in the ground to your left	SE	79
10.023	90	6.2	At the T-junction with a broad track, turn left	House visible ahead, GR sign	NE	90
10.024	180	6.4	At the T-junction with a pasture ahead, turn left	Yellow VF sign	N	86
10.025	300	6.7	At the junction turn sharp left, downhill	Yellow VF sign	NW	75
10.026	180	6.9	Take the left fork, uphill	GR sign	NW	64

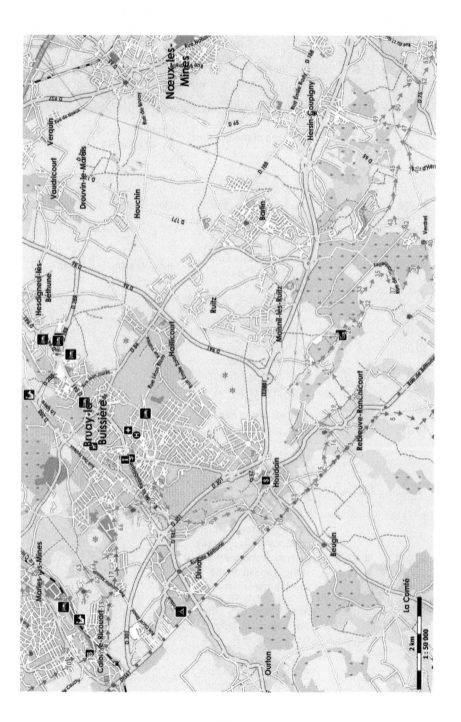

Waypoint	Distance between waypoints	Total km	Directions	Verification Point	Compass	Altitude m
10.027	180	7.0	At the top of the hill, turn left	Keep the trees close on your right, GR sign	SW	73
10.028	80	7.1	At the T-junction with the broad level track, turn right	Yellow VF sign	N	75
10.029	1600	8.7	Turn sharp right onto a partially obscured track, downhill and bearing right	Yellow VF sign	SE	51
10.030	170	8.9	At the T-junction, turn right. Note:- the stone memorial marks the place where the bodies of the murdered Irish Saints Lugle and Luglien where discovered in 696AD	Yellow VF sign	S	46
10.031	40	8.9	Turn left onto a narrow track, pass wooden barrier	GR sign	SE	47
10.032	260	9.2	At the T-junction with a broad gravel track, turn left towards the main road	Yellow VF sign	E	62
10.033	80	9.3	At the crossroads with the D916, carefully cross the main road and continue straight ahead on the small tarmac road	Towards the cemetery, GR sign	SE	64
10.034	600	9.8	At the crossroads with the main road, continue straight ahead	Rue du 11 Novembre, GR sign	SE	57
10.035	400	10.2	At the T-junction,with a pasture directly ahead, turn right	Rue Bois Rimbert, GR sign	SW	49

Waypoint	Distance between waypoints	Total km	Directions	Verification Point	Compass	Altitude m
10.036	60	10.3	Take the left fork towards the grassy track. Note:- ahead there is a barrier that may not be passable by some horses. Riders should continue on rue du Bois Rimbert, turn left just before reaching the parking area, climb the hill, turn left at the T-junction with the broad track and rejoin the "Official Route" at the crossroads, where they should turn right	House n° 26b on your right, GR sign	S	50
10.037	80	10.4	Continue straight ahead on the track	Pass barrier	SE	53
10.038	400	10.7	At the crossroads in the tracks, approaching the top of the hill, continue straight ahead. At the end of the fence bear left towards the road signs on the skyline ahead	Wire fence on your right	SE	82
10.039	300	11.0	At the crossroads with the tarmac road, continue straight ahead on the stony track	Towards the television tower on the horizon, GR sign	SE	91
10.040	400	11.4	At the T-junction, turn right on the stony track	Keep the large industrial buildings on your right, yellow VF sign	SE	88
10.041	600	12.0	With the water tower and industrial buildings on your right, turn left downhill on the broad stony track	Towards the church spire in Allouagne, yellow VF sign	NE	83
10.042	500	12.5	At the junction at the foot of the hill, bear right on the broad stony track	Towards the church spire, GR sign	E	58

Waypoint	Distance between waypoints	Total km	Directions	Verification Point	Compass	Altitude m
10.043	230	12.7	At the junction, turn right and right again	Towards a prominent church, GR sign	SE	47
10.044	700	13.4	At the junction, continue straight ahead	Towards the church, yellow VF sign	SE	51
10.045	270	13.7	At the end of rue Achille Hibon, bear left towards the Stop sign and then continue straight ahead over the pedestrian crossing	Direction Marles les M. on the D188, towards the church	SE	56
10.046	700	14.4	Turn right onto rue des Champs Dorés. Note:- there is a metal barrier on the path ahead which is not passable by horses. To avoid this, remain on the road and take the first road to the right and then rejoin the "Official Route" at the exit from the playing fields	Small parking area on the left of the junction, yellow VF sign	S	67
10.047	290	14.7	At the end of the road, bear right on the track, uphill	Pass the football field on your left	SW	79
10.048	90	14.8	At the end of the hedgerow, turn left and pass through the metal barriers into the playing fields	GR sign, at the time of writing the VF sign had been vandalised	S	84
10.049	110	14.9	On reaching the road turn right and then quickly turn right again on the footpath at the rear of the houses	At the time of writing this VF sign had also been vandalised	SW	86

Waypoint	Distance between waypoints	Total km	Directions	Verification Point	Compass	Altitude m
10.050	300	15.2	At the end of path turn left on the road	Pass house n° 14 on your left, GR sign	SE	88
10.051	90	15.3	At the crossroads, turn right beside the road. Note:- there is again a barrier which makes the route ahead impassable by horses. Riders should continue straight ahead on rue de Cracovie and rejoin the "Official Route" at the foot of the hill	Towards the spoil heap, GR sign	W	85
10.052	230	15.5	Turn left through a gap in the crash barriers onto the pathway into the woods	Yellow VF sign	S	80
10.053	190	15.7	At the T-junction with the rue de Cracovie, turn right	Follow the sign for Centre Ville, GR sign	SE	54
10.054	600	16.3	At the crossroads with the archway and post office directly ahead, turn left	Direction Centre Ville, GR sign	E	64
10.055	210	16.6	Turn right and pass directly in front of the Mairie	Yellow VF sign	SE	57
10.056	130	16.7	At the junction with the road, turn right and then immediately left downhill. Note:- to avoid difficulties in the park ahead, horse-riders should remain on rue Jean Jaurés and then take the next left turn on rue de la Fosse and rejoin the "Official Route" beside the river bridge	Rue de l'Egalité, GR sign	SE	48

Waypoint	Distance between waypoints	Total km	Directions	Verification Point	Compass	Altitude m
10.057	200	16.9	Shortly before reaching the church, turn right on the small road	Pass through the barriers into the park, Yellow VF sign	SE	39
10.058	90	17.0	At the top of the short rise, turn right on the tarmac path	Pass through the park parallel to the river on your left	SW	38
10.059	400	17.4	At the T-junction with the road, turn left over the bridge and then immediately right on the track	GR sign	SW	42
10.060	700	18.0	At the T-junction with the road, turn left beside the road, uphill	Lake to the right at the junction, yellow VF sign	SE	41
10.061	210	18.2	At the crossroads after crossing the railway tracks, continue straight ahead up the hill	Centre Equestre to the right	SE	48
10.062	600	18.9	At the T-junction at the top of the hill, turn left	Pass bus stop on your left, yellow VF sign	NE	92
10.063	300	19.2	Turn right and remain on the road, uphill	Large spoil heap on your left at the junction, yellow VF sign	S	91
10.064	100	19.3	Bear left initially on a track and then joining a tarmac road behind the crash barriers	Towards the twin spoil heaps, GR sign	SE	95
10.065	700	20.0	At the T-junction with the road, turn left. Note:- the Alternate Route rejoins from the right	Continue with the hedge on your right, yellow VF sign	E	84
10.066	600	20.5	At the No-entry sign, continue straight ahead with caution	Pass grass area on your left, GR sign	E	78

Waypoint	Distance between waypoints	Total km	Directions	Verification Point	Compass	Altitude m
10.067	400	20.9	At the crossroads, turn right on rue Gaston Blot	Pass a boulangerie on your left, GR sign	S	73
10.068	600	21.5	At the junction at the foot of the long descent, carefully cross the D302 and take the pathway into the parc de la Lawe and bear left over the wooden bridge. Note:- horse riders should turn left and skirt the park and then rejoin the "Official Route" at the end of the section at the road junction after the petrol station	Allée Martin Luther King, GR sign	S	40
10.069	80	21.6	At the top of the steps turn left on the cinder path	Skirt the lake on your right, GR sign	S	38
10.070	170	21.8	Turn left on the uphill path towards the main road	Pass hippo sculpture on your right, GR sign	SE	41
10.071	60	21.9	At the road junction, take the pedestrian crossing and turn left	Towards the petrol station, yellow VF sign	NE	40
10.072	30	21.9	Arrive at Bruay-la-Buissière at the junction between rue de la République and rue Chopin. Note:- the town centre is straight ahead	Petrol station ahead		40

Alternate Route #10.A1   Length: 7.7km

Stage Summary: direct route to Bruay-la-Buissièr saving 8km. The route is largely undertaken on suburban roads, parallel to the Chaussée Brunehaut

Stage Ascent: 112m   **Stage Descent: 120m**

Waypoint	Distance between waypoints	Total km	Directions	Verification Point	Compass	Altitude m
10A1.001	0	0.0	Turn right and proceed on the grass beside the main road		SE	92
10A1.002	900	0.9	At the T-junction with the main road, turn left	Pass small park on your left	NE	92
10A1.003	40	0.9	Turn right	Pass second park on your right	SE	92
10A1.004	1100	2.0	At the crossroads, continue straight ahead	Boulevard Emile Basly	SE	87
10A1.005	400	2.4	At the traffic lights, continue straight ahead	Pass the Lycée on your right	SE	90
10A1.006	400	2.7	At the roundabout, bear right into place Jules Guesde	Pass between the church and la Poste	S	97
10A1.007	130	2.9	Leave the car park and turn left on rue Roger Salengro	Road immediately bears right	SE	101
10A1.008	1500	4.4	At the T-junction, turn left	Rue de Colmar	NE	89
10A1.009	130	4.5	At the T-junction, turn right	School ahead at the junction	S	88
10A1.010	180	4.7	Keep right on the small road	Pass under the main road	S	72
10A1.011	300	5.0	At the T-junction, turn left	Leave rue de la Cavée	E	48
10A1.012	30	5.0	At the "Stop" sign turn right	Direction Centre Ville	SE	48
10A1.013	210	5.2	At the roundabout continue straight ahead, up the hill	Pass under railway bridge	SE	47

Waypoint	Distance between waypoints	Total km	Directions	Verification Point	Compass	Altitude m
10A1.014	300	5.6	Bear left on the road, rue de Katowice	Embankment on the right	E	71
10A1.015	1000	6.6	At the crossroads turn right on rue du Bois Rietz	Turn just before the supermarket	SE	95
10A1.016	300	6.9	At the crossroads go straight ahead on rue Paul Langevin	Water tower behind houses to the right	E	110
10A1.017	500	7.4	At the crossroads go straight ahead on rue du Maréchal Léclerc	Pass bus stop on the right	E	94
10A1.018	400	7.7	At the junction, continue straight ahead and rejoin the "Official Route"	Field on your right		85

Accommodation & Facilities .... Amettes - Bruay-la-Buissière

Gîte d'Etape du Presbytère,Place de l'Église,62151 Burbure,Pas de Calais,France; Tel:+33(0)3 21 61 02 00; Email:mairie.burbure@wanadoo.fr; Web-site:burbureviagite.wordpress.com; Note:Contact the Mairie,

Dolce Vita,2049 rue de la Libération,62700 Bruay-la-Buissière,Pas de Calais,France; Tel:+33(0)3 21 62 00 22; Email:dolcevita-bruay@orange.fr; Price:B

Hôtel Ibis Styles,Parc de la Porte Nord, rue des Frères Lumière,62700 Bruay-la-Buissière,Pas de Calais,France; Tel:+33(0)3 21 01 11 11; Web-site:accorhotels.com; Price:B

Auberge des Gourmets,Rue du Mont Saint Eloi,62470 Calonne-Ricouart,Pas de Calais,France; Tel:+33(0)3 21 62 26 58; Email:lesgourmetscalonnix@free.fr; Price:B

Liberty Hotel,Parc de la Falande, avenue de la Liberation,62700 Bruay-la-Buissière,Pas de Calais,France; Tel:+33(0)3 21 62 90 00; Email:hl6214@inter-hotel.com; Price:B

Hotel le Cottage,292 avenue Libération,62700 Bruay-la-Buissière,Pas de Calais,France; Tel:+33(0)3 21 53 14 14; Email:lecottagehotel@wanadoo.fr; Web-site:lecottagehotel.com; Price:B

Hôtel Saint-Hubert,925 rue Louis Dussart,62700 Bruay-la-Buissière,Pas de Calais,France; Tel:+33(0)3 21 62 40 32; Price:B

Camping de la Biette,Chausée Brunehaut,62460 Divion,Pas de Calais,France; +33(0)6 85 83 81 43; Email:parcbiette.divion@orange.fr; Web-site:domaine-de-la-biette.wifeo.com/le-camping.php; Price:C; Note:Chalets available for rent,

Les Crinieres au Vent,32 rue Aire,62190 Lières,Pas de Calais,France; Tel:+33(0)9 65 00 11 98

Poney Club du Bois,100 Ruelle Herlin,62700 Bruay-la-Buissière,Pas de Calais,France; Tel:+33(0)3 91 80 41 07

Centre Équestre - Ecurie Hazout,Parc André Mancey,62470 Calonne-Ricouart,Pas de Calais,France; Tel:+33(0)3 21 62 92 92; Email:postmaster@centre-equestre-calonne-ricouart.fr

Syndicat d'Initiative Bruay et Environs,32 rue Henri Hermant,62700 Bruay-la-Buissière,Pas de Calais,France; Tel:+33(0)3 21 57 61 13

BNP Paribas,63 rue Jean Jaurès,62260 Auchel,Pas de Calais,France; Tel:+33(0)8 20 82 00 01; Web-site:www.bnpparibas.net

Caisse d'Epargne,19 Bis rue André Mancey,62470 Calonne-Ricouart,Pas de Calais,France; Tel:+33(0)8 20 82 13 35

Société Générale,64 rue République,62700 Bruay-la-Buissière,Pas de Calais,France; Tel:+33(0)3 21 62 43 49

Crédit du Nord,111 rue Alfred Leroy,62700 Bruay-la-Buissière,Pas de Calais,France; Tel:+33(0)3 91 80 13 20

Crédit Mutuel,16 rue Roger Salengro,62150 Houdain,Pas de Calais,France; Tel:+33(0)8 20 35 21 11

Clinique Médico-Chirurgicale de Bruay,200 rue Auvergne,62700 Bruay-la-Buissière,Pas de Calais,France; Tel:+33(0)3 21 64 66 66

Kiczynski Caron Anne,237 rue Louis Dussart,62700 Bruay-la-Buissière,Pas de Calais,France; Tel:+33(0)3 21 53 08 62

Schepkens Etienne,241 rue Florent Evrard,62700 Bruay-la-Buissière,Pas de Calais,France; Tel:+33(0)3 21 53 69 59

Intersport,Parc de la Porte Nord,62700 Bruay-la-Buissière,Pas de Calais,France; Tel:+33(0)3 21 52 01 90

Pascal Benault Maréchal-Ferrant,166 Bis rue Philippe Van Tieghem,59270 Bailleul,Nord,France; +33(0)6 17 46 24 71

Allo Bruay Taxi,1254 rue Pierre Brossolette,62700 Bruay-la-Buissière,Pas de Calais,France; Tel:+33(0)3 21 54 03 57

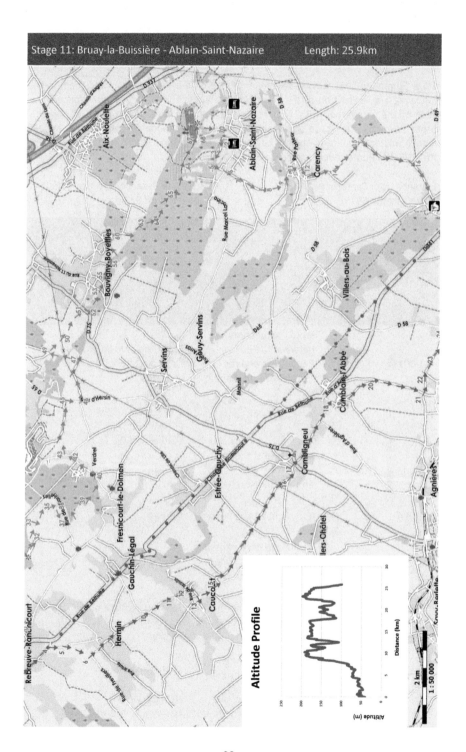

Altitude Profile

Stage Summary: after leaving Bruay-la-Buissière on a disused railway and then briefly following a quiet section of the Chaussée Brunehaut the "Official Route" follows the path of the established GR127, climbing the wooded ridge to the north of Sigeric's probable route. The route passes the cemetery Notre Dame de Lorette – the largest French military cemetery – before beginning the descent to return to the Douai plain. An Alternate Route reduces the distance to Arras by 12km.

Distance from Canterbury: 191km   Distance to Besançon: 719km
Stage Ascent: 597m   Stage Descent: 538m

Waypoint	Distance between waypoints	Total km	Directions	Verification Point	Compass	Altitude m
11.001	0	0.0	From the junction between rue de la République and rue Chopin take rue Chopin, uphill	Leave the parc de la Lawe directly behind you	SE	40
11.002	240	0.2	At the top of the hill, turn left	Pass a row of miner's cottages on your right, GR sign	NE	55
11.003	130	0.4	At the end of the road, go down the flight of steps and continue on the road	GR sign	E	50
11.004	60	0.4	Turn right on rue Rossini	GR sign	SE	48
11.005	100	0.5	At the end of rue Rossini, climb the embankment and turn right on the track	Yellow VF sign	SW	55
11.006	80	0.6	At the T-junction, turn right on the grit track that follows the former railway	Pass a petrol station on your left, yellow VF sign	SW	60
11.007	900	1.5	Continue straight ahead under the road bridge	Yellow VF sign	S	51
11.008	700	2.2	At the crossroads with a tarmac road, continue straight ahead	Pass beside the barriers, yellow VF sign	S	49

Waypoint	Distance between waypoints	Total km	Directions	Verification Point	Compass	Altitude m
11.009	1100	3.2	Take the pedestrian crossing over the busy D341 and continue straight ahead on the old railway	Beside the former Houdain railway station, yellow VF sign	SW	55
11.010	700	3.9	At the road crossing turn left and leave the railway	Beside the rue Ville Juif bus stop, yellow VF sign	SE	56
11.011	40	3.9	At the crossroads, continue straight ahead, uphill	Chaussée Brunehaut	SE	55
11.012	500	4.4	At the roundabout, just before the top of the hill, continue straight ahead	Rue du Bon Val, GR sign	SE	63
11.013	280	4.7	At the crossroads with the track, continue straight ahead on the tarmac, towards the brow of the hill	Yellow VF sign	SE	71
11.014	400	5.0	At the crossroads in the hollow, continue straight ahead on the road	Yellow VF sign	SE	69
11.015	500	5.5	Turn left onto the small tarmac road. Note:- the "Official Route" makes a major loop climbing to the ridge top on your left and then meandering on woodland and farm tracks before returning to the historic route near the ruins of the Abbaye de Mont St Eloi. The "Official Route" involves some steep climbs and can be treacherous in wet conditions. The Alternate Route proceeds more directly and saves 12km	Yellow VF sign	E	72

Waypoint	Distance between waypoints	Total km	Directions	Verification Point	Compass	Altitude m
11.016	600	6.1	At the T-junction, turn left and follow the road as it skirts the château on the left	Pass large metal building on your right, yellow VF sign	E	65
11.017	400	6.5	At the T-junction with the main road, turn left on the gravel path beside the road	Yellow VF sign	NE	75
11.018	210	6.7	At the mini-roundabout take the first exit, slightly uphill	Rue d'Olhain, yellow VF sign	SE	74
11.019	600	7.3	As the road narrows at the top of the hill, continue straight ahead	Basketball court on your left	SE	85
11.020	400	7.7	At the crossroads in the tracks directly under the power line, turn left towards the forest	Yellow VF sign	NE	84
11.021	700	8.4	At the entry to the woods, take the left fork	Yellow VF sign	N	123
11.022	300	8.7	At the top of the hill continue straight ahead on the path	Pass camp site on your right	NE	157
11.023	200	8.9	At the T-junction with the road, turn right, uphill	Entrance to parc d'Olhain, yellow VF sign	S	147
11.024	150	9.0	Beside the camping reception, continue straight ahead on the road	Towards parcours Aventure, passing red and white metal barrier	SE	165
11.025	800	9.8	Bear left in front of the central reception building	GR sign	E	181
11.026	130	9.9	After passing the reception area, bear right on the tarmac	Towards the Salle Polyvalente, yellow VF sign	SE	181

Waypoint	Distance between waypoints	Total km	Directions	Verification Point	Compass	Altitude m
11.047	1000	17.4	At the crossroads in the tracks, with the television tower to your right ahead, turn left between the fields	Yellow VF sign	N	180
11.048	700	18.1	Join a tarmac road and turn sharp right	Yellow VF sign	E	114
11.049	100	18.2	At the junction in the tracks continue straight ahead, avoid the track on your left	Towards the television tower	SE	115
11.050	400	18.6	At the junction in the tracks under the power line, continue straight ahead	House on the horizon on the left of the track	SE	120
11.051	800	19.4	At the T-junction at the end of the chemin de la Claire Fontaine, turn right beside the busy road. Note:- the route ahead is not passable by horses. Riders should turn left and then take the next road to the right and skirt the school on their right and rejoin the route on rue des Ferronniers	GR sign	SW	147
11.052	100	19.5	With house n° 52 on your right, turn left between the metal posts	Yellow VF sign	SE	152
11.053	600	20.1	At the T-junction with the road at the end of the path, turn left and then immediately right on rue des Ferronniers	No-Entry sign, yellow VF sign	E	137
11.054	170	20.3	At the T-junction, turn left and then immediately right	GR sign	E	144

Waypoint	Distance between waypoints	Total km	Directions	Verification Point	Compass	Altitude m
11.055	220	20.5	At the end of the tarmac, continue straight ahead on the narrow path with the woods on your right	Water tower visible ahead to your left	E	144
11.056	250	20.7	At the crossroads in the tracks, continue straight ahead	Fields on the left and woods on the right, yellow VF sign	SE	155
11.057	280	21.0	At the T-junction in the tracks, turn left, slightly downhill, between fields	Water towers visible on both left and right, yellow VF sign	NE	142
11.058	300	21.3	After joining the tarmac road, take the first turning on the right	GR sign	SE	123
11.059	160	21.5	At the T-junction, turn left	Stables on your right	E	120
11.060	60	21.6	At the crossroads at the end of rue Ampére , turn right	Pass EHPAD on your left, GR sign	S	118
11.061	270	21.8	As the road turns left, bear right on the tarmac track towards the trees	Pass between houses n° 2 on 76, GR sign	SE	122
11.062	500	22.4	Take the right fork, steeply uphill	GR sign	S	152
11.063	160	22.5	At the junction in the tracks, continue straight ahead, uphill	Yellow VF signs	S	180
11.064	120	22.6	At the crossroads at the top of the hill, turn left	GR sign	SE	188
11.065	900	23.5	Beside the No-Entry sign, take the left fork	Yellow VF sign	E	184

Waypoint	Distance between waypoints	Total km	Directions	Verification Point	Compass	Altitude m
11.066	700	24.1	At the junction in the tracks, continue straight ahead in the edge of the woods	Yellow VF sign	SE	180
11.067	700	24.8	At the T-junction with the road beside Cimetière de Notre Dame de Lorette, turn right on the pathway that skirts the cemetery	Yellow VF sign	S	174
11.068	50	24.8	At the road junction, bear left remaining beside the cemetery. Note:- at the time of writing the pathway ahead was closed because of the discovery of unexploded ordnance. To avoid this path, bear right on the road, down the hill in the direction of Ablain St Nazaire. The "Official Route" will join from the left in 500m		E	170
11.069	260	25.1	Shortly before reaching the main entrance to the cemetery, turn right down the steep wooded track	Yellow VF sign	S	168
11.070	400	25.5	At the T-junction with the road, turn left and continue downhill	Yellow VF sign	S	125
11.071	150	25.7	As the road turns to the left, turn right on the unmade track into the trees	Ruins of the old church of Ablain-Saint-Nazaire below, yellow VF sign	W	111

Waypoint	Distance between waypoints	Total km	Directions	Verification Point	Compass	Altitude m
11.072	200	25.9	Arrive at Ablain-Saint-Nazaire outskirts. Note:- the most direct route to the village centre is to leave the "Official Route" and turn left down the hill on rue Ponthiers and then right at the subsequent T-junction, horse riders are advised to follow this route to avoid barriers ahead on the "Official Route"	T-junction with road, sports field directly ahead		99

Alternate Route #11.A1   **Length: 17.2km**

Stage Summary: a more direct route following minor roads closer to the historic route and reducing total distance by 12km. The route remains on largely level ground.

Stage Ascent: 175m   **Stage Descent: 174m**

Waypoint	Distance between waypoints	Total km	Directions	Verification Point	Compass	Altitude m
11A1.001	0	0.0	Continue straight ahead	Chaussée Brunehaut	SE	74
11A1.002	600	0.6	At the crossroads go straight ahead	Modern houses on both side of the road	SE	74
11A1.003	300	0.9	At the crossroads at the bottom of the hill, continue straight ahead	Uphill between trees	SE	80
11A1.004	800	1.7	At the Stop sign turn right	D72, direction Hermin	S	90
11A1.005	400	2.1	On the crown of the bend to the left, bear right onto track towards the water tower	Beside semi-buried building	S	103

Waypoint	Distance between waypoints	Total km	Directions	Verification Point	Compass	Altitude m
11A1.006	600	2.7	At the road junction beside the water tower turn left on the road towards Hermin	Pass cemetery on the left	SE	116
11A1.007	290	3.0	In the centre of Hermin bear left and immediately turn right onto a smaller road	Pass the church on your left and Mairie on your right	SE	112
11A1.008	250	3.3	At fork in the road bear left	Rue du Calvaire	SE	105
11A1.009	250	3.5	At the junction, continue straight ahead	Towards the brow of the hill	SE	115
11A1.010	900	4.4	At the junction go straight ahead	D73, direction Caucourt	SE	117
11A1.011	700	5.1	On the entry to Caucourt fork left on rue du Parc	Calvaire to the left	SE	112
11A1.012	300	5.4	At the T-junction after crossing a small bridge turn right	Stream on your right	SW	101
11A1.013	400	5.8	At the T-junction with the main road, turn sharp left on the D73	Uphill, embankment on the right	SE	111
11A1.014	600	6.5	After leaving the village take the first road to the left	Towards the transmission mast on the horizon	NE	139
11A1.015	130	6.6	Bear right on the road		SE	137
11A1.016	2800	9.4	At the junction with the D73e2 turn left	Enter Cambligneul	E	134
11A1.017	300	9.7	At the crossroads with the D75 continue straight ahead	Direction Camblain-l'Abbé	SE	133

Waypoint	Distance between waypoints	Total km	Directions	Verification Point	Compass	Altitude m
11A1.018	1600	11.4	At the T-junction in Camblain-l'Abbé bear right on rue de l'Eglise and then left on rue Cojon	Follow sign for Cycle Route	S	122
11A1.019	400	11.7	Take the left fork	Direction Acq	SE	122
11A1.020	800	12.5	At the junction, bear right	Between open fields	S	118
11A1.021	1100	13.7	At the crossroads, shortly before entering Frévin-Capelle turn left	Chemin de Mont Saint Eloi	E	97
11A1.022	500	14.1	At the crossroads continue straight ahead	Uphill	SE	94
11A1.023	500	14.6	Take the left fork	Chemin d'Aubigny	E	99
11A1.024	600	15.2	At the crossroads in Acq, go straight ahead on rue de l'Egalité	Public toilet to the left	SE	94
11A1.025	260	15.4	Continue straight ahead on farm track	Large farm buildings on the right	SE	93
11A1.026	600	16.0	At the road junction go straight ahead on the main road, D49	The ruins of Mont St Eloi visible on the left	SE	82
11A1.027	300	16.3	On the outskirts of Ecoivres, take the left fork, rue de Douai	Pass wooden sign on the left	E	85
11A1.028	600	16.8	Take the right fork	Rue Oboeuf	E	83
11A1.029	140	17.0	At the T-junction turn right	Towards church	SE	83
11A1.030	110	17.1	Continue straight ahead on rue Oboeuf	Pass a stone wall and church on the right	SE	78
11A1.031	100	17.2	Turn right into place d' Eglise. Note:- the "Official Route" rejoins from the left	Church on right		75

Résidence de Séjour Ethic Étapes - Parc d'Olhain,Parc de Loisirs d'Olhain,62150 Houdain,Pas de Calais,France; Tel:+33(0)3 21 27 91 79; Email:reservation@parcdolhain.fr; Price:B; Note:Open all year,

Chambre d'Hôtes - le Gout des Hôtes,68 rue Marcel Lancino,62153 Ablain-Saint-Nazaire,Pas de Calais,France; Tel:+33(0)3 21 72 56 18; +33(0)6 77 13 48 43; Email:contact@legoutdeshotes.eu; Price:B

Ferme Auberge du Pré Molaine,9 rue Marcel Lancino,62153 Ablain-Saint-Nazaire,Pas de Calais,France; Tel:+33(0)3 21 45 20 01; Email:fermeaubergedupremolaine@orange.fr; Price:B

Bataille Valentin,23 Impasse rue de Lille,59840 Lompret,Nord,France; Tel:+33(0)6 85 69 92 93

Panel Laurent,25 rue de la Croix Rouge,62190 Lillers,Pas de Calais,France; Tel:+33(0)3 21 62 33 96

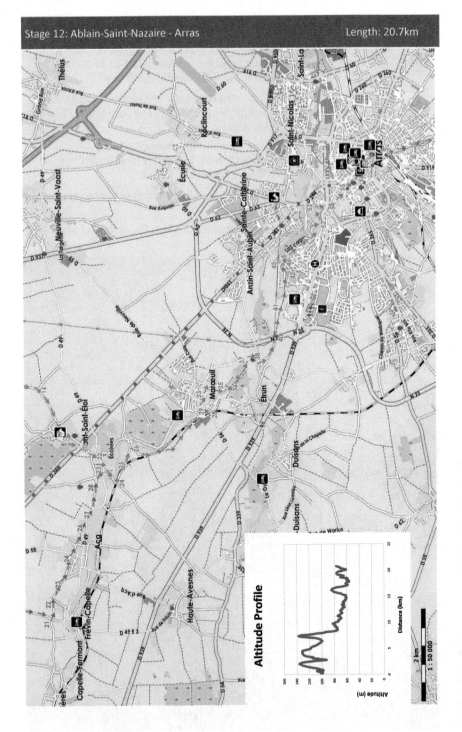

Stage Summary: the route continues on farm tracks and minor roads, crossing a further ridge before climbing to pass the ruins of the Abbey of Mont Saint Eloi and then returning to the Douai plain. The entry to Arras initially uses cycle tracks beside the main roads and then pathways through the park of Les Grandes Prairies before following the busy roads through the town centre to the Place des Héros

Distance from Canterbury: 217km   Distance to Besançon: 693km
Stage Ascent: 260m   Stage Descent: 283m

Waypoint	Distance between waypoints	Total km	Directions	Verification Point	Compass	Altitude m
12.001	0	0.0	At the T-junction with the road, turn right on the road which quickly becomes a stony track. Note:- if leaving from the centre of the village the most direct route is to briefly follow the D57, with the church on your left, and then rejoin the "Official Route" by turning left on rue des Vauxchaux	Wire fencing on the left, GR sign	W	99
12.002	110	0.1	At an oblique crossroads, continue straight ahead with the open field on your left	Church steeple on the left at the junction, GR sign	W	100
12.003	200	0.3	As the main track bears right, continue straight ahead through the wooden barriers	GR127 sign	W	99
12.004	400	0.7	Turn left over the small bridge and continue with the fence on your left	Yellow VF sign	S	108
12.005	70	0.7	Continue straight ahead on the tarmac road	Pass house n°10 on your left, GR sign	SW	97

Waypoint	Distance between waypoints	Total km	Directions	Verification Point	Compass	Altitude m
12.006	190	0.9	At the crossroads with the D57, continue straight ahead on rue des Vauxchaux	GR sign	SW	101
12.007	500	1.4	Keep left on the smaller road	Yellow VF sign	SW	121
12.008	500	1.9	At the top of the hill, continue straight ahead avoid the turning to the left	Mont St Eloi visible ahead, yellow VF sign	S	134
12.009	600	2.5	At the T-junction with a tarmac road, turn left and enter the village of Carency	Yellow VF sign	E	118
12.010	210	2.7	At the road junction, bear left continuing downhill	Rue du Moulin	SE	99
12.011	230	2.9	At the T-junction at the top of the hill, turn right and then immediately left	Direction Mont St Eloi, GR127 sign	S	101
12.012	160	3.1	At the crossroads with a church on your left, turn right	Rue Jules Ferry, GR sign	SW	112
12.013	210	3.3	At the road junction, turn left on rue du Général Barbot	GR sign	S	113
12.014	600	3.9	Take the left fork towards the woods	Mont St Eloi ahead, yellow VF sign	SE	130
12.015	1000	4.8	At the junction in the track, initially continue straight ahead and then immediately turn right. Note:- at the time of writing there was a misplaced yellow VF sign at this point	Woods on your left at the junction, GR sign	S	119

Waypoint	Distance between waypoints	Total km	Directions	Verification Point	Compass	Altitude m
12.016	1400	6.2	At the junction with the road, continue straight ahead	Yellow VF sign	SW	100
12.017	1200	7.4	At the top of the hill, continue straight ahead	Ruins of Mont St Eloi on your left, yellow VF sign	SW	136
12.018	90	7.5	With the entrance to the ruins immediately on your left, turn right	Rue des Tours	W	134
12.019	130	7.6	At the T-junction at the foot of the hill, turn left	GR sign	SW	121
12.020	300	7.9	At the junction with the main road, Chaussée Brunehaut,carefully cross the road and continue straight ahead on the pathway between the houses	GR sign	S	100
12.021	180	8.1	At the T-junction with the tarmac road, turn right, downhill	Towards the church spire, yellow VF sign	SW	94
12.022	260	8.4	At the T-junction turn right towards Acq	Stone calvaire at the junction, GR sign	SW	76
12.023	400	8.8	At the road junction beside the church, bear left and then right. Note:- the Alternate Route rejoins from the right	Rue de l'Eglise, GR sign	SW	75
12.024	400	9.2	Turn left on the tarmac road immediately after going under the railway bridge	GR sign	SE	80
12.025	500	9.7	Turn left over the bridge	GR sign	E	82
12.026	400	10.0	On entering the village of Bray, turn right on rue de l'Ecole	GR sign	S	74

Waypoint	Distance between waypoints	Total km	Directions	Verification Point	Compass	Altitude m
12.027	500	10.5	Immediately after re-crossing the railway, turn left on the stony track	Initially parallel to railway, yellow VF sign	SE	71
12.028	1700	12.2	At the T-junction turn left over the level-crossing	Yellow VF sign	NE	70
12.029	90	12.3	Bear right on D56, towards Maroeuil Centre	GR sign	E	69
12.030	100	12.4	Bear left on D56 again towards Maroeuil Centre	GR sign	NE	68
12.031	160	12.6	At the road junction, turn right on rue du Vert Bocage	Keep the iron railings on your left, GR sign	E	67
12.032	180	12.7	At the Stop sign, turn left	Cross the river la Scarpe, GR sign	NE	66
12.033	10	12.8	Turn right on rue de la Marlière	Parallel to river on the right	E	66
12.034	150	12.9	Turn right on rue de la Source	GR sign	S	63
12.035	500	13.4	Shortly after passing La Source de Sainte Bertille, turn right	Pass through the car park	SW	64
12.036	100	13.5	Turn left on a narrow grass path to continue beside river - do not cross the bridge	River on right	SE	65
12.037	800	14.3	At the T-junction with the road, turn right	Enter Louez, yellow VF sign	SE	61
12.038	140	14.4	Turn right towards Louez military cemetery	Direction Aubigny en A., GR sign	S	62
12.039	400	14.8	As the road bears right, turn left on rue des Maçons (marked No Through Road) - road becomes track	Yellow VF sign	SE	61
12.040	500	15.3	Proceed straight ahead under the road bridge	GR sign	E	67

Waypoint	Distance between waypoints	Total km	Directions	Verification Point	Compass	Altitude m
12.041	700	16.0	Continue straight ahead on the track	Golf course in the valley to the left, commercial area to the right	E	82
12.042	700	16.7	At the T-junction, bear left on the gravel path	New houses immediately on your left	NE	70
12.043	140	16.9	Continue straight ahead. Note:- the path ahead is blocked for horse riders, who should turn left onto the road and then turn right and right again to regain the "Official Route" at the T-junction with the main road	Down the steps	NE	64
12.044	90	17.0	Pass through metal turnstile gate and then bear right	Towards the main road	NE	61
12.045	70	17.0	At the T-junction with the main road, turn right on the footpath and bike track	D64, rue du 8 Mai 1945	SE	59
12.046	100	17.1	At the traffic lights, continue straight ahead and take the pedestrian crossing	Continue to follow the bike track	SE	59
12.047	900	18.0	At the end of the soccer pitch turn left into the park and then immediately right on the tarmac. Note:- a number of GR routes pass through the park and as a result the GR markings can be confusing	Yellow VF sign	SE	58
12.048	80	18.1	Continue straight ahead on the gravel path into the trees	GR sign	SE	60

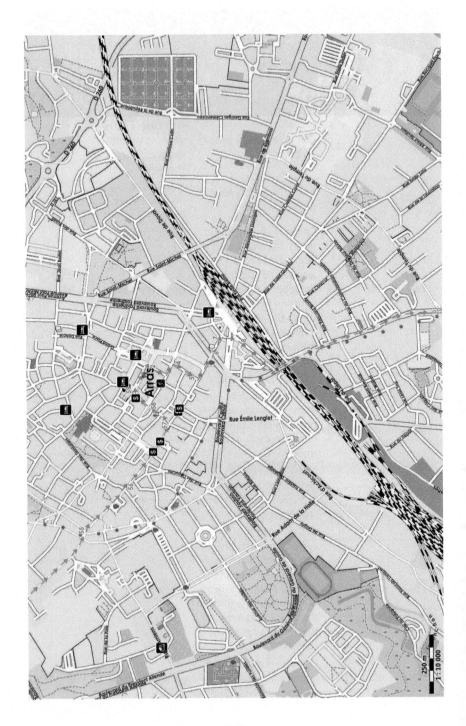

Waypoint	Distance between waypoints	Total km	Directions	Verification Point	Compass	Altitude m
12.049	40	18.1	At the T-junction, turn left on the tree lined tarmac road	GR sign	NE	60
12.050	130	18.2	With the pond directly ahead, bear right on the tarmac road	GR sign	SE	59
12.051	100	18.4	Beside the sign for l'histoire de la cité, turn right	Remain on the tarmac	S	58
12.052	90	18.4	Bear left, downhill, bear right to cross the bridge and then bear left	GR sign on the bridge	E	62
12.053	500	18.9	Turn right and climb the steps	Beware multiple GR signs	S	64
12.054	260	19.2	At the complex junction at end of chemin de la Baudimont, take the pedestrian crossings to follow the road towards Centre Ville	Rue Baudimont	SE	75
12.055	700	19.9	At the traffic lights, continue straight ahead towards Centre Ville	Rue Saint Aubert	SE	65
12.056	260	20.1	At the crossroads, continue straight ahead	Direction les Places	SE	63
12.057	400	20.5	Turn left on rue Désiré Delansorne	Direction Les Places, bell tower ahead	NE	70
12.058	120	20.6	At the traffic lights, continue straight ahead	Towards bell tower	NE	73
12.059	110	20.7	Arrive at Arras (LXXV) place des Héros	Beside bell tower		77

Maison Diocésaine Saint Vaast,103 rue Amiens,62000 Arras,Pas de Calais,France; Tel:+33(0)3 21 21 40 00; Web-site:arras.catholique.fr/maison-diocesaine-arras

Presbytère,16 rue Raoul Briquet,62223 Saint-Nicolas,Pas de Calais,France; Tel:+33(0)3 21 55 41 36

Chambres d'Hôtes - la Grenouillère,(Olivier Demoulin),15 rue Marechal Léclerc,62690 Frévin-Capelle,Pas de Calais,France; Tel:+33(0)3 21 48 52 47; +33(0)6 82 44 40 88; Email:contact@lagrenouillere-maisondhote.com; Price:B

Chambres d'Hôtes - Domaine de la Tillièr,113 Chemin de Bray,62161 Maroeuil,Pas de Calais,France; Tel:+33(0)3 21 58 79 30; +33(0)6 71 27 97 74; Email:contact@domainedelatilliere.com; Web-site:domainedelatilliere.com; Price:B; Note:Hunting centre,

Chambres d'Hôtes - la Ferme des 4 Vents,(Antoinette Lesueur),Route de Roclincourt,62223 Saint-Nicolas,Pas de Calais,France; Tel:+33(0)3 21 55 27 85; Email:antoinette.lesueur@orange.fr; Price:B; PR

Chambre d'Hôtes - le Clos Grincourt,18 rue du Château,62161 Duisans,Pas de Calais,France; Tel:+33(0)3 21 48 68 33; Email:contact@leclosgrincourt.com; Web-site:www.leclosgrincourt.com; Price:B

B&B Hôtel Arras,Parc des Bonnettes, avenue du Mal Koenig,62022 Arras,Pas de Calais,France; Tel:+33(0)8 92 70 22 13; Web-site:www.hotel-bb.com/en/hotels/arras.htm; Price:B

Chambres d'Hôtes - Laure Blanchet,6 rue de Jérusalem,62000 Arras,Pas de Calais,France; Tel:+33(0)3 21 71 56 78; Price:B

Hotel les Trois Luppars,49 Grand'place,62000 Arras,Pas de Calais,France; Tel:+33(0)3 21 60 02 03; Web-site:www.hotel-les3luppars.com; Price:A

Hôtel Diamant,5 place Héros,62000 Arras,Pas de Calais,France; Tel:+33(0)3 21 71 23 23; Email:info@arras-hotel-diamant.com; Web-site:www.arras-hotel-diamant.com; Price:A

Hotel Ibis Arras,Place Ipswich, 11 rue de Justice,62000 Arras,Pas de Calais,France; Tel:+33(0)3 21 23 61 61; Email:H1567@accor.com; Web-site:www.ibis.com/Arras; Price:A

Le Passe Temps,1 place Mar Foch,62000 Arras,Pas de Calais,France; Tel:+33(0)3 21 50 04 04; Web-site:www.hotelrestaurantlepassetemps.com; Price:B

Hotel Formula 1,27 avenue d'Immercourt,62217 Tilloy-Lès-Mofflaines,Pas de Calais,France; Tel:+33(0)8 91 70 51 67; Email:H2284@accor.com; Price:C

Earl Nollet Olivier,0 rue de la Warde,62144 Mont-Saint-Éloi,Pas de Calais,France; Tel:+33(0)9 81 08 85 15

Pony Pouce,37 route Nationale Lens,62223 Sainte-Catherine,Pas de Calais,France; Tel:+33(0)3 21 50 10 45; Web-site:www.infoloisirs.fr/pony-pouce-10587.html

K'Val Cad - Centre Équestre,5 rue Pierre Bérégovoy,62217 Beaurains,Pas de Calais,France; Tel:+33(0)3 21 15 07 41; Email:k.val.cad@orange.fr

Office de Tourisme,Place des Héros,62000 Arras,Pas de Calais,France; Tel:+33(0)3 21 51 26 95

Crédit Mutuel,10 rue Désiré Delansorne,62000 Arras,Pas de Calais,France; Tel:+33(0)8 20 35 20 13

Société Générale,19 place Théâtre,62000 Arras,Pas de Calais,France; Tel:+33(0)3 21 21 28 50

BNP Paribas,21 rue Ernestale,62000 Arras,Pas de Calais,France; Tel:+33(0)8 20 82 00 01

Banque Populaire,31 rue Gambetta,62000 Arras,Pas de Calais,France; Tel:+33(0)8 20 00 09 15

Crédit du Nord,64 rue Gambetta,62000 Arras,Pas de Calais,France; Tel:+33(0)3 21 24 37 00

Gare SNCF,Place du Maréchal Foch,62000 Arras,Pas de Calais,France; Tel:+33(0)8 92 33 53 35; Web-site:www.sncf.fr

Centre Hospitalier,57 avenue Winston Churchill,62000 Arras,Pas de Calais,France; Tel:+33(0)3 21 21 10 10; Web-site:fo.ch.arras.over-blog.com

Capsule Cycle,3 rue Copernic,62000 Arras,Pas de Calais,France; Tel:+33(0)3 21 71 03 67

Cycle Devis,7 Bis rue Emile Legrelle,62000 Arras,Pas de Calais,France; Tel:+33(0)3 21 15 37 87

Maréchal Ferrant Norbert Laga,13 Résidence Maurice Lemaître,62217 Beaurains,Pas de Calais,France; +33(0)6 68 65 08 89

Chuffart Grégory,4 Chaussée Brunehaut,62144 Mont-Saint-Éloi,Pas de Calais,France; Tel:+33(0)3 21 22 90 93

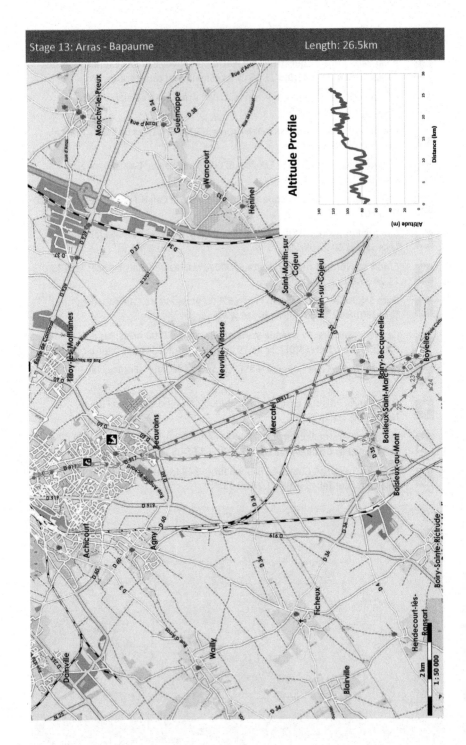

Stage Summary: after leaving Arras progress is easy using straight and generally level minor roads and tracks across farmland and first world war battlefields. There are no intermediate facilities.

Distance from Canterbury: 238km

Distance to Besançon: 672km

Stage Ascent: 271m

Stage Descent: 2226m

Waypoint	Distance between waypoints	Total km	Directions	Verification Point	Compass	Altitude m
13.001	0	0.0	From Arras centre with the bell tower behind, follow the right hand side of the place des Héros	Car park on the left	SE	77
13.002	70	0.1	Turn right to leave the place	Rue des Balançes	SW	76
13.003	100	0.2	At the T-junction, turn left	Rue Emile Legrelle	SE	75
13.004	60	0.2	Take the first turning to the right	Narrow street, rue Briquet Tailliander	SW	75
13.005	130	0.4	At the T-junction, turn left	No Entry sign, rue Gambetta	SE	74
13.006	130	0.5	At the traffic lights continue straight ahead	Towards the railway station	SE	74
13.007	70	0.6	Turn right in place du Maréchal Foch	Station ahead	S	75
13.008	80	0.7	Bear right into rue du Dr Brassart	Pass the hotel on your right and railway on your left	SW	72
13.009	200	0.9	At the T-junction, turn left on the avenue du Maréchal Léclerc	Cross over railway	S	71
13.010	800	1.7	Continue straight ahead at the crossroads	D917 (former N17) direction Beaurains	S	85
13.011	1600	3.2	At the traffic lights, continue straight ahead	Direction Bapaume	S	90
13.012	800	4.0	Turn right onto rue Robespierre, towards the water tower	Restaurant La Nouvelle Auberge on the corner, yellow VF sign	S	95
13.013	500	4.4	Continue straight ahead on the tarmac, pass under the highway bridge	GR sign	S	88

Waypoint	Distance between waypoints	Total km	Directions	Verification Point	Compass	Altitude m
13.014	1600	6.0	Take the right fork and remain on the tarmac	Keep the church and trees on your left, GR sign	S	74
13.015	600	6.6	At the crossroads in Mercatel continue straight ahead on rue de l'Abbiette	Small chapel to the left of the junction, GR sign	S	76
13.016	800	7.4	Continue straight ahead on the road	Pass under the TGV track	S	93
13.017	1400	8.8	Continue straight ahead and avoid the path to the right	Pass Montaigu Chapelle on your right	S	87
13.018	500	9.3	At the T-junction in Camblain-l'Abbé bear right on rue de l'Eglise and then left on rue Cojon		W	74
13.019	140	9.4	Turn left onto a pathway into the woods	Yellow VF sign	SE	75
13.020	500	9.9	At the junction with a tarmac road, continue straight ahead on the grassy track between the trees	Cemetery on your right, GR sign	SE	78
13.021	230	10.2	At the crossroads with a further tarmac road, continue straight ahead on the disused railway track	Brick built house on your right, ignore the GR cross	SE	84
13.022	240	10.4	Continue straight ahead on the old railway track, avoid turning to the right	Radio tower visible on your right	SE	90
13.023	900	11.3	At the crossroads with the tarmac road, turn right on the road	Yellow VF sign	SW	75
13.024	220	11.5	At the junction in the tracks, continue straight ahead on the grassy track	Towards the wind generators and church steeple on the horizon	SW	76
13.025	800	12.2	At the junction with the broader track, turn left and continue slightly uphill	Towards the church, yellow VF sign	S	79

Waypoint	Distance between waypoints	Total km	Directions	Verification Point	Compass	Altitude m
13.026	900	13.1	At the junction in the tracks, continue straight ahead on the tarmac	Pass small chapel on your right	S	101
13.027	130	13.3	At the crossroads with the D12, continue straight ahead on the track	Pass the village of Hamelincourt on your right, yellow VF sign	S	102
13.028	700	14.0	At the T-junction in the tracks, turn right	Yellow VF sign	W	105
13.029	250	14.2	At the crossroads with the D12, continue straight ahead on the tarmac road and then immediately turn left on the track	Yellow VF sign	S	107
13.030	2100	16.4	At the T-junction with the road, turn right on the road towards the village of Courcelles-le-Comte	Chapelle Saint Sulpice ahead	W	112
13.031	400	16.8	At the road junction, turn sharp left and pass beside the Chapelle Saint Sulpice	Direction Gomiécourt, C9	SE	109
13.032	1300	18.0	At the T-junction in Gomiécourt turn right, direction Achiet-le-Grand and then immediately turn left	Direction Gomiécourt South Cemetery, GR sign	SE	114
13.033	900	18.9	At the T-junction, turn left	Towards Gomiécourt South Cemetery, yellow VF sign	NE	108
13.034	210	19.1	Just before reaching the cemetery, turn right on the tarmac road	Slightly uphill, between embankments	SE	105
13.035	700	19.9	At the junction, continue straight ahead on the tarmac	Hedgerow on your left, GR sign	SE	99
13.036	1000	20.8	Just before the brow of the hill, continue straight ahead on the tarmac	Pass large barns on your right	SE	110

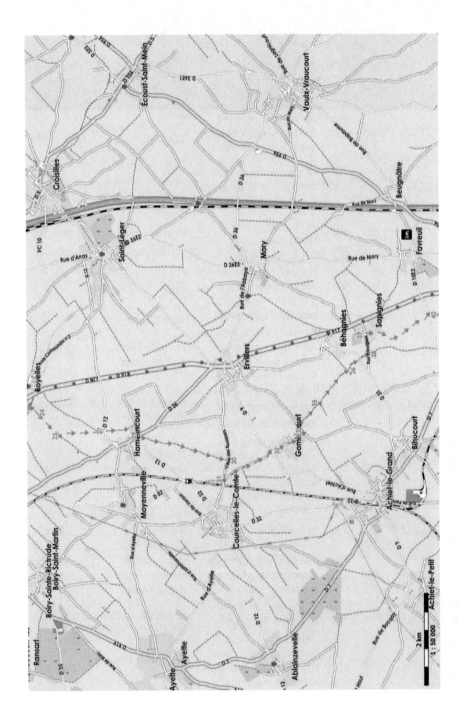

Waypoint	Distance between waypoints	Total km	Directions	Verification Point	Compass	Altitude m
13.037	400	21.2	At the crossroads, continue straight ahead on the track	Towards Bapaume on the horizon, GR sign	SE	119
13.038	250	21.4	At the crossroads with the tarmac road, turn left	Towards the church spire	E	119
13.039	400	21.8	At the crossroads beside the church in Sapignies, turn right	Towards the German military cemetery, GR sign	S	120
13.040	1700	23.5	At the crossroads with a tarmac road, continue straight ahead on the track	Yellow VF sign	S	109
13.041	1500	24.9	At the T-junction with a road and with an ivy covered house ahead, turn left and immediately right	Yellow VF sign	S	114
13.042	300	25.3	At the T-junction with a tarmac road, turn left	GR sign	SE	112
13.043	270	25.5	At the T-junction with D929 turn right, cross the disused railway and then turn left	Pass Mr Bricolage on your right. At the time of writing the yellow VF sign was pointing in the wrong direction	SE	116
13.044	500	26.0	At the crossroads, turn left towards the green spire	GR sign	E	122
13.045	170	26.2	At the crossroads, turn right	Rue Oribus, GR sign	SE	123
13.046	120	26.3	At the T-junction, turn left and continue straight ahead towards the centre of Bapaume	GR sign points to the right	E	124
13.047	190	26.5	Arrive at Bapaume centre	At the crossroads with rue de Péronne		122

Paroisse Notre Dame Pitie,3 rue Eglise,62450 Bapaume,Pas de Calais,France; Tel:+33(0)9 60 51 20 69; +33(0)3 21 07 13 37; Price:D

Chambre d'Hôtes- Aux Portes de l'Artois,30 rue de Beugnatre,62450 Favreuil,Pas de Calais,France; Tel:+33(0)3 21 48 77 37; Price:B

Chambre d'Hôtes - la Villa de Victoria,8 rue Favreuil,62450 Biefvillers-Lès-Bapaume,Pas de Calais,France; Tel:+33(0)3 21 07 13 48; +33(0)6 13 50 27 31; Email:lavilladevictoria@yahoo.fr; Price:A

Hôtel Restaurant le Gourmet,10 rue Gare,62450 Bapaume,Pas de Calais,France; Tel:+33(0)3 21 07 20 00; Email:legourmet.bapaume@wanadoo.fr; Web-site:www.le-gourmet.fr; Price:B

Syndicat d'Initiative,10 place Faidherbe,62450 Bapaume,Pas de Calais,France; Tel:+33(0)3 21 59 89 84

Crédit Mutuel,23 place Faidherbe,62450 Bapaume,Pas de Calais,France; Tel:+33(0)8 20 35 20 27

Crédit du Nord,11 place Sadi Carnot,62450 Bapaume,Pas de Calais,France; Tel:+33(0)3 21 16 85 40

Caisse d'Epargne,1 place République,62450 Bapaume,Pas de Calais,France; Tel:+33(0)8 20 82 18 14

CIC,57 rue Péronne,62450 Bapaume,Pas de Calais,France; Tel:+33(0)3 21 16 17 80

Centre Hospitalier,55 rue République,62450 Bapaume,Pas de Calais,France; Tel:+33(0)3 21 59 88 11

Cabinet Médical Faidherbe Scm,11 place Faidherbe,62450 Bapaume,Pas de Calais,France; Tel:+33(0)3 21 07 14 33

Pouillaude Xemar,13 rue Faubourg de Péronne,62450 Bapaume,Pas de Calais,France; Tel:+33(0)3 21 07 11 14

Albers Sports,15 rue Arras,62450 Bapaume,Pas de Calais,France; Tel:+33(0)3 21 50 23 37

Escoriza Manuel,21 rue de Bihucourt,62121 Béhagnies,Pas de Calais,France; Tel:+33(0)3 21 24 99 25

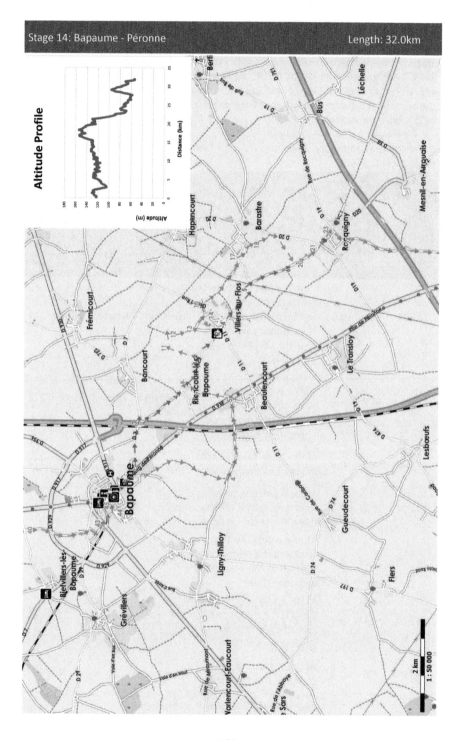

Stage Summary: the route uses quiet country roads and farm tracks and makes for easy going for all groups. The VF and GR145 signposting cease in the village of Roquiny and will not restart until a little after Berry-au-Bac in the region of Champagne-Ardennes. At the expense of using some minor roads, the distance to Péronne can be reduced by 5km by following the Alternate Routes.

Distance from Canterbury: 264km   Distance to Besançon: 645km
Stage Ascent: 269m   Stage Descent: 338m

Waypoint	Distance between waypoints	Total km	Directions	Verification Point	Compass	Altitude m
14.001	0	0.0	From the junction between rue de Péronne and rue de l'Eglise in the centre of Bapaume, take rue de Péronne, D917	Direction Péronne	SE	122
14.002	600	0.5	Turn right on rue de Lesboeufs. Note:- 2.5km may be saved by continuing straight ahead on the more direct Alternate Route	Yellow VF sign	S	122
14.003	400	0.9	At the stone calvaire, take the left fork on the track	Yellow VF sign	S	126
14.004	2000	2.9	At the T-junction with the road, turn left on the road towards the church spire	Military cemeteries on your left and right, yellow VF sign	E	104
14.005	1800	4.7	After crossing the TGV track and the motorway, turn left at the T-junction with the D11e2	GR sign	NE	117
14.006	80	4.8	At the crossroads with the D917, turn left and immediately right onto a small tarmac road		N	116
14.007	700	5.5	At the junction in tracks, continue straight ahead		N	127
14.008	160	5.6	Take the right fork on the stony track	Towards the farmhouse	NE	128

Waypoint	Distance between waypoints	Total km	Directions	Verification Point	Compass	Altitude m
14.009	300	5.9	At the T-junction beside the farmhouse on the edge of Riencourt lès Bapaume, turn right on the road. The Alternate Route joins from the left	Rue Principale, GR sign	SE	124
14.010	600	6.5	Shortly after passing the Manchester military cemetery, turn left on the track. Note:- 2.2km may be saved by continuing straight ahead and following the Alternate Route	Yellow VF sign	N	124
14.011	800	7.3	Turn right on the grass track between open fields	Sign "Turn right in 300m on the VF"	E	116
14.012	300	7.6	At the T-junction in the tracks, turn right	Large farm building on the right of the track ahead	S	124
14.013	700	8.2	Take the left fork	Yellow VF sign	SE	118
14.014	400	8.6	Turn left on rue du Calvaire	Calvaire ahead, GR sign	E	122
14.015	250	8.8	At the crossroads beside the calvaire, continue straight ahead on the track	Towards the trees, yellow VF sign	SE	119
14.016	1300	10.1	At the T-junction with the road, turn left	Towards the copse of trees, yellow VF sign	E	120
14.017	100	10.2	At the crossroads, turn right on the stony track	Yellow VF sign	SE	122
14.018	400	10.6	At the junction with a small tarmac road, continue straight ahead	Church spire on your left, GR sign	SE	125
14.019	500	11.1	At the T-junction with the road, turn right and then immediately right again	Pass the calvaire on your right, yellow VF sign	SW	127
14.020	900	12.0	At the T-junction with a gravel track, turn left. Note:- Alternate Route joins from the right	Towards the modern church tower, GR sign	SE	126

Waypoint	Distance between waypoints	Total km	Directions	Verification Point	Compass	Altitude m
14.021	700	12.6	The track joins a tarmac road in front of cemetery, continue straight ahead at the junction	Village of Roquigny, GR sign	SE	133
14.022	290	12.9	Beside the bell tower, continue straight ahead, direction Betancourt, D19, rue du Calviere	Café on the left, GR sign	SE	132
14.023	200	13.1	Turn right on rue de Sailly	GR sign	SW	130
14.024	400	13.5	At the junction bear left on the road. Note:- at the time of writing the yellow VF signs and the GR145 signs cease at this point	Leave the village	S	129
14.025	3100	16.6	At the junction with the D172, continue straight ahead	Towards the village	S	151
14.026	280	16.9	On entering Sailly-Saillisel, take the first turning to the left	Rue de Moislains	SE	152
14.027	2500	19.3	At the crossroads turn right, direction Moislains on the D184	Pass Bois des Vaux, on the left	S	142
14.028	3600	22.9	At the bottom of the hill in Moislains, bear right on rue Verte	Direction Bouchavesnes, D149, ivy covered buildings on your right	S	73
14.029	400	23.3	At the junction, continue straight ahead	D149 turns right	S	71
14.030	80	23.4	Turn left on rue Carré	Towards the church	E	70
14.031	250	23.6	At the T-junction, turn right and then bear left	Pass church on the hill to the left	SE	72
14.032	100	23.7	At the crossroads continue straight ahead and then immediately take the right fork	D184, rue de l'Ecluse, direction Templeux	SE	77
14.033	220	23.9	Turn right and continue with the canal du Nord on your left	Towards the lock	S	79

Waypoint	Distance between waypoints	Total km	Directions	Verification Point	Compass	Altitude m
14.034	500	24.4	At the junction, following the lock, continue straight ahead	Remain beside the canal	SW	75
14.035	600	25.0	Continue straight ahead	Under the metal bridge	SW	73
14.036	1700	26.6	Immediately before the next bridge, bear right and then turn left to cross the bridge	Pass the centre equestre on your right	S	62
14.037	400	27.1	At the road junction in Allaines, continue straight ahead	Grande Rue	SW	60
14.038	500	27.5	At the road junction, after passing the church, turn left	Rue du Pont	S	60
14.039	220	27.7	At the T-junction, turn right on rue du Mont Saint Quentin	Pass a garage with a "stork" on the roof	SW	59
14.040	1600	29.3	Cross over main road, and take gravel track ahead	Pass a camping sign and house n°145 on the left	SW	93
14.041	80	29.4	Turn left at the rear of the house	Trees to the left and open fields to the right	S	90
14.042	60	29.4	Bear right and proceed between two concrete pillars	Grassy track	S	89
14.043	500	29.9	Cross the car park towards main road	Pass a supermarket on your left	S	78
14.044	200	30.1	Cross the main road and take rue de Madrid	MacDonald's to the right	W	76
14.045	300	30.4	At the crossroads, turn left	Avenue de l'Europe	SW	69
14.046	500	30.9	At the roundabout turn left	Direction "Historia de la Grande Guerre"	SE	65
14.047	600	31.5	At the mini-roundabout continue straight ahead	Avenue de la République	SE	61
14.048	400	32.0	Arrive at Péronne centre	Beside Musée de la Grande Guerre		53

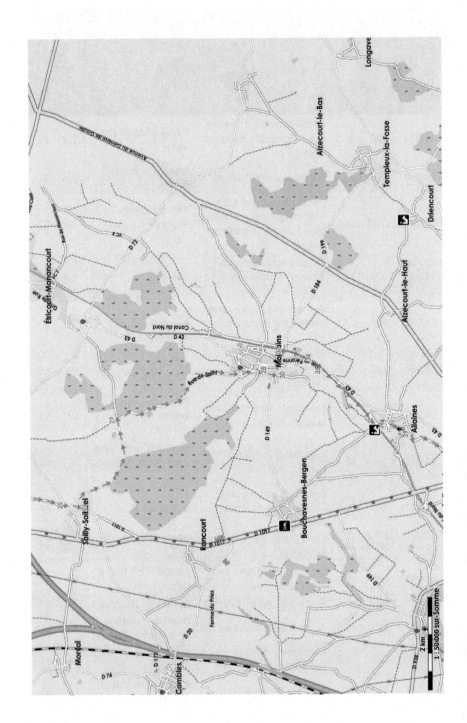

Alternate Route #14.A1				Length: 2.8km		
Stage Summary: a more direct route to Riencourt lès Bapaume following a minor road.						
Stage Ascent: 26m				Stage Descent: 23m		

Waypoint	Distance between waypoints	Total km	Directions	Verification Point	Compass	Altitude m
14A1.001	0	0.0	Continue straight ahead	Chaussée Brunehaut	SE	74
14A1.002	120	0.1	At the crossroads go straight ahead	Modern houses on both side of the road	SE	74
14A1.003	1200	1.3	At the crossroads at the bottom of the hill, continue straight ahead	Uphill between trees	SE	80
14A1.004	1300	2.5	At the Stop sign turn right	D72, direction Hermin	S	90
14A1.005	220	2.8	Continue straight ahead on the road. Note:- the "Official Route" rejoins from the right"	Rue Principale		126

Alternate Route #14.A2				Length: 3.2km		
Stage Summary: more direct route via Villers au Flos using small country roads.						
Stage Ascent: 26m				Stage Descent: 24m		

Waypoint	Distance between waypoints	Total km	Directions	Verification Point	Compass	Altitude m
14A2.001	0	0.0	Continue straight ahead on the road	Towards the village	SE	125
14A2.002	900	0.8	At the crossroads, beside the Mairie in Villers-au-Flos, bear left	Direction Bancourt, D11	E	123
14A2.003	160	1.0	In the centre of the village, turn right	Rue du Transloy	SE	122
14A2.004	130	1.1	Beside the cemetery take the left fork	Pass cemetery on right	SE	122
14A1.005	220	2.8	Continue straight ahead on the road. Note:- the "Official Route" rejoins from the right"	Rue Principale		126

Paroisse de Péronne,16 rue Saint-Jean,80200 Péronne,Somme,France; Tel:+33(0)3 22 84 16 90; Price:D

Hotel - le Prieuré,24 route Nationale 17,80360 Rancourt,Somme,France; Tel:+33(0)3 22 85 04 43; Email:contact@hotel-le-prieure.fr; Web-site:www. hotel-le-prieure.fr; Price:A

Le Provençal,15 Faubourg Bretagne,80200 Péronne,Somme,France; Tel:+33(0)3 22 84 06 16; Price:B

La Picardière,7 Faubourg Bretagne,80200 Péronne,Somme,France; Tel:+33(0)3 22 84 02 36; Price:B

L'Auberge des Remparts,17 rue Beaubois,80200 Péronne,Somme,France; Tel:+33(0)3 22 88 41 10; +33(0)9 64 12 51 21; Email:contact@ aubergedesremparts.fr; Web-site:www.aubergedesremparts.fr; Price:B

Hotel Campanile,Route de Paris,80200 Péronne,Somme,France; Tel:+33(0)3 22 84 22 22; Web-site:www.campanile.com; Price:B

Camping du Port de Plaisance,80200 Péronne,Somme,France; Tel:+33(0)3 22 84 19 31; Email:contact@camping-plaisance.com; Web-site:www.camping-plaisance.com; Price:C; Note:Chalets also available,

Crampon Sebastien,6 rue Riencourt,62450 Villers-au-Flos,Pas de Calais,France; Tel:+33(0)3 21 71 48 02

Centre Equestre - Allaines,7 rue Bouchavesnes,80200 Allaines,Somme,France; Tel:+33(0)3 22 84 19 99; +33(0)6 69 51 05 81; Web-site:www. centreequestreallaines.ffe.com

Office du Tourisme,16 place André Audinot,80200 Péronne,Somme,France; Tel:+33(0)3 22 84 42 38

LCL,4 rue Saint-Sauveur,80200 Péronne,Somme,France; Tel:+33(0)3 22 73 38 41

BNP Paribas,16 place Louis Daudré,80200 Péronne,Somme,France; Tel:+33(0)8 20 82 00 01

Crédit du Nord,23 place Louis Daudré,80200 Péronne,Somme,France; Tel:+33(0)3 22 73 01 55

Centre Hospitalier,Place Jeu de Paume,80200 Péronne,Somme,France; Tel:+33(0)3 22 83 61 94

Chennoufi Mohamed,10 rue Juifs,80200 Péronne,Somme,France; Tel:+33(0)3 22 84 13 86

Clinique Veterinaire,1 Fbg de Bretagne,80200 Péronne,Somme,France; Tel:+33(0)3 22 84 60 00

Auranasport,Rue Madrid,80200 Péronne,Somme,France; Tel:+33(0)9 63 44 31 30

Cycles Nicolas Dubois,9 Faubourg Bretagne,80200 Péronne,Somme,France; Tel:+33(0)3 22 84 42 47

A2 Taxi,18 rue des Bouleaux,80200 Péronne,Somme,France; Tel:+33(0)3 22 84 59 22

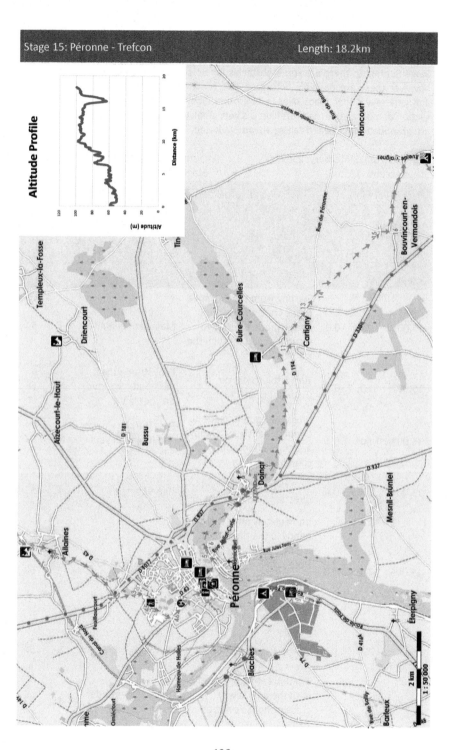

Altitude Profile

Stage Summary: there are some obstacles for horse riders on the exit from Péronne, however these are passable with care. The remainder of the route combines tracks and generally minor roads over level ground. Shortly before Trefcon there is a short section of more major road. Trefcon is a very small village, with very limited facilities. If accommodation is needed calling ahead is advised.

Distance from Canterbury: 296km   Distance to Besançon: 614km
Stage Ascent: 183m   Stage Descent: 138m

Waypoint	Distance between waypoints	Total km	Directions	Verification Point	Compass	Altitude m
15.001	0	0.0	Starting from the entrance to the château, Musée de la Grande Guerre, go straight ahead through the car par	Main gate behind	E	54
15.002	50	0.1	Turn left into rue du Gladimont, uphill	Pedestrian zone, pass Hotel St Cloud on your left	NE	56
15.003	60	0.1	Cross the square, place du Commandant Louis Daudré and turn left in front of the church of St Jean	Pass the clock tower and Maire on your left	NE	57
15.004	290	0.4	Turn right at traffic lights direction Flamicourt, D199	Rue Béranger	E	57
15.005	700	1.0	Immediately after the road bends to the right, turn left onto the gravel track. Note:- riders wishing to avoid the obstacles on the track should remain on rue Joliot-Curie until reaching Doingt	Pass house n° 45 on your left	E	50
15.006	300	1.3	Continue straight ahead	Former railway track	SE	52
15.007	1200	2.5	Continue straight ahead with the old railway crossing house on your right	Track passes under the main road	SE	53

Waypoint	Distance between waypoints	Total km	Directions	Verification Point	Compass	Altitude m
15.008	500	3.0	At the crossroads following the Doingt railway station, continue straight ahead	Remain on the old railway track	SE	58
15.009	700	3.7	At the crossroads with a tarmac road, continue straight ahead on the old railway track	Crash barriers to your left	E	61
15.010	2500	6.2	On meeting a partially tarmac track, turn right on the track and continue straight ahead uphill on rue du Puissard	Between the houses	SE	60
15.011	260	6.4	At the T-junction at the top of the hill, turn left into the village of Cartigny	D194	SE	73
15.012	900	7.3	Continue straight ahead at crossroads	Direction Hancourt	SE	66
15.013	270	7.6	Just before the Cartigny exit sign, continue straight ahead and pass the chapel on the hill to your left	Ivy covered brick wall on right	SE	68
15.014	280	7.9	After passing the chapel, bear right on the initially tarmac track between the fields	Water tower visible on the skyline to the left at the junction	SE	75
15.015	2000	9.9	At the top of the hill, bear left at the fork and immediately turn right at the crossroads	Village of Bouvincourt-en-Vermandois, rue de Beaumetz	S	97
15.016	300	10.2	In the village centre, with house n° 1 on your right, turn left on the road	Pass the war memorial on your left	E	94
15.017	1700	11.8	At the junction with the D15, turn right into the village of Vraignes-en-Vermandois	Signpost for Bouvincourt on the right	S	93

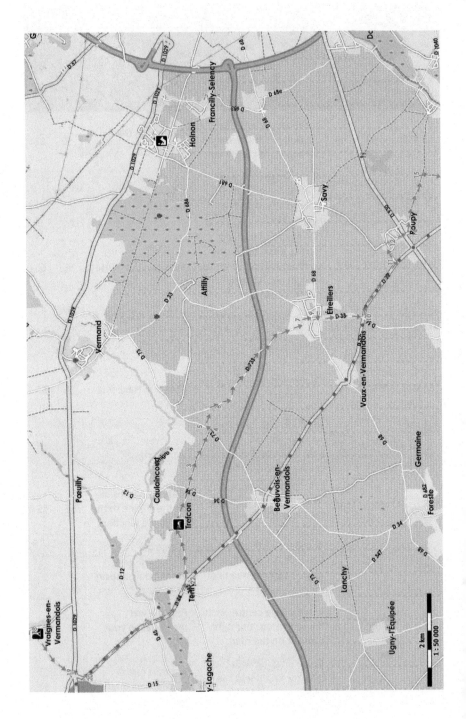

Waypoint	Distance between waypoints	Total km	Directions	Verification Point	Compass	
15.018	300	12.1	Pass through Vraignes and continue straight ahead	D15	SW	94
15.019	1500	13.6	At the roundabout take the 3rd exit, direction Tertry, D15	Large industrial complex and airfield to right	SW	95
15.020	260	13.8	Turn left	Direction Tertry, D44	SE	93
15.021	2000	15.8	At the crossroads in Tertry, continue straight ahead on the D44	Downhill	SE	78
15.022	1300	17.1	At the top of the hill, turn left	Direction Trefcon, pass under power lines	E	94
15.023	1100	18.2	Arrive at Trefcon centre	Crossroads with Allée de l'Eglise		99

Accommodation & Facilities .... Péronne - Trefcon

Champs d'Hôtes - le,Moulin de Binard,80200 Buire-Courcelles,Somme,France; Tel:+33(0)3 22 83 00 16; +33(0)6 09 71 20 34; Email:joel.bleriot@wanadoo.fr; Web-site:www.moulin-de-binard.fr; Price:B

Chambres d'Hôtes - le Val d' Omignon,(M. Hubert Wynands),3 rue Principale,02490 Trefcon,Aisne,France; Tel:+33(0)3 23 66 58 64; +33(0)6 99 19 95 47; Email:le.val-domignon@wanadoo.fr; Web-site:www.picardie-val-domignon.com; Price:B; Note:Will accept horses,

Le Château de Monchy - Chambres d'Hôtes,2 rue du Huit Mai 1945,80200 Monchy-Lagache,Somme,France; Tel:+33(0)3 22 85 08 49; Price:B

Camping des Hortensias,22 rue Basse,80240 Vraignes-en-Vermandois,Somme,France; Tel:+33(0)0 32 28 56 46 8; Email:campinghortensias@free.fr; Web-site:www.campinghortensias.com; Price:C

Centre Equestre de Driencourt,11 rue Aizecourt le Haut,80240 Driencourt,Somme,France; Tel:+33(0)3 22 83 14 03

Poney-Club du Vermandois,7 rue Charles Vavasseur,02760 Holnon,Aisne,France; Tel:+33(0)3 23 09 66 75

Azur Taxi,25 rue de la Chapelle,02590 Beauvois-en-Vermandois,Aisne,France; Tel:+33(0)3 23 64 12 12

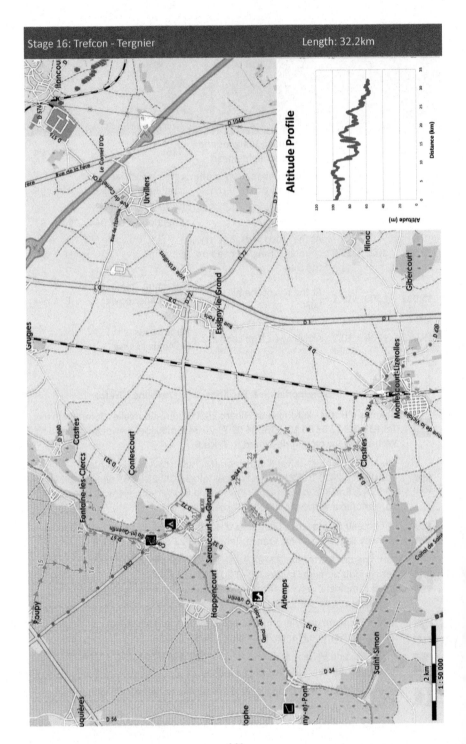

Altitude Profile

Stage Summary: Tergnier is a former railway hub with some unusual choices of accommodation. The route has some very pleasant off-road sections that are excellent for all groups, but with short stretches on potentially busy roads. The large town of St Quentin is 7 kilometres off the Main Route and can be reached by a short train journey from Tergnier.

Distance from Canterbury: 315km   Distance to Besançon: 595km
Stage Ascent: 209m   Stage Descent: 251m

Waypoint	Distance between waypoints	Total km	Directions	Verification Point	Compass	Altitude m
16.001	0	0.0	From the centre of Trefcon follow the D345 to the east	Pass the water tower on your right	E	99
16.002	900	0.9	At the crossroads, proceed straight ahead on a part made road	Sign for the Trefcon British cemetery on the left	E	96
16.003	600	1.5	Continue straight ahead	Between the fields	SE	92
16.004	900	2.3	At the T-junction, turn left	Direction Villevêque, D73	NE	93
16.005	140	2.5	Turn right on the part made road	Between fields, towards the spire on the horizon	E	94
16.006	500	2.9	At the T-junction with the road, turn right	Between fields and across motorway bridge	SE	93
16.007	3000	5.9	Bear right on rue Maurice Dallongeville	Village of Etreillers	SE	95
16.008	210	6.1	At the crossroads, continue straight ahead	Rue des Docteurs	S	97
16.009	140	6.3	At the T-junction turn right on Avenue du Général de Gaulle and then take the first turning to the left	Direction Seraucourt-le-Grand	S	98

Waypoint	Distance between waypoints	Total km	Directions	Verification Point	Compass	Altitude m
16.010	1100	7.4	At the crossroads, shortly after passing under a bridge, turn left with great care beside the busy road	D32, towards Roupy	SE	98
16.011	1400	8.8	Turn left on the small road towards the village. Note:- the D32 can be very busy, but if you are content to continue on the road to Seraucourt-le-Grand you will reduce your distance by 2km	Rue du moulin	NE	93
16.012	500	9.3	At the crossroads, turn right into the village of Roupy	Walled garden on the right	SE	98
16.013	500	9.7	At crossroads in Roupy, continue straight ahead on rue Barette	Church on the left of the junction	S	98
16.014	110	9.9	On the edge of Roupy turn left onto rue de Fontaine	Pass large barn on your right	E	97
16.015	1300	11.2	While climbing the hill on the stony track, turn right and continue beside a line of trees on your right	Château visible on the left of the junction	S	82
16.016	1000	12.1	Track bends to the left	Towards the woods	E	72
16.017	900	13.0	At the T-junction turn right onto the road	Towards the water tower	S	70
16.018	1400	14.4	At the crossroads, turn left direction Seraucourt-le-Grand, D32	Road crosses the canal	SE	81
16.019	900	15.3	In Seraucourt-le-Grand (LXXIII) bear right direction Artemps, D32	Church on your left	S	71

Waypoint	Distance between waypoints	Total km	Directions	Verification Point	Compass	Altitude m
16.020	270	15.5	At the crossroads beside the Madonna continue straight ahead on the D72. Note:- the GR signs relate to the GR655 which briefly crosses our route	Direction Essigny-le-Grand, GR sign	SE	73
16.021	500	16.0	Where the road turns sharply to the left, continue straight ahead on the stony track	GR sign	SE	90
16.022	1000	17.0	At the T-junction with the road, turn left and follow the road. Note:- the GR turns right at this point and leaves the VF	Towards church spire on the horizon	SE	89
16.023	800	17.8	At the crossroads continue straight ahead		SE	91
16.024	800	18.6	Bear right	Remain on the road	SW	84
16.025	900	19.4	As the road bears right, fork left on the left most track	Grassy track, towards the church	S	84
16.026	600	20.0	At the junction with the tarmac road, continue straight ahead	Towards the church	S	74
16.027	100	20.1	At the junction keep left	Pass the church on your right	S	75
16.028	150	20.2	At the T-junction, turn left	Beside the church	E	73
16.029	130	20.4	Bear right	Remain on D34	SE	72
16.030	1400	21.7	At the roundabout, bear right on D8, direction Jussy	Railway track on your left	SW	73
16.031	200	21.9	Turn left on rue de Missemboeuf	Towards the Stade Municipal	S	72
16.032	400	22.3	Bear left on rue du Lieutenant Brunehant	Towards the railway, No-Entry	SE	72
16.033	120	22.5	At the T-junction, turn left under railway bridge	Rue Louis Sébline	E	73

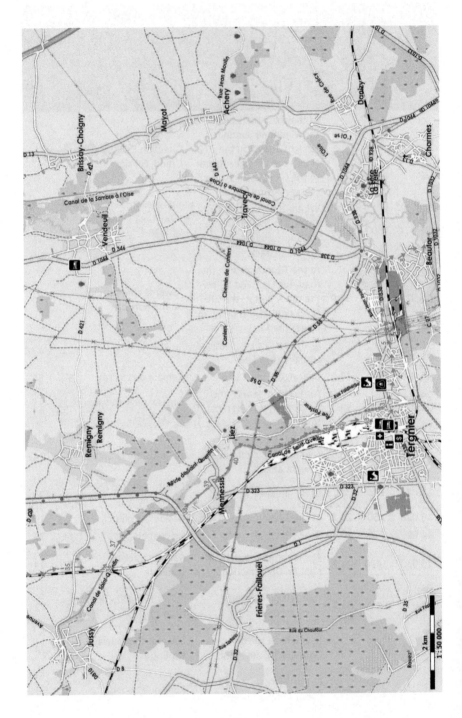

145

Waypoint	Distance between waypoints	Total km	Directions	Verification Point	Compass	Altitude m
16.034	70	22.5	At traffic lights turn right onto the gravel path	Close beside railway	S	75
16.035	1600	24.1	Cross the road and continue on track	Towards the woods, then beside the railway	S	76
16.036	700	24.8	Bear left to continue on track	Keep the canal close on your right	SE	69
16.037	600	25.4	Continue straight ahead	Canal lock on right	SE	64
16.038	1700	27.1	Follow the tow path under the highway		SE	65
16.039	900	28.0	Continue along the tow-path under the bridge	Beside lock	SE	60
16.040	700	28.7	After passing the lock continue straight ahead on the grass	Beside canal	S	55
16.041	2600	31.3	The tow-path emerges onto a road. Turn right	Over the bridge	S	56
16.042	160	31.4	Immediately after crossing the canal turn left	Follow the road between the railway and canal	S	58
16.043	800	32.2	Arrive at Tergnier	Beside the railway station		57

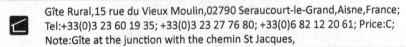

Gîte Rural,15 rue du Vieux Moulin,02790 Seraucourt-le-Grand,Aisne,France;
Tel:+33(0)3 23 60 19 35; +33(0)3 23 27 76 80; +33(0)6 82 12 20 61; Price:C;
Note:Gîte at the junction with the chemin St Jacques,

Halte Compostelle,2 rue du Pont,02640 Tugny-et-Pont,Aisne,France;
Tel:+33(0)3 23 68 78 93; +33(0)6 65 72 22 87; Email:graffitichinon@orange.fr ;
Web-site:composteltugnyetpont.over-blog.com; Price:D

Presbytère Fargniers,47 avenue Jean Jaurès,02700 Tergnier,Aisne,France;
Tel:+33(0)3 23 57 21 61

Auberge de Jeunesse,91 Boulevard Jean Bouin,02100 Saint-
Quentin,Aisne,France; Tel:+33(0)3 23 06 94 05; +33(0)3 23 06 94 19; Price:C;
Note:Open June to September,

Hôtel le Florence,42 rue Emile Zola,02100 Saint-Quentin,Aisne,France;
Tel:+33(0)3 23 64 22 22; Web-site:www.hotel-le-florence.fr; Price:B

Auberge de Vendeuil,D1044,02800 Vendeuil,Aisne,France;
Tel:+33(0)2 03 02 79 77 9; Price:B

Hotel des Voyageurs,60 rue Pierre Sémard,02700 Tergnier,Aisne,France;
Tel:+33(0)3 23 57 20 68; Price:B; Note:Curious place,

Le Paon,55 avenue Jean Jaurès,02700 Tergnier,Aisne,France; Tel:+33(0)3 23 57
04 13; Web-site:traiteur-lepaon.com; Price:B

Hotel Restaurant Indian Haweli,10 rue Pierre Semard,02700
Tergnier,Aisne,France; Tel:+33(0)3 23 52 49 61; Price:B

La Petite Auberge,17 rue Gaston Trioux,02300 Viry-Noureuil,Aisne,France;
Tel:+33(0)3 23 52 06 62; Email:contact@lapetite-auberge.fr;
Web-site:www.lapetite-auberge.fr; Price:B

Le Camping du Vivier Aux Carpes,10 rue Charles Voyeux,02790 Seraucourt-
le-Grand,Aisne,France; Tel:+33(0)3 23 60 50 10; Email:contact@camping-
picardie.com; Web-site:www.camping-picardie.com; Price:C; Note:Chalets
also available,

Gueny Philippe,35 Grande rue,02480 Artemps,Aisne,France;
Tel:+33(0)3 23 65 30 06

Pate Christopher,32 rue Faidherbe,02700 Tergnier,Aisne,France;
Tel:+33(0)6 28 52 53 35

Herbulot Yves,7 rue J et M Toussaint,02700 Tergnier,Aisne,France;
Tel:+33(0)3 23 39 91 60

Office de Tourisme,27 rue Victor Basch,02100 Saint-Quentin,Aisne,France;
Tel:+33(0)3 23 67 05 00

Mairie,Rue des 4 Fils Paul Doumer,02700 Tergnier,Aisne,France;
Tel:+33(0)3 23 57 11 27

$ Crédit du Nord,16 rue Isle,02100 Saint-Quentin,Aisne,France; Tel:+33(0)3 23 62 88 66

$ Credit Agricole,2 Boulevard Gustave Grégoire,02700 Tergnier,Aisne,France; Tel:+33(0)3 23 57 25 11

$ LCL,18 Boulevard Gambetta,02700 Tergnier,Aisne,France; Tel:+33(0)3 23 37 20 71

🚉 Gare SNCF,Avenue Léo Lagrange,02100 Saint-Quentin,Aisne,France; Tel:+33(0)8 92 33 53 35; Web-site:www.sncf.fr

🚉 Gare SNCF,2 Boulevard Gambetta,02700 Tergnier,Aisne,France; Tel:+33(0)8 92 33 53 35; Web-site:www.sncf.fr

Ⓗ Centre Hospitalier,1 avenue Michel de l'Hospital,02321 Saint-Quentin,Aisne,France; Tel:+33(0)3 23 06 71 71

Ⓗ Centre Hospitalier,94 rue Anciens Combattants Afn,02300 Chauny,Aisne,France; Tel:+33(0)3 23 38 55 00; Web-site:www.ch-chauny.fr

✚ Docteur Perrin Jean-Jacques,7 rue d'Estienne d'Orves,02100 Saint-Quentin,Aisne,France; Tel:+33(0)3 23 05 19 99

✚ Monsigny Marcel,29 place Herment,02700 Tergnier,Aisne,France; Tel:+33(0)3 23 56 39 52

🐾 Clinique Vétérinaire,49 rue Gabriel Péri,02100 Saint-Quentin,Aisne,France; Tel:+33(0)3 23 62 24 39

☎ Dussaux Philippe,16 rue Franklin,02700 Tergnier,Aisne,France; Tel:+33(0)3 23 57 00 06

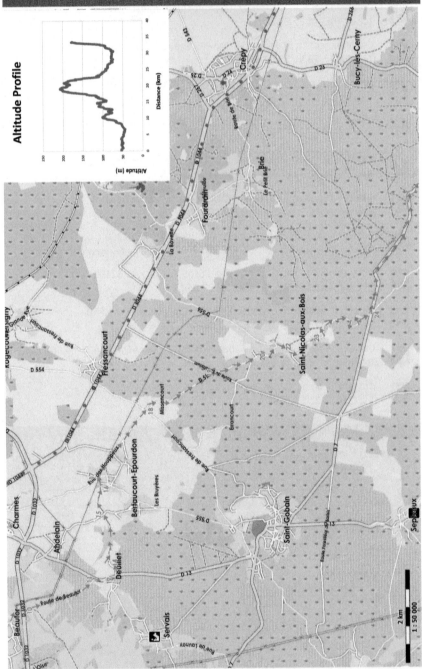

Stage Summary: another long section between accommodation points. The route quickly leaves Tergnier and crosses the huge forest of St Gobain. The route is almost exclusively on roads, but these are rarely busy before reaching Laon. There is a stiff climb near the Abbaye of St Nicolas, but you will be rewarded with good views of the Abbaye, the forest and lakes. Laon has a full range of facilities. There is also a frequent train service between Tergnier and Laon.

Distance from Canterbury: 347km
Stage Ascent: 480m

Distance to Besançon: 563km
Stage Descent: 357m

Waypoint	Distance between waypoints	Total km	Directions	Verification Point	Compass	Altitude m
17.001	0	0.0	From the railway station, continue straight ahead and then bear left on rue Marceau	Pass the cultural centre on your left	SE	55
17.002	500	0.5	At the T-junction, turn left	Towards the canal bridge	E	54
17.003	180	0.7	After crossing the canal, bear right on rue Carnot	Direction "Musée de la Resistance"	E	53
17.004	600	1.3	At the roundabout take the third exit	Long, straight road, rue Raymond Poincaré	E	52
17.005	700	2.0	At roundabout continue straight ahead on the D338	Pass the centre commercial on right	E	53
17.006	2000	4.0	At the traffic lights, turn right	Rue des Caves, D553, sign Beautor	S	53
17.007	400	4.4	Shortly after passing under the railway, bear left over the canal, then bear right	Canal on your right	S	51
17.008	180	4.6	Bear left towards St Gobain	Grande Rue	S	49
17.009	700	5.3	Turn left remaining on D553	Cross canal bridge	SE	48
17.010	500	5.7	Continue straight ahead across the main road	D553, direction Deuillet	S	48
17.011	1800	7.5	Turn right	Direction Servais, D13	S	51
17.012	180	7.7	Fork left, direction St. Gobain, D13	Pass "Au Rendezvous des Passants" on right	S	51

Waypoint	Distance between waypoints	Total km	Directions	Verification Point	Compass	Altitude m
17.013	300	8.0	Immediately after passing the exit sign from Deuillet, turn left onto the small road	White house on left	NE	53
17.014	400	8.4	The road deteriorates into a track	Farm on left	E	54
17.015	1100	9.5	Cross over the road to remain on the track	Woodland on right	E	74
17.016	600	10.1	Take the left fork	Route skirts Bertacourt-Epourdon	E	96
17.017	300	10.4	At the complex road junction take the second road on the right	Direction Missancourt,D55	SE	102
17.018	1800	12.2	At the crossroads in Missancourt, continue straight ahead	D55, towards forest	SE	87
17.019	1900	14.0	At the Stop sign, continue straight ahead on the D55	Route Forestière du Mont-Tortu	S	108
17.020	1000	15.0	Continue straight ahead, direction St Nicolas aux Bois, D55	Hamlet of le Moulin	SE	102
17.021	600	15.7	At the junction, continue straight ahead	Direction Centre Village, D55	S	95
17.022	140	15.8	Continue straight ahead on the D55	12th century church on right	S	99
17.023	1100	16.9	Continue uphill on D55	Abbaye de St Nicolas aux Bois on the right	SE	118
17.024	1800	18.7	At the crossroads, at the top of the hill, turn left	Direction Cessières, D7	SE	200
17.025	4900	23.6	In Cessières, continue straight ahead, direction Laon	Restaurant Le Rustique	E	104
17.026	6900	30.5	At the roundabout with the N44, continue straight ahead, direction la Neuville	The citadel and the high town of Laon ahead and to the right	E	74

Waypoint	Distance between waypoints	Total km	Directions	Verification Point	Compass	Altitude m
17.027	600	31.1	At the crossroads with D54, continue straight ahead on rue Gabriel Péri over the railway track	Signs for camping and hotels	E	79
17.028	1000	32.1	At the roundabout, continue straight ahead	Direction Centre Ville	E	94
17.029	170	32.3	At the traffic lights, turn right	Rue Jean Baptiste Lebas	SE	93
17.030	30	32.3	Immediately bear right on the smaller one-way road	Pass willow tree on left, towards cathedral in high town	SE	93
17.031	400	32.6	At the T-junction, bear right	Uphill, Rampe Saint Marcel	SE	106
17.032	400	33.1	Bear right on the steep road	Rue de l'Eperon	E	153
17.033	140	33.2	At the T-junction with the main road, turn right	Pass funicular (POMA) station on your left	W	168
17.034	130	33.3	Take the left fork, rue Franklin Roosevelt	Pass a hotel on your right, No Entry	SW	171
17.035	80	33.4	At the T-junction, turn left and left again	Direction Hôtel de Ville	E	176
17.036	90	33.5	Arrive at Laon (LXXII) old town in front of the Mairie	Place du Général Léclerc		178

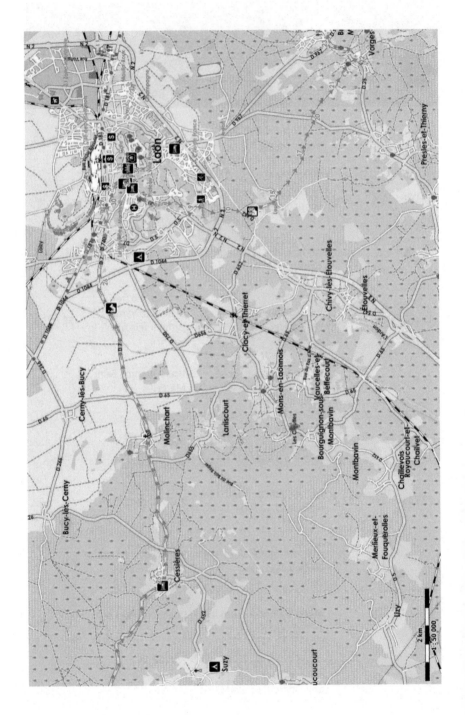

Presbytère Cathédrale,8 rue du Cloître,02000 Laon,Aisne,France; Tel:+33(0)3 23 20 26 54

Chambres d'Hôtes - Ferme de Brellemont,4 route de Brellemont,02410 Septvaux,Aisne,France; Tel:+33(0)3 23 52 57 45; Email:daniel.steichen@orange.fr; Price:B; Note:Pension for horses possible,

Chambre d'Hotes Laon Cathedrale,12 rue Milon de Martigny,02000 Laon,Aisne,France; Tel:+33(0)3 23 79 32 39; +33(0)6 62 06 32 39; Email:yb.joannoteguy@gmail.com; Web-site:www.chambre-hotes-laon-cathedrale.com; Price:B

Hotel les Chevaliers,3 rue Sérurier,02000 Laon,Aisne,France; Tel:+33(0)3 23 27 17 50; Email:hotelchevaliers@aol.com; Price:A

Chambres d'Hôtes - la Maison des 3 Rois,17 rue Saint-Martin,02000 Laon,Aisne,France; Tel:+33(0)3 23 20 74 24; +33(0)6 43 45 48 53; Email:lamaisondes3rois@gmail.com; Web-site:www.lamaisondes3rois.com; Price:A

Chambres d'Hôtes - la Forestière,7 Ruelle Buet,02320 Cessières,Aisne,France; Tel:+33(0)3 23 24 19 07; Email:jjdru@orange.fr; Web-site:chambres-hotes-laon.jimdo.com; Price:B

Chambres d'Hôtes - Frion Gérard,7 rue Marguerites,02000 Laon,Aisne,France; Tel:+33(0)3 23 20 21 27; Email:gerard.frion@laposte.net; Web-site:marguerites.voila.net; Price:B

Camping la Chênaie,Allée de la Chênaie,02000 Laon,Aisne,France; Tel:+33(0)3 23 20 25 56; Email:contact-camping-laon@gmail.com; Web-site:www.camping-laon.com; Price:C

Les Etangs du Moulin,7 Bis rue de l'Arbre Rond,02320 Suzy,Aisne,France; Tel:+33(0)3 23 80 92 86; Web-site:www.etangsdumoulin.fr; Price:C; Note:Tipis, gipsy caravans and chalets also available,

Monsieur Frederic Wibaut,7 rue du Petit Marais,02700 Servais,Aisne,France; +33(0)6 75 53 81 25

Compere Jeremy,Ferme Avin,02000 Laon,Aisne,France; Tel:+33(0)3 23 79 07 88

Club Hippique de Laon,Ruelle Harengs,02000 Laon,Aisne,France; Tel:+33(0)3 23 20 34 32

Ferme du Moulin,Faubourg Leuilly,02000 Laon,Aisne,France; Tel:+33(0)3 23 20 34 32

Ferme du Moulin,Club Hippique Fbg Leuilly,02000 Laon,Aisne,France; Tel:+33(0)3 23 20 34 32

Office du Tourisme,Place du Parvis G.de Mortagne,02000 Laon,Aisne,France; Tel:+33(0)3 23 20 28 62

Mairie,1 Ruelle Buet,02320 Cessières,Aisne,France; Tel:+33(0)3 23 24 14 49

Credit Agricole,50 Boulevard Pierre Brossolette,02000 Laon,Aisne,France; Tel:+33(0)3 23 28 41 00

LCL,12 avenue Carnot,02000 Laon,Aisne,France; Tel:+33(0)3 23 23 63 89

BNP Paribas,2 avenue Carnot,02000 Laon,Aisne,France; Tel:+33(0)8 20 82 00 01

Crédit Mutuel,10 rue Eugène Leduc,02000 Laon,Aisne,France; Tel:+33(0)8 20 35 21 19

Banque de France,18 rue John Fitzgérald Kennedy,02000 Laon,Aisne,France; Tel:+33(0)3 23 27 38 00

Gare SNCF,Place Droits de l'Homme,02000 Laon,Aisne,France; Tel:+33(0)8 92 33 53 35; Web-site:www.sncf.fr

Centre Hospitalier,Rue Marcelin Berthelot,02000 Laon,Aisne,France; Tel:+33(0)3 23 24 33 33

Vignon Gérard,8 rue Paul Doumer,02000 Laon,Aisne,France; Tel:+33(0)3 23 23 16 34

Clinique Vétérinaire des Epinettes,118 avenue Pierre Mendès France,02000 Laon,Aisne,France; Tel:+33(0)3 23 23 37 47

Intersport,Rue Romanette,02000 Laon,Aisne,France; Tel:+33(0)3 23 26 02 19

Méga Cycles,1134 avenue Georges Pompidou,02000 Laon,Aisne,France; Tel:+33(0)3 23 20 29 29

Aisne Taxi Lharch,126 Boulevard Pierre Brossolette,02000 Laon,Aisne,France; Tel:+33(0)3 23 79 09 01

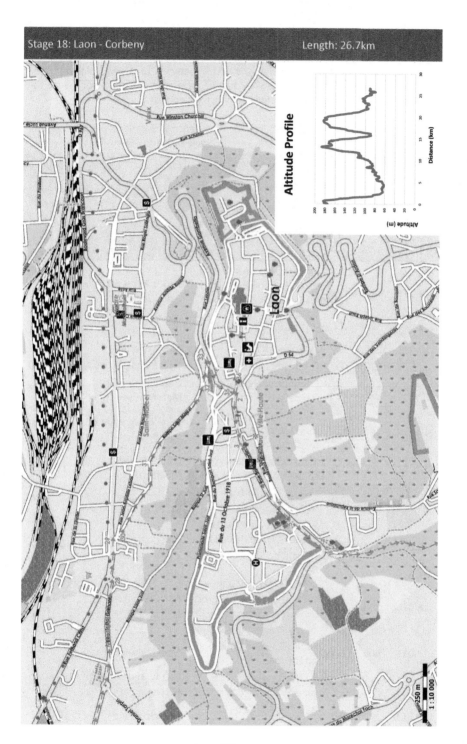

Stage Summary: the route will follow the GR142 between Laon and Vorge and then briefly follow the GR12A. The route will continue on farm tracks and minor roads. The woodland sections can be very muddy and difficult for cyclists.

Distance from Canterbury: 380km   Distance to Besançon: 529km
Stage Ascent: 377m   Stage Descent: 465m

Waypoint	Distance between waypoints	Total km	Directions	Verification Point	Compass	Altitude m
18.001	0	0.0	From the Mairie in the place du Général Léclerc return to the right on rue du Bourg	Pass la Poste on your right	W	178
18.002	120	0.1	Take the left fork	Rue Saint Jean	W	175
18.003	200	0.3	Take the left fork	Rue St Martin	SW	182
18.004	270	0.6	Keep right	Towards the abbey	SW	180
18.005	130	0.7	Continue straight ahead on rue de la Libération	L'Abbaye de Saint Martin on your right	SW	183
18.006	180	0.9	At the junction at the exit from the city walls, follow the road to the left	Porte de Suissons on your left	S	174
18.007	90	1.0	Keep right, downhill on the cobblestones	Rue de la Vieille Montagne	S	163
18.008	1000	2.0	At the crossroads at the foot of the hill, turn left	Rue Romanette	SE	84
18.009	260	2.2	Immediately after passing house n°17 on the left, turn right, on the small road	GR sign	S	82
18.010	700	2.8	At the crossroads with the very busy main road, cross over with great care and continue straight ahead	Commercial centre to the left	S	64
18.011	400	3.3	At the T-junction, turn right on the road	Metal calvaire ahead	S	65
18.012	260	3.5	Bear left on rue le Coq, towards the church spire	GR142, sign for Club Hippique	SE	65
18.013	170	3.7	Bear left on rue de la Ferme	Church on left	SE	66

Waypoint	Distance between waypoints	Total km	Directions	Verification Point	Compass	Altitude m
18.014	500	4.2	At the T-junction, turn left	Pass between the metal barn and the equestrian centre	E	62
18.015	150	4.4	Turn right on the gravel track between fields. Avoid the turning to the left at the rear of the gîte	Gîte - le Moulin de Leuilly on left	SE	62
18.016	1000	5.3	Continue straight ahead into the trees. Note:- it may be necessary to divert briefly to the left to bypass gulley		SE	67
18.017	190	5.5	At the junction in the tracks, bear left	Deeply rutted track, GR sign	E	75
18.018	600	6.1	At the T-junction in the tracks, bear left	Continue in the edge of the woods	SE	71
18.019	230	6.4	At the T-junction with the road, turn left, D54	GR sign, pass farm la Christopherie to the right	NE	71
18.020	100	6.5	Turn right, into the woods	GR and yellow signs	SE	71
18.021	1000	7.4	At the junction in tracks, bear left towards the houses	GR and yellow signs	SE	78
18.022	700	8.1	At the crossroads in the centre of Vorges turn left, D25 direction Bruyères-et-Montbérault	Pass Mont Pigeon on the right	NE	84
18.023	800	8.9	At the roundabout, take the second exit	Towards Centre Ville and the church tower	E	85
18.024	400	9.3	At the crossroads in the centre of Bruyères-et-Montbérault, turn right	Towards the church	SE	85
18.025	400	9.7	At the mini roundabout, continue straight ahead	High wall on your right	S	89

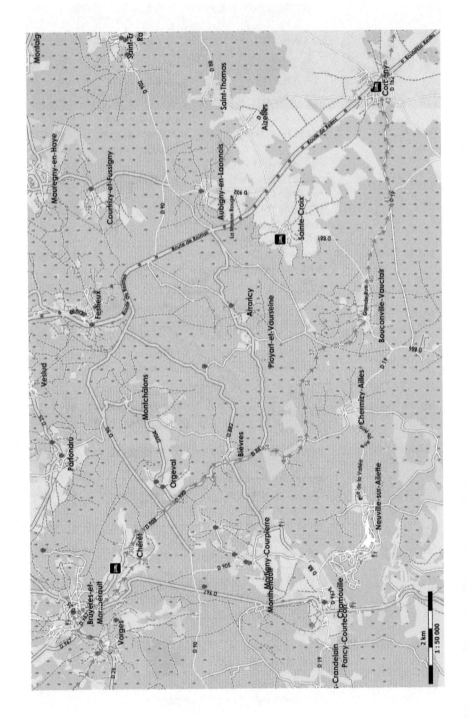

Waypoint	Distance between waypoints	Total km	Directions	Verification Point	Compass	Altitude m
18.026	100	9.8	At the next roundabout, keep to the broad pavement on the left and then fork left on the small road with the No Through Road sign		SE	89
18.027	600	10.3	At the fork, keep left on the smaller track	GR sign	SE	98
18.028	1000	11.3	Bear left and keep the wood on your right	GR sign	E	110
18.029	60	11.3	At the T-junction in the tracks, turn left, towards the village of Chérêt	Keep the woods on your left	NE	113
18.030	400	11.8	At the T-junction with the road facing house n° 6, turn right on D903 and leave the GR	Pass large house on the left	SE	112
18.031	1500	13.2	At the crossroads, continue straight ahead	Direction Bièvres, D890	SE	187
18.032	300	13.5	At the junction, continue straight ahead	Direction Bièvres	SE	166
18.033	1900	15.4	After passing through Bièvres, bear left	Direction Chermizy Ailles, D88	SE	112
18.034	800	16.2	Fork right	Direction Chermizy Ailles	S	91
18.035	1500	17.7	Shortly before the top of the hill, where the road makes a right turn, turn left on the broad track along the ridge	Keep the forest on your right	E	169
18.036	1300	18.9	At the T-junction in the tracks, bear right		SE	182
18.037	800	19.7	Fork right from the main track	Keep close to the forest on your right	SE	180
18.038	400	20.1	At the T-junction with the tarmac road, turn right and remain on the road. Note:- leaving the GR12	Downhill	SE	176

Waypoint	Distance between waypoints	Total km	Directions	Verification Point	Compass	Altitude m
18.039	1200	21.2	At the Stop sign, turn left	Pass the Mairie on your left	E	112
18.040	900	22.1	Keep right on the D19	Direction Corbeny	E	94
18.041	1900	24.0	At the road junction in the forest, bear left	Direction Corbeny, D62	E	101
18.042	2300	26.3	At the T-junction, bear left on D18 towards Corbeny centre	Place Saint Marcoul	E	90
18.043	400	26.7	Arrive at Corbeny (LXXI) centre	Beside the church		91

Accommodation & Facilities .... Laon - Corbeny

B&B - le Clos,(Michel & Monique Simonnot),18 rue Principale,02860 Chérêt,Aisne,France; Tel:+33(0)3 23 24 80 64; Email:leclos.cheret@club-internet.fr; Web-site:www.lecloscheret.com; Price:B

Chambres d' Hôtes - le Besace,21 rue Haute,02820 Sainte-Croix,Aisne,France; Tel:+33(0)3 23 22 48 74; Email:la.besace@wanadoo.fr ; Web-site:la-besace.fr; Price:B

Hôtel du Chemin des Dames,22 rue de Laon,02820 Corbeny,Aisne,France; Tel:+33(0)3 23 23 95 70; Email:hotel.chemindesdames@wanadoo.fr; Web-site:www.hotelchemindesdames.com; Price:B

Mairie,10 rue Pierre Curtil,02820 Corbeny,Aisne,France; Tel:+33(0)3 23 22 41 40

Marechalerie J.Leveaux,36 rue Principale,02350 Cuirieux,Aisne,France; Tel:+33(0)3 23 79 35 70

Duhant Herve,49 Tour de Ville,02860 Bruyères-et-Montbérault,Aisne,France; Tel:+33(0)3 23 24 54 31

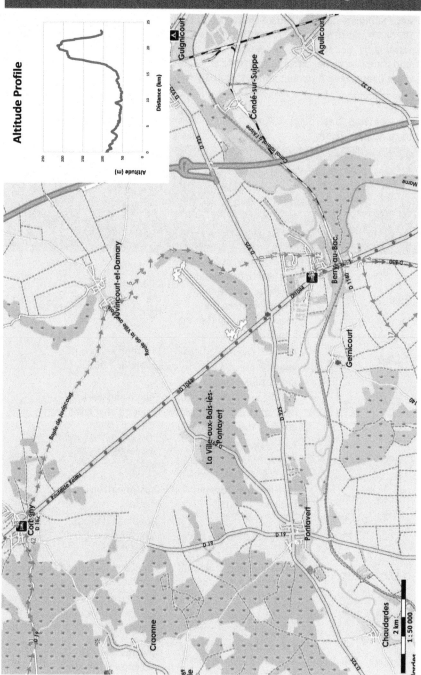

Altitude Profile

Stage Summary: after an initial 5km stretch of tarmac this section uses a good deal of off-road tracks to eventually reach the hill-side vineyards of Champagne. All sections are passable by mountain-bike and horse riders, however there are a number of stiff off-road climbs to be negotiated. The "Official" GR145 signposting restarts on the border of the Champagne-Ardennes region shortly after passing through the town of Berry-au-Bac.

Distance from Canterbury: 407km   Distance to Besançon: 503km
Stage Ascent: 257m   Stage Descent: 242m

Waypoint	Distance between waypoints	Total km	Directions	Verification Point	Compass	Altitude m
19.001	0	0.0	From the crossroads of the D18 and D1044, beside the church in the centre of Corbeny, take the pavement beside the very busy D1044	Direction Reims, pass the church on your right	SE	91
19.002	170	0.2	Turn left and immediately bear right	Direction Juvincourt-et-Damary, D62	E	87
19.003	5000	5.2	At the T-junction in Jouvincourt-et-Damay, turn right and then immediately left onto rue de l'Abreuvoir	Church and clock tower on your left	SE	62
19.004	500	5.7	After passing the agricultural machinery store, bear left	Pass large barn on right	E	60
19.005	300	6.0	Fork left and cross the bridge	Cross the river, la Miette	E	61
19.006	270	6.3	Turn right after the bridge	Woodland on your right, large open field on the left	SE	57
19.007	1100	7.4	At tye junction, continue straight ahead on the track	Wood and marshland on right	S	57
19.008	1200	8.6	Continue straight ahead	Pass a strip of uncultivated ground on your left	SW	54
19.009	110	8.7	Follow the grassy track as it turns left and climbs the hill	Towards the road and circular road sign	SE	54

Waypoint	Distance between waypoints	Total km	Directions	Verification Point	Compass	Altitude m
19.010	700	9.4	Cross straight over the D925 and continue on the road in the direction of the village	Large grain silo in the distance. No Entry signs	S	66
19.011	600	10.0	At the crossroads, continue straight ahead on the tarmac	Metal fence on your right	S	53
19.012	700	10.7	At the crossroads turn right	Towards centre of Berry-au-Bac	W	54
19.013	400	11.1	At the junction with the main road, avenue Gènèral de Gaulle, turn left	Restaurant de la Mairie and Hotel des Nations to the right	S	54
19.014	600	11.7	Cross the 3 bridges and continue straight ahead beside the road. Note:- at the time of writing the signposting for the GR145	Pass grain silos on your left	S	52
19.015	400	12.0	Turn right on rue de Cormicy, D530	Yellow VF sign	S	56
19.016	140	12.2	At the crossroads, turn right and then bear left on the stony track. Note:- the "Official Route" makes a dog leg through the fields before returning to this road. 1.5km may be saved by remaining on the D530 to the crossroads at the entrance to Cormicy	Between the fields	SW	55
19.017	1900	14.0	At the crossroads in the tracks, turn left on the grass track	Towards the church spire, GR sign	SE	65
19.018	900	14.9	At the crossroads in the track, continue straight ahead	Towards the village	SE	64
19.019	1000	15.9	At the crossroads with the tarmac road, continue straight ahead	Pass the sign "Bienvenue à Cormicy" on your right, GR sign	SE	74

Waypoint	Distance between waypoints	Total km	Directions	Verification Point	Compass	Altitude m
19.020	140	16.0	At the junction take the second turning to the right	Wall to the cemetery on your left, yellow VF sign	SW	76
19.021	210	16.2	At the crossroads, continue straight ahead towards the church	Direction "Maison des Jeunes", GR sign	S	80
19.022	190	16.4	At the crossroads with the D32, turn right	Church on your right, GR sign	SW	84
19.023	400	16.8	Shortly after passing the pharmacy, turn left on rue du Bois de Pré	Yellow VF sign	SW	90
19.024	150	16.9	Beside house n° 1, turn left on the concrete track, uphill	GR sign	S	96
19.025	160	17.1	At the T-junction, turn left and immediately bear right on the concrete track	GR sign	SW	106
19.026	280	17.4	Approaching the top of the hill, at the end of the concrete track, bear left on the stony track	Towards the trees, GR sign	SW	129
19.027	300	17.7	At the crossroads in the tracks, continue straight ahead on the grass track between the woods and the vines	GR sign	W	148
19.028	110	17.8	At the fork in the track, continue straight ahead on the main track	Into the woods	SW	156
19.029	500	18.3	At the crossroads in the woods continue straight ahead		SW	186
19.030	700	18.9	At the T-junction in the track, turn left on the broad track		S	190
19.031	500	19.4	At the crossroads in the tracks, continue straight ahead, slightly uphill	GR sign	S	194

Waypoint	Distance between waypoints	Total km	Directions	Verification Point	Compass	Altitude m
19.032	150	19.6	Avoid the track on the left and continue straight ahead	Towards the field on your right, GR sign	S	200
19.033	700	20.3	At the T-junction, turn left, initially towards the corner of the forest	Continue on track between fields as it bears right	S	211
19.034	700	21.0	Turn left on the grass track between the fields	Direction le Mont Chatte, yellow VF sign	NE	205
19.035	300	21.3	Bear right, downhill	Towards the trees	SE	202
19.036	210	21.5	At the junction with the broad gravel track, continue straight ahead. Downhill, into the trees		E	183
19.037	300	21.8	Emerge from the trees and continue straight ahead on the track between the vines	Parallel to the road, below	E	160
19.038	230	22.0	At the crossroads in the tracks, continue straight ahead	Towards the silos	E	135
19.039	500	22.5	At the junction in the tracks, continue straight ahead	Pass a reservoir on your right	E	109
19.040	140	22.7	At the the junction with the tarmac road, turn right	Keep the hedgerow on your left and the field on your right	S	105
19.041	110	22.8	At the junction with house n° 12 on your left, continue straight ahead	GR sign	SE	103
19.042	230	23.0	At the end of rue de la Bonne Fontaine, bear left on rue du Temple	Keep the trees on your right, GR sign	E	103
19.043	220	23.2	At the T-junction with rue de l'Eglise, turn right	GR sign	S	104
19.044	40	23.3	With the church on your left, turn left	Place de l'Eglise	E	104

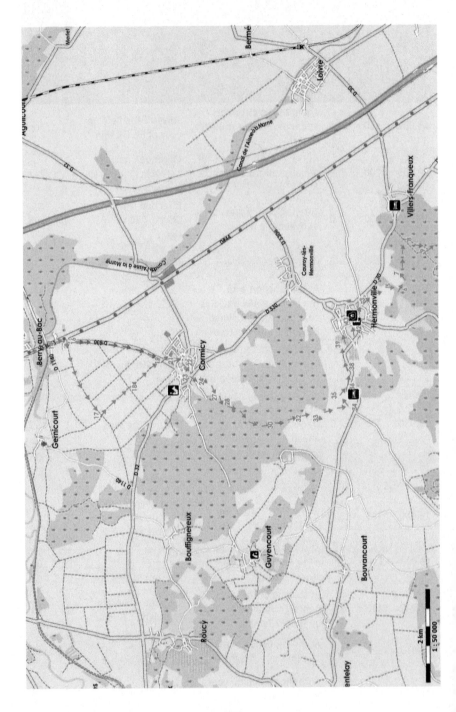

Waypoint	Distance between waypoints	Total km	Directions	Verification Point	Compass	Altitude m
19.045	80	23.3	At the T-junction, turn right and then right again	Rue Thomas Picotin	SW	105
19.046	60	23.4	Arrive at Hermonville centre	Place de la Mairie		106

Accommodation & Facilities .... Corbeny - Hermonville

🏠 Presbytère,6 rue Thomas Picotin,51220 Hermonville,Marne,France; Tel:+33(0)3 26 61 58 36

👥 M.et Mme Menninga,La Grange Aux Coleurs,51220 Hermonville,Marne,France; Tel:+33(0)3 26 61 57 57; +33(0)6 82 30 14 59; Email:ln.spanneut@orange.fr

🛏 Logis des Nations,19 avenue du Général de Gaulle,02190 Berry-au-Bac,Aisne,France; Tel:+33(0)3 23 21 33 65; Email:contact@hotel-des-nations.com; Web-site:www.hotel-des-nations.com; Price:B

🛏 B&B - Domaine des Grattières,Les Grattières,51220 Hermonville,Marne,France; Tel:+33(0)3 26 02 10 60; +33(0)6 22 69 49 52; Email:dg@domainedesgrattieres.com; Web-site:www.domainedesgrattieres.com; Price:A

🛏 Chambre d'Hôtes - la Champenoise,7 rue Pouillon,51220 Villers-Franqueux,Marne,France; Tel:+33(0)3 26 61 55 77; +33(0)6 12 65 49 05; Price:B

⛺ Camping Guignicourt,14 Bis rue Godins,02190 Guignicourt,Aisne,France; Tel:+33(0)3 23 79 74 58; Email:camping-guignicourt@wanadoo.fr; Web-site:www.camping-aisne-picardie.fr; Price:C

🐴 Dumez Marc,26 rue Franklin Roosevelt,51220 Cormicy,Marne,France; Tel:+33(0)3 26 08 21 90

🐴 ABC Cheval Poney,Route d26,51140 Trigny,Marne,France; Tel:+33(0)3 26 03 11 31

ℹ Mairie,4 place Truchon,51220 Hermonville,Marne,France; Tel:+33(0)3 26 61 51 23

🔧 Sylvain Censier - Maréchal Ferrant,14 rue du Carrefour,02160 Guyencourt,Aisne,France; Tel:+33(0)3 23 25 69 59

📞 Taxis Foulon,4 rue des Bois,02190 Guignicourt,Aisne,France; Tel:+33(0)3 23 79 85 09

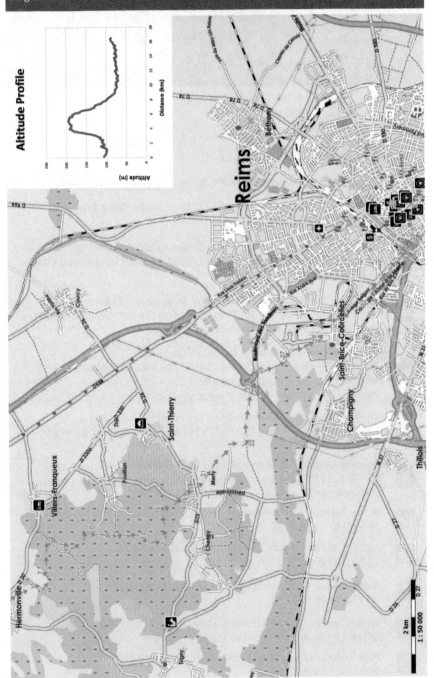

Stage Summary: this section is substantially off-road through woodland and vineyards, finally approaching Reims by the tow-path of the Canal de l'Aisne et la Marne. Expect to see GR654/St James Way/chemin de St Jacques cockleshell signs as the two pilgrimage routes converge. The routes will share the same paths for the next stages until reaching the village of Amance in the south of Champagne-Ardennes.

Distance from Canterbury: 431km   Distance to Besançon: 479km
Stage Ascent: 184m   Stage Descent: 202m

Waypoint	Distance between waypoints	Total km	Directions	Verification Point	Compass	Altitude m
20.001	0	0.0	From the centre of Hermonville, take the D30 rue de Reims	Pass la Poste on your left	E	106
20.002	230	0.2	In front of the bank, turn right and then keep left on rue de Toussicourt	Yellow VF sign	SE	105
20.003	240	0.5	At the crossroads with the tarmac road, continue straight on the track	GR sign on the kerbstone	SE	102
20.004	600	1.1	Take the left fork into the trees	GR sign	SE	99
20.005	80	1.2	With the field straight ahead, turn right	Keep the woods close on your right	SW	100
20.006	160	1.3	In the corner of the field, bear left on the track	Keep the field on your left and the woods on your right, GR sign	E	104
20.007	400	1.7	Take the left fork	Into the woods	E	106
20.008	800	2.5	At intersection of tracks cross over and then bear right	Forest close on left and field on right	SW	112
20.009	600	3.1	At the T-junction turn left, slightly uphill	House, Toussicourt, on your left, GR sign	SE	133
20.010	600	3.7	At the T-junction at the top of hill, turn right on the stony track	GR sign	S	182

Waypoint	Distance between waypoints	Total km	Directions	Verification Point	Compass	Altitude m
20.011	700	4.3	At the crossroads in the track, continue straight ahead on the broad track	GR sign	S	187
20.012	500	4.9	At the junction in the tracks, continue straight ahead on the broad track	Ignore the track to the left, GR sign	S	194
20.013	500	5.4	Bear left onto a small track and immediately bear right parallel to the main track		E	193
20.014	700	6.0	At the T-junction with a small track, turn left	GR sign	E	182
20.015	200	6.2	At the T-junction with a broad track, turn right, downhill	GR sign	SE	167
20.016	400	6.6	At the T-junction with the road, turn right onto road, downhill	GR sign	SE	141
20.017	210	6.8	At the crossroads, continue straight ahead into the village of Merfy	Remain on rue de Pouillon, GR sign	SE	132
20.018	230	7.1	At the crossroads, continue straight ahead	No Entry sign, rue de Pouillon, GR sign	S	128
20.019	60	7.1	At the crossroads with the D26, continue straight ahead	Pass a school on your right, GR sign	S	127
20.020	90	7.2	At the next crossroads, again continue straight ahead downhill	Between walled gardens, chemin des Jardins	SE	126
20.021	300	7.5	At the crossroads with the track, continue straight ahead on the tarmac road, downhill	Yellow VF sign – Reims 5.5km	SE	111
20.022	1200	8.7	At the T-junction, in the hamlet of Les Maretz, turn left	GR sign	E	82
20.023	1200	9.9	Continue straight over autoroute bridge	Crash barriers on both sides	E	75

Waypoint	Distance between waypoints	Total km	Directions	Verification Point	Compass	Altitude m
20.024	400	10.3	Turn right under the power lines. Note:- to avoid barriers in the track ahead, horse-riders should remain parallel to the main road to the canal then turn right on the tow path and rejoin the "Official Route" at the next bridge	Yellow VF sign - Port Colbert 3km	S	76
20.025	200	10.5	Pass through the metal gates and continue straight ahead on the track	GR sign	S	72
20.026	500	11.0	Turn left with the water treatment plant on your left	GR sign	E	72
20.027	180	11.2	Pass through a metal barrier and continue straight ahead	GR sign	S	71
20.028	800	12.0	At the crossroads in the tracks, turn left on the small track	Towards the radio tower, GR sign	E	76
20.029	70	12.1	At the T-junction with the road in the industrial zone, turn right on the pavement	Continue towards the radio mast, GR sign	E	73
20.030	110	12.2	At the crossroads with the road, continue straight ahead on the tarmac path	Pass metal barriers, GR sign	E	72
20.031	250	12.4	At the T-junction, turn right on the path beside the canal l'Aisene à la Marne	GR sign	SE	74
20.032	1000	13.4	Continue straight ahead	Under the road bridge	SE	78
20.033	2000	15.4	To reach the cathedral and the centre of Reims, climb the steps on the right and cross the bridge over the canal. Note:- the "Official Route" will return to the canal-side after passing the city centre and cathedral	Continue beside the tramway	NE	77

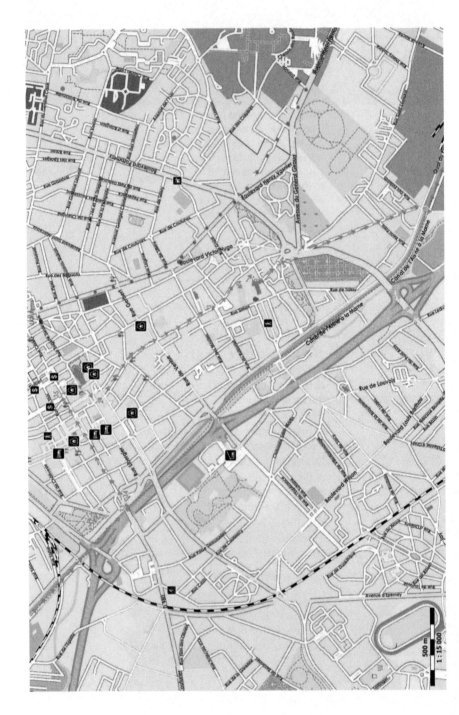

Waypoint	Distance between waypoints	Total km	Directions	Verification Point	Compass	Altitude m
20.034	170	15.5	At the junction continue straight ahead into the pedestrian zone	Pass 3 black obelisks on your right, GR sign	NE	80
20.035	800	16.3	After passing the Tribunal, immediately turn right and continue towards the cathedral	Rue du Trésor	S	89
20.036	170	16.5	Arrive at Reims (LXX) centre	Beside Cathédral doors		87

Accommodation & Facilities .... Hermonville - Reims

Monastère des Bénédictines,2 place Abbaye,51220 Saint-Thierry,Marne,France; Tel:+33(0)3 26 03 99 37; +33(0)6 18 97 55 24; Email:hotellerie-st-thierry@wanadoo.fr; Web-site:www.benedictines-ste-bathilde.fr/-Saint-Thierry-; Price:D

Paroisse Notre Dame et Saint Jacques,1 rue Guillaume de Machault,51100 Reims,Marne,France; Tel:+33(0)3 26 47 55 34

Eglise Saint Jacques,12 rue Marx Dormoy,51100 Reims,Marne,France; Tel:+33(0)3 26 47 06 40

Association Diocésaine de Reims,3 rue Cardinal de Lorraine,51100 Reims,Marne,France; Tel:+33(0)3 26 47 05 33

Vicariat Général de l'Archevêché,1 rue d'Anjou,51100 Reims,Marne,France; Tel:+33(0)3 26 47 69 55

Soeurs Auxiliatrices,46 rue des Capucins,51100 Reims,Marne,France; Tel:+33(0)3 26 47 65 80

Association Saint Sixte,6 rue du Lieut Herduin,51100 Reims,Marne,France; Tel:+33(0)3 26 02 04 61; +33(0)3 26 82 72 50; +33(0)6 80 38 25 89

François Louviot,51100 Reims,Marne,France; Tel:+33(0)3 26 51 61 05; +33(0)6 09 42 93 76; Note:President French via Francigena Association - AVFF,

Centre International de Séjour,Parc Léo Lagrange - Chaussée Bocquaine 21,51100 Reims,Marne,France; Tel:+33(0)3 26 40 52 60; Email:info@cis-reims.com; Web-site:www.cis-reims.com; Price:B

Hôtel Azur,9 rue des Ecrevées ,51100 Reims,Marne,France; Tel:+33(0)3 26 47 43 39; Email:contact@hotel-azur-reims.com ; Web-site:www.hotel-azur-reims.com; Price:A

Hôtel Victoria,1 rue Buirette,51100 Reims,Marne,France; Tel:+33(0)3 26 47 21 79

Hotel le Bon Moine,14 rue Capucins,51100 Reims,Marne,France;
Tel:+33(0)3 26 47 33 64; Price:B

Hôtel de la Cathédrale,Place du Cardinal Luçon,51100 Reims,Marne,France;
Tel:+33(0)3 26 47 28 46; Web-site:www.hotel-cathedrale-reims.fr; Price:B

Société Hippique de Reims,46 rue de Mars,51100 Reims,Marne,France;
Tel:+33(0)3 26 82 03 99

Office du Tourisme,2 rue Guillaume de Machault,51100 Reims,Marne,France;
Tel:+33(0)8 92 70 13 51

Crédit Mutuel,8 Bis rue Edouard Mignot,51100 Reims,Marne,France;
Tel:+33(0)8 20 35 22 46

Caisse d'Epargne,6 rue Grosse Ecritoire,51100 Reims,Marne,France;
Tel:+33(0)8 21 01 05 65

Credit Agricole,9 place Forum,51100 Reims,Marne,France;
Tel:+33(0)3 26 35 56 10

HSBC,17 Cours Jean Baptiste Langlet,51100 Reims,Marne,France;
Tel:+33(0)3 26 05 42 42

Société Générale,2 place Royale,51100 Reims,Marne,France;
Tel:+33(0)3 26 50 85 06

Gare SNCF,Place de la Gare,51100 Reims,Marne,France;
Tel:+33(0)8 92 33 53 35; Web-site:www.sncf.fr

Centre Hospitalier Universitaire,45 rue Cognacq-Jay,51092
Reims,Marne,France; Tel:+33(0)3 26 78 78 78

Cabinet de Médecine Générale Luton,35 place Luton,51100
Reims,Marne,France; Tel:+33(0)3 26 47 32 93

Clinique Vétérinaire Pommery,226 Boulevard Pommery,51100
Reims,Marne,France; Tel:+33(0)3 26 85 85 85

Go Sport,2 rue de l'Étape,51100 Reims,Marne,France; Tel:+33(0)8 25 10 60 60

Saint Rémi Sport,27 Esplanade Flechambault,51100 Reims,Marne,France;
Tel:+33(0)3 26 05 19 39

Cycles 2000,21 rue Martin Peller,51100 Reims,Marne,France;
Tel:+33(0)3 26 08 45 29

Taxis de Reims,1 Cour de la Gare,51100 Reims,Marne,France;
Tel:+33(0)3 26 47 05 05

Josselin Frederic,29 rue du Gen Leclerc,51220 Loivre,Marne,France;
Tel:+33(0)3 26 61 02 45

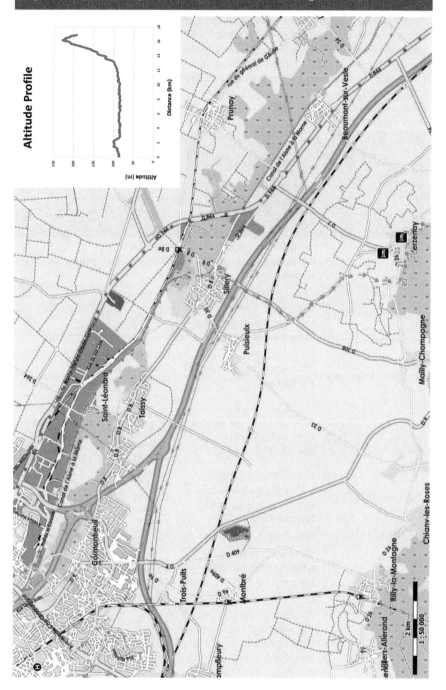

Stage Summary: this section continues to share the route with the chemin de Saint Jacques - GR654. The route passes the Basilica of Saint Rémi before returning to the canal-side and then climbing the tracks through the champagne vineyards and passing through the woods of the Parc Naturel de la Montagne de Reims. Expect some steep climbs with woodland muddy tracks in wet conditions.

Distance from Canterbury: 447km   Distance to Besançon: 463km
Stage Ascent: 237m   Stage Descent: 131m

Waypoint	Distance between waypoints	Total km	Directions	Verification Point	Compass	Altitude m
21.001	0	0.0	From the entrance to the Cathédral take rue Rockefeller	Pass the Médiathèque on the left	SW	86
21.002	70	0.1	At the crossroads, turn left and continue on rue Chanzy and rue Gambetta through numerous intersections	GR sign	SE	86
21.003	1100	1.1	Continue straight ahead on rue Gambetta	Pass the city of Reims administration buildings on your right	SE	89
21.004	200	1.3	Turn right into the wooded gardens surrounding the Basilica of Saint Rémi	Skirt the Basilica on your right and the statue of Clovis on your left	S	93
21.005	220	1.6	Shortly after passing the statue of Clovis, turn left, cross rue Saint Julien and take rue Fery	Towards narrow brick building in the centre of the road	SE	98
21.006	150	1.7	Take the right fork	Rue Kalas	S	98
21.007	40	1.8	Carefully pass around the large roundabout and take the small No-Entry road rue Albert Thomas	Pass the cemetery on your right, Veuve Cliquot plant on your left	S	98
21.008	1000	2.8	At the traffic lights beside the pharmacy, continue straight ahead over the canal bridge and then turn left to rejoin the canal-side path	Pass the canal lock on your left	E	84

177

Waypoint	Distance between waypoints	Total km	Directions	Verification Point	Compass	Altitude m
21.009	1500	4.3	Continue straight ahead on the canal-side path	Pass under the highway bridge	E	84
21.010	2300	6.5	Continue straight ahead on the grassy track	Pass the restaurant - Saint Léonard - on your right	SE	84
21.011	3900	10.4	Beside the lock, continue straight ahead under the road bridge	GR sign	S	87
21.012	500	10.9	Beside the boat dock in Sillery, turn right. Note:- there is a chain across the exit and a turnstile gate that the marina staff will open	GR sign	SW	87
21.013	90	11.0	At the T-junction, turn left on rue du Canada	Large stone house directly in front	SE	89
21.014	90	11.1	Turn right onto rue de Mailly, direction Mailly - Champagne, D308	Cross the motorway and the railway track, GR654	SW	88
21.015	2100	13.2	At the crossroads in Le Puits, turn left	Yellow GR145 sign - Verzenay 2km	SE	100
21.016	1700	14.8	At the top of the hill, turn sharp right on the tarmac track	Yellow sign - Verzenay	W	156
21.017	70	14.9	Turn left onto gravel track, uphill between vines	Pass le Moulin de Verzenay on your left, GR sign	S	156
21.018	1000	15.8	Cross straight over the road and continue on the track up the hill	GR and St Jacques signs	SW	208
21.019	70	15.9	At the next crossroads, turn left	Calvaire, GR sign	S	211
21.020	180	16.1	At the crossroads continue straight ahead into the woods	Village of Verzenay on left	SE	223
21.021	500	16.5	Fork left after leaving the woods, downhill	GR sign, avenue de Champagne	E	214

Waypoint	Distance between waypoints	Total km	Directions	Verification Point	Compass	Altitude m
21.022	210	16.7	Continue straight ahead, avoid the turning to the left	GR sign	NE	205
21.023	150	16.9	Arrive at Verzenay centre	Crossroads beside the wine press		192

Accommodation & Facilities ....   Reims - Verzenay

Celine Rousseaux,51360 Verzenay,Marne,France; Tel:+33(0)3 26 04 88 05

M Dubois,51360 Verzenay,Marne,France; Tel:+33(0)3 26 49 43 21

Alain Mallement,51380 Verzy,Marne,France; Tel:+33(0)3 26 97 92 32

Pierre & Veronique Barbier,51380 Verzy,Marne,France; Tel:+33(0)3 26 97 90 29; Price:C

Jean-Marie Henry,51100 Reims,Marne,France; Tel:+33(0)3 26 47 25 21; +33(0)6 89 22 76 66

Eliane Rampont,51100 Reims,Marne,France; Tel:+33(0)3 26 47 36 41; +33(0)6 29 52 37 85

Chambres d'Hôtes - Champagne Jacques Rousseaux,5 rue Puisieulx,51360 Verzenay,Marne,France; Tel:+33(0)3 26 49 42 73; +33(0)6 78 55 33 16; Price:B

Chambres d'Hotes - Dubois,(Dubois Jean-Marc),9 rue Grossats,51360 Verzenay,Marne,France; Tel:+33(0)3 26 49 43 21

Chambre d'Hôte - le Tihlia,1 rue de Louvois,51380 Verzy,Marne,France; Tel:+33(0)3 26 97 90 29; Email:athos0997@aol.com; Web-site:www.letihlia. com/chambre-hote.php; Price:B

Credit Agricole,5 rue Chanzy,51380 Verzy,Marne,France; Tel:+33(0)3 26 48 41 20

Taxi de Mailly Champagne,19 rue Haute des Carrières,51500 Mailly-Champagne,Marne,France; Tel:+33(0)3 26 49 45 85

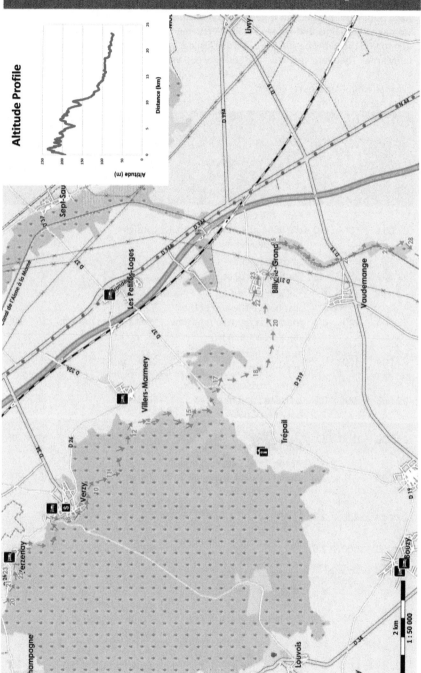

Stage Summary: the section is generally off-road. The route re-enters the Forêt de la Montagne de Reims and passes beside Verzy, but then continues through open farm land to find the paths beside the canal de l'Aisne à la Marne for the approach to Condé-sur-Marne. There are very few facilities between Verzy and Condé.

Distance from Canterbury: 464km   Distance to Besançon: 446km
Stage Ascent: 277m   Stage Descent: 391m

Waypoint	Distance between waypoints	Total km	Directions	Verification Point	Compass	Altitude m
22.001	0	0.0	From the crossroads beside the wine press take the small road, rue Frédéric Bin	GR sign	SE	192
22.002	300	0.3	At the end of the tarmac, continue straight ahead on the gravel track		E	204
22.003	140	0.4	Just before the end of the road, turn right onto narrow track up a steep hill	White House on left	SE	209
22.004	100	0.5	Turn left onto a broad track at the top of the slope	Towards vines	E	226
22.005	90	0.6	At the crossroads in track proceed straight ahead between vines	GR sign	SE	222
22.006	1300	1.9	After leaving woods continue through a builder's yard	GR sign	SE	205
22.007	70	1.9	At the crossroads, continue straight ahead on rue de la Croix de Mission	GR sign	S	204
22.008	200	2.1	Continue straight ahead into woods	Route Forestière de CBR	SE	207
22.009	800	2.9	At the crossroads, continue straight ahead on Track	GR sign	E	214
22.010	500	3.3	Continue straight ahead. Ignore the left fork	GR sign	SE	202
22.011	800	4.1	Continue straight ahead	Avoid the left turn - route Forestière Saint Basle	E	204
22.012	1100	5.2	At the junction, continue straight ahead	Avoid the right turn, route Forestière de Coutron	SE	185

Waypoint	Distance between waypoints	Total km	Directions	Verification Point	Compass	Altitude m
22.013	400	5.6	At intersection with road, continue straight ahead	Village of Villers-Marmery on the left	S	170
22.014	60	5.6	At the end of the line of trees, fork left	Towards the forest	S	175
22.015	1600	7.2	At the crossroads in the tracks, continue straight ahead on the broad track	Continue to skirt the forest	SE	197
22.016	1000	8.2	At the T-junction with the road, turn left on the road and then immediately turn right on track beside trees	Yellow VF sign - Billy-le-Grand	E	184
22.017	240	8.4	At the junction in the tracks, turn right on the gravel track	Parallel to the road, GR sign	S	188
22.018	700	9.1	At the crossroads in the tracks, continue straight ahead, downhill	Grass track, towards the woods	SE	177
22.019	400	9.5	At the junction, after emerging from the woods, bear left on the broad track	Yellow VF sign	E	154
22.020	1000	10.5	At junction with tarmac road, continue straight downhill on the tarmac	Vines on your right, GR sign	E	161
22.021	400	10.9	Bear left on the road	Keep village on right	N	136
22.022	300	11.2	Bear right on the road	Enter the village of Billy-le-Grand	E	129
22.023	600	11.8	At the junction beside the Mairie, turn right	Direction Vaudemange on the D319, GR sign	S	122
22.024	200	12.0	Just before reaching the sign for the exit from Billy-le-Grand, turn left on the road	Rue de la Voûte, GR sign	E	119
22.025	800	12.8	Pass over the canal and immediately turn right on the grass track	Keep the canal to your right, GR sign	S	109
22.026	1600	14.4	At junction with the tarmac road, pass around the crash barrier and continue straight ahead on the track nearest to the canal	Bridge on the right, yellow VF sign for Condé-sur-Marne 8km	S	99

Waypoint	Distance between waypoints	Total km	Directions	Verification Point	Compass	Altitude m
22.027	1400	15.7	Immediately after passing the lock and with a bridge on your right, turn left on the gravel track	Yellow VF sign - Condé-sur-Marne, 7km	SE	94
22.028	400	16.1	As the main track bears left, turn right between the trees	GR sign	SW	95
22.029	1500	17.6	At the crossroads with the tarmac road, continue straight ahead on the grass track	Hedgerow on the left	SW	95
22.030	1000	18.6	At the next crossroads with a gravel track, turn right	Track bears left	W	94
22.031	500	19.0	At the T-junction, turn right	Cross the canal bridge	N	84
22.032	200	19.2	After crossing the canal bridge, turn sharp left and then right on the tarmac track beside the canal	Keep canal on your left, GR sign	SW	82
22.033	700	19.9	Continue straight ahead on the canal-side path	Under the bridge	SW	80
22.034	2900	22.8	At the crossroads with a major road, after passing the lock, continue straight ahead remaining beside the canal. Note:- accommodation on the road to the right	Condé-sur-Marne, yellow VF sign	S	75
22.035	220	23.0	Turn sharp right onto the road	Pass sign boards for the canal on your right, GR sign	N	73
22.036	130	23.2	At the T-junction, turn left towards the church	House number 8 on the right, GR sign	W	74
22.037	150	23.3	Arrive at Condé-sur-Marne centre in place Alexandre Batilliot	Beside the Mairie		78

Francis Chaviére,51100 Reims,Marne,France; Tel:+33(0)3 26 88 56 42;
+33(0)6 80 67 03 53

Mme Jacqueminet,4 rue Saint-Martin,51380 Trépail,Marne,France;
Tel:+33(0)3 26 57 82 29; +33(0)6 19 81 22 52; Price:D

Mme Meuret,51150 Ambonnay,Marne,France; Tel:+33(0)3 26 57 01 13

Mme Horneck,51150 Condé-sur-Marne,Marne,France;
Tel:+33(0)3 26 67 98 97

Chambres d'Hotes - le Trilogis,3 rue de Villers Marmery,51400 Les-Petites-
Loges,Marne,France; Tel:+33(0)3 26 03 98 57; +33(0)6 80 93 21 19;
Email:ch51400@gmail.com; Web-site:letrilogis.free.fr; Price:B; Note:Reduced
price room available to hikers and cyclists,

Hotel le Soleil d'Or,1 rue Pasteur,51380 Villers-Marmery,Marne,France;
Tel:+33(0)3 26 97 95 80; Email:soleildor51@hotmail.fr; Price:B

Chambre d'Hote- les Barbontines,10 rue Jeanne d'Arc,51150
Bouzy,Marne,France; Tel:+33(0)3 26 57 07 31; +33(0)3 26 51 70 70;
Email:contact@lesbarbotines.com ; Web-site:www.lesbarbotines.com ;
Price:A

Chambres d'Hôtes - la Pélerine,13 rue Gambetta,51150 Bouzy,Marne,France;
Tel:+33(0)3 26 52 90 19; Web-site:pelerine.fr; Price:B

Chambres d'Hôtes - la Cle des Champs,(Denis Wolter),2 rue Albert
Barre,51150 Condé-sur-Marne,Marne,France; Tel:+33(0)3 26 68 94 75;
+33(0)6 85 66 53 64; Email:denis.wolter@orange.fr; Price:B

Hôtel du Soleil d'Or,9 rue Châlons,51150 Condé-sur-Marne,Marne,France;
Tel:+33(0)3 26 67 98 97; Price:B; Note:Good price and pilgrim friendly, ; PR

Chambres d'Hôtes - Barrault,(Bruno & Jeanne Barrault),7 rue Albert
Barre,51150 Condé-sur-Marne,Marne,France; Tel:+33(0)3 26 66 90 61;
Email:barrault.home@wanadoo.fr; Price:B

Mairie,Rue Mairie,51380 Trépail,Marne,France; Tel:+33(0)3 26 57 05 55

Mairie,Place de La mairie,51400 Les-Petites-Loges,Marne,France;
Tel:+33(0)3 26 03 90 87

Mairie,Place Mairie,51150 Isse,Marne,France; Tel:+33(0)3 26 67 99 44

Mairie,Place Alexandre Batilliot,51150 Condé-sur-Marne,Marne,France;
Tel:+33(0)9 60 52 69 01

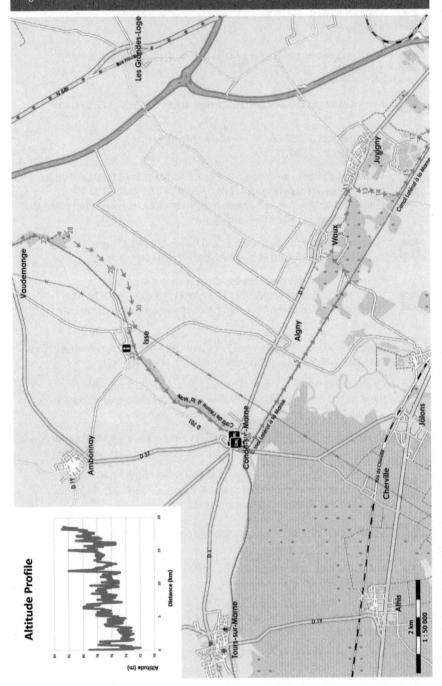

Altitude Profile

Stage Summary: the route follows the tow-path of the Canal Latéral à la Marne, remaining on the GR145/654. The town of Châlons-en-Champagne was formerly known as Châlons-sur-Marne and still appears as this on older signs.

Distance from Canterbury: 487km   Distance to Besançon: 423km
Stage Ascent: 118m   Stage Descent: 114m

Waypoint	Distance between waypoints	Total km	Directions	Verification Point	Compass	Altitude m
23.001	0	0.0	From place Alexandre Batilliot, take rue du 8 Mai	Pass the church on your right	NW	78
23.002	100	0.1	At the T-junction, turn left	Large arch doorway on your left, GR sign	SW	78
23.003	130	0.2	At the crossroads with impasse de Silo , continue straight ahead over the bridge	GR sign	SW	73
23.004	40	0.3	After crossing the bridge, immediately turn left and continue on the canal-side track	Between canal and river	SE	73
23.005	2300	2.6	At the road junction, continue straight ahead on the canal-side track	GR sign, bridge on the left	SE	74
23.006	2100	4.6	At the road junction, turn left on the road and cross the bridge	Lock - ecluse de Vraux - on the right of the bridge	NE	75
23.007	800	5.3	Just before reaching the bridge, turn right on the track	Juvigny 2km, yellow VF sign	E	77
23.008	500	5.9	At the crossroads with a gravel track, continue straight ahead	Bridge on the left, GR sign	SE	76
23.009	900	6.8	At the T-junction with a gravel track, turn left over the bridge	GR sign	NE	78
23.010	150	6.9	At the T-junction with the busy road, turn right on the D1	Enter Juvigny, GR sign	SE	79

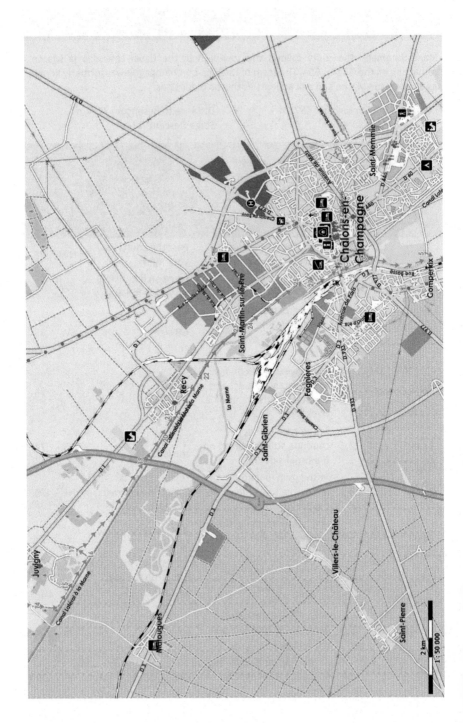

Châlons-en-Champagne

Saint-Memmie

Compertrix

Fagnières

Saint-Gibrien

Saint-Martin-sur-le-Pré

Recy

Juvigny

Villers-le-Château

Saint-Pierre

La Marne

2 km
1 : 50 000

Waypoint	Distance between waypoints	Total km	Directions	Verification Point	Compass	Altitude m
23.011	190	7.1	At the crossroads, turn right on rue St Martin	Towards house n° 4, GR sign	S	77
23.012	100	7.2	Continue straight ahead on the grassy track	Cross the field	S	75
23.013	400	7.6	At the T-junction with the road, turn right on the road over the bridge	Yellow VF sign - Châlons 11km	SW	77
23.014	50	7.7	Turn left onto the track shortly before crossing another bridge	Between trees	SE	78
23.015	1200	8.8	With a road to the left, continue straight ahead on the track	GR sign	SE	76
23.016	800	9.6	At the T-junction, turn left onto a wider gravel road	Towards copse of trees, GR sign	NE	75
23.017	210	9.8	At the crossroads, turn right	GR sign	SE	79
23.018	2100	11.9	At the junction with a broader track, bear right on the broad track through the woods	GR sign, pass under motorway	SE	79
23.019	400	12.3	At the junction in the tracks, continue straight ahead on the broad gravel track		SE	78
23.020	600	12.9	At the junction in the tracks, continue straight ahead towards the church	Trees on your right, GR sign	SE	76
23.021	600	13.5	The track joins a road, continue ahead and then turn right over 2 bridges and then turn left beside the canal	GR sign, church on left	SE	78
23.022	1200	14.6	At the crossroads with a gravel, proceed straight ahead on the concrete track with bridge on left	GR sign	SE	77

Châlons-en-Champagne

Waypoint	Distance between waypoints	Total km	Directions	Verification Point	Compass	Altitude m
23.023	1400	16.0	With bridge and tarmac road on left, continue straight on concrete track	Canal on left	SE	75
23.024	90	16.1	Take right fork - gravel track	GR sign	SE	77
23.025	1600	17.7	At the junction with a tarmac road, continue straight ahead	Pass rue de l' Association Foncière on your right, GR sign	SE	78
23.026	120	17.8	Take right fork beside house n°25	GR sign	SW	78
23.027	300	18.1	At T-junction at end of rue des Frères Navlet, turn left	Keep the river and railway on right	SE	79
23.028	600	18.7	Arrive at Châlons-en-Champagne (LXIX). Note:- to gain access to the town centre turn left	Crossroads with rue Jean Jaurès		82

Accommodation & Facilities .... Condé-sur-Marne - Châlons-en-Champagne

Presbytère Notre Dame,5 place Notre-Dame,51000 Châlons-en-Champagne,Marne,France; Tel:+33(0)3 26 64 18 30; +33(0)3 26 65 63 17; Price:D

Cathédrale Saint Etienne,1 place Monseigneur Tissier,51000 Châlons-en-Champagne,Marne,France; Tel:+33(0)3 26 65 63 17; +33(0)3 26 64 18 30

Auberge de Jeunesse,4 avenue du Général Patton,51000 Châlons-en-Champagne,Marne,France; Tel:+33(0)3 26 26 46 28; Email:ajchalons@orange.fr; Price:C; Note:Open May to October,

Hotel le Montreal,Avenue du Général Sarrail,51000 Châlons-en-Champagne,Marne,France; Tel:+33(0)3 26 26 99 09; Web-site:www.hotel-lemontreal.com; Price:B

Hôtel de la Cité,12 rue de la Charrière,51000 Châlons-en-Champagne,Marne,France; Tel:+33(0)3 26 64 31 20; Email:contact@hotel-de-la-cite.com; Web-site:www.hotel-de-la-cite.com; Price:B; PR

Hotel d'Angleterre,19 place Monseigneur Tissier,51000 Châlons-en-Champagne,Marne,France; Tel:+33(0)3 26 68 21 51; Email:hot.angl@wanadoo.fr; Web-site:www.hotel-dangleterre.fr; Price:A

Hotel d'Angleterre,19 place Monseigneur Tissier,51000 Châlons-en-Champagne,Marne,France; Tel:+33(0)3 26 68 21 51; Email:hot.angl@wanadoo.fr; Web-site:www.hotel-dangleterre.fr; Price:A

Hôtel Pasteur,46 rue Pasteur,51000 Châlons-en-Champagne,Marne,France; Tel:+33(0)3 26 68 10 00; Email:contact@hotel-pasteur.fr; Web-site:www.hotel-pasteur.fr; Price:B

Hôtel Bristol,77 avenue Pierre Semard,51510 Fagnières,Marne,France; Tel:+33(0)3 26 68 24 63; Email:contact@hotelbristol-marne.com; Website:www.hotelbristol-marne.com; Price:A

Camping Municipal,Rue de Plaisance,51000 Châlons-en-Champagne,Marne,France; Tel:+33(0)3 26 68 38 00; Email:camping.chalons@orange.fr; Price:C

Centre Équestre le Haras des Essordilles,Route de Louvois,51520 Recy,Marne,France; Tel:+33(0)3 26 64 93 43

Centre Equestre Poney Club le Destrier,Rue Stéphane Mallarmé,51000 Châlons-en-Champagne,Marne,France; Tel:+33(0)3 26 68 56 03

Ecuries de Coolus,4 rue des Sources,51510 Coolus,Marne,France; Tel:+33(0)3 26 65 97 32

Office du Tourisme,3 Quai des Arts,51000 Châlons-en-Champagne,Marne,France; Tel:+33(0)3 26 65 17 89

Credit Agricole,4 rue Vaux,51000 Châlons-en-Champagne,Marne,France; Tel:+33(0)3 26 26 32 14

Banque Populaire,00000 2 rue Garinet,51000 Châlons-en-Champagne,Marne,France; Tel:+33(0)8 20 38 66 05

CIC,1 rue Marne,51000 Châlons-en-Champagne,Marne,France; Tel:+33(0)8 20 01 67 74

LCL,25 rue Marne,51000 Châlons-en-Champagne,Marne,France; Tel:+33(0)3 26 69 23 60

BNP Paribas,31 rue Marne,51000 Châlons-en-Champagne,Marne,France; Tel:+33(0)8 20 82 00 01

Société Générale,45 rue Marne,51000 Châlons-en-Champagne,Marne,France; Tel:+33(0)3 26 69 35 40

Gare SNCF,Avenue Gare,51000 Châlons-en-Champagne,Marne,France; Tel:+33(0)8 92 33 53 35; Web-site:www.sncf.fr

Centre Hospitalier,51 rue du Commandant Derrien,51000 Châlons-en-Champagne,Marne,France; Tel:+33(0)3 26 69 60 60

Metivet François,10 Quai Eugène Perrier,51000 Châlons-en-Champagne,Marne,France; Tel:+33(0)3 26 68 20 36

Clinique Vétérinaire Mont Héry,31 rue du Docteur Pellier,51000 Châlons-en-Champagne,Marne,France; Tel:+33(0)3 26 68 38 31

Go Sport,Rue Michel Menard, Zac des Escarnotieres,51000 Châlons-en-Champagne,Marne,France; Tel:+33(0)8 25 10 60 60

Lehmann Olivier Liliane,5 avenue de Valmy,51000 Châlons-en-Champagne,Marne,France; +33(0)6 07 45 40 43

Guiset Jacques,7 route de Louvois,51150 Vraux,Marne,France; Tel:+33(0)3 26 64 45 46

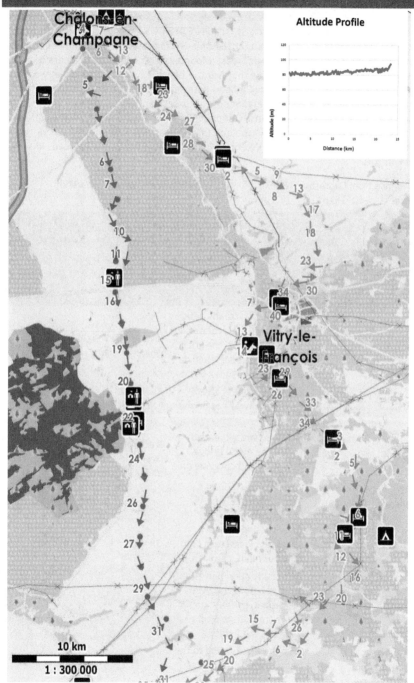

Altitude Profile

Stage Summary: ahead there is a major decision on routes. The "Official Route" continues to follow the chemin de St Jacques/GR654 via Vitry-le-François. This route is reasonably well sign-posted, but, at the time writing, there were a number of signs missing in the exposed agricultural areas. Mountain bikers need to be aware that the clay surfaces of many paths beside the river can be extremely slippery in wet weather. The "Official Route", which initially follows pathways beside the banks of the Marne, offers more choices in accommodation, but adds substantially to distance (48km) and bypasses 2 further Sigeric locations. Our preferred Alternate Route is generally off-road and with long atmospheric sections along the vestiges of a Roman road. Horse-riders are recommended to follow the Alternate Route to avoid the very busy roads in Vitry-le-François.

Distance from Canterbury: 506km   Distance to Besançon: 404km
Stage Ascent: 157m   Stage Descent: 145m

Waypoint	Distance between waypoints	Total km	Directions	Verification Point	Compass	Altitude m
24.001	0	0.0	From the crossroads beside bridge over the river on rue Jean Jaurés, take the grit pathway beside chemin du Barrage	River on your right, yellow VF sign	S	83
24.002	500	0.5	Continue straight ahead on the pathway beside the river	GR654 sign	S	79
24.003	210	0.7	Continue straight ahead across the metal bridge, turn right and continue on the track	Track returns to the river-side and passes under a highway	S	84
24.004	1400	2.1	Facing an embankment, bear left on the gravel track		E	81
24.005	110	2.2	After passing between concrete blocks, turn right on an unmade path	GR sign	SE	81
24.006	2500	4.7	A little after the river turns left and before the river turns right, turn left on the more distinct track, between the fields	Railway visible to the right at the junction	NE	80
24.007	290	5.0	Take the first turning to the right, towards the trees	GR sign	SE	79

Waypoint	Distance between waypoints	Total km	Directions	Verification Point	Compass	Altitude m
24.008	700	5.6	Turn left on the track. Initially the woods are on your right with a field to the left	GR sign	SE	83
24.009	500	6.1	Continue on the broad track	Keep the woods to your right	E	80
24.010	400	6.5	At the junction in the tracks, continue straight ahead on the broad track with the woods on your right	Canal bridge visible on your extreme left	SE	81
24.011	800	7.3	Turn right, keep the fields on your right, trees on your left	Church visible slightly to your right, GR sign	SE	82
24.012	400	7.7	At the crossroads with the D80, cross the road with care and continue straight ahead on the gravel track. Note:- to take the shorter Alternate Route turn right towards the church	Yellow VF sign	NE	83
24.013	260	7.9	Bear right on the broad track	Pass a lake on your left, GR sign	E	81
24.014	170	8.1	At the junction in the tracks, continue straight ahead beside the fence	Avoid the track to the right	E	81
24.015	230	8.3	At the T-junction in the tracks, turn right	Yellow VF sign	SE	82
24.016	1000	9.3	At the crossroads in the track, turn right through a gap in the trees	Pass field on your left, GR sign	S	81
24.017	1000	10.3	With the river close on your right, take the left fork through the trees on a broad track, then immediately turn right	GR 145	E	83
24.018	1100	11.4	With a canal bridge visible ahead, turn right on the broad track	Between fields	SE	81

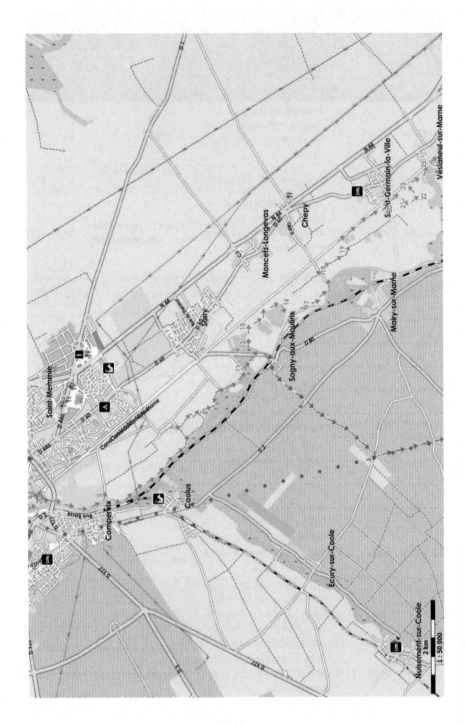

Waypoint	Distance between waypoints	Total km	Directions	Verification Point	Compass	Altitude m
24.019	800	12.3	At the junction in the tracks, turn left and then turn right parallel to the canal	GR sign	SE	84
24.020	1500	13.7	At the crossroads with the D280, continue straight ahead on the tarmac track	Silos to the left of the track, GR sign	S	84
24.021	800	14.5	At the junction in the track, turn left on the well defined track	Football field on the right at the junction	SE	83
24.022	280	14.8	At the T-junction in the tracks, turn left	GR sign	NE	83
24.023	300	15.1	At the junction in the tracks, turn right	Pass a conifer plantation on your left, GR sign	SE	85
24.024	400	15.5	At the T-junction with a broad gravel track turn left and then bear right	GR sign	SE	87
24.025	300	15.8	At the crossroads with the D202, continue straight ahead on the tarmac track beside the canal	Village of Vésigneul-sur-Marne on your left, GR sign	SE	86
24.026	2600	18.3	At the crossroads with the D54, turn right on the bridge over the river Marne	Village of Pogny on the left, GR sign	SW	87
24.027	130	18.5	Immediately after crossing the bridge, turn left on the small tarmac road and then bear right	GR sign	SW	86
24.028	300	18.8	At the T-junction with the main road, turn left, cross the bridge and then turn left again on the track	GR sign and yellow VF sign	S	87
24.029	1000	19.8	At the junction in the track, continue straight ahead with the river on your left. Note:- in wet conditions the track ahead can be very slippery	Avoid the broad track on your right, GR sign	SE	89

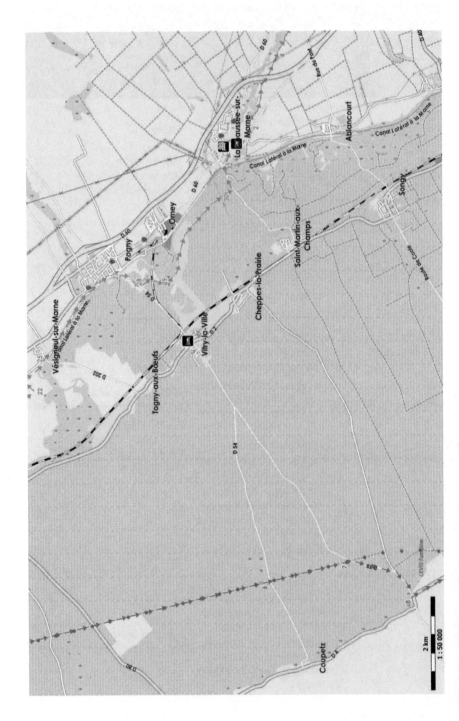

Waypoint	Distance between waypoints	Total km	Directions	Verification Point	Compass	Altitude m
24.030	2200	22.0	At the junction in the tracks, under the power lines, continue straight ahead towards the main road	GR sign	SE	88
24.031	400	22.4	At the T-junction with the D302, turn left	Pass a football field on your right, GR sign	E	89
24.032	600	22.9	After crossing the canal bridge, turn right on rue d'el Biar	GR sign	E	91
24.033	500	23.4	Arrive at La-Chaussée-sur-Marne centre	Hôtel du Midi on your left		95

Accommodation & Facilities ....   Châlons-en-Champagne - La-Chaussée-sur-Marne

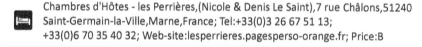

Chambres d'Hôtes - les Perrières,(Nicole & Denis Le Saint),7 rue Châlons,51240 Saint-Germain-la-Ville,Marne,France; Tel:+33(0)3 26 67 51 13; +33(0)6 70 35 40 32; Web-site:lesperrieres.pagesperso-orange.fr; Price:B

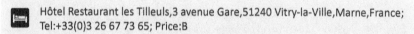

Hôtel Restaurant les Tilleuls,3 avenue Gare,51240 Vitry-la-Ville,Marne,France; Tel:+33(0)3 26 67 73 65; Price:B

Hôtel du Midi,1 rue du Colonel Caillot,51240 La-Chaussee-sur-Marne,Marne,France; Tel:+33(0)3 26 72 94 77; Email:hoteldumidi51@wanadoo.fr; Price:B

Hôtel Clos de Mutigny,17 avenue du Docteur Justin Jolly,51240 La-Chaussee-sur-Marne,Marne,France; Tel:+33(0)3 26 72 94 20; Email:closdemutigny@free.fr; Price:B

Vatry Airport,51320 Bussy-Lettrée,Marne,France; Tel:+33(0)3 26 64 82 00; Web-site:www.vatry.com

Waypoint	Distance between waypoints	Total km	Directions	Verification Point	Compass	Altitude m

Alternate Route #24.A1 **Length: 54.2km**

Stage Summary: shorter and more historically accurate route using vestiges of the Roman road and passing the Sigeric locations of Fontaine-sur-Coole (LXVIII) and Donnement (LXVIII). The substantially off-road Alternate Route is shown as a single section for consistency of layout, but the journey may be broken with accommodation available in Coole, Humbauville and Le-Miex-Tiercelin.

Stage Ascent: 620m **Stage Descent: 541m**

Waypoint	Distance between waypoints	Total km	Directions	Verification Point	Compass	Altitude m
24A1.001	0	0.0	Turn right beside the D80	Towards the church	S	83
24A1.002	400	0.4	At the T-junction after crossing the river bridge, turn right	Grande rue in Sogny-aux-Moulins	NW	85
24A1.003	110	0.5	Turn left on rue d'Ecury, uphill	Direction Châlons-en-Champagne	SW	90
24A1.004	1200	1.7	At the crossroads with the busy D2, continue straight ahead on the track	Between open fields	SW	125
24A1.005	1900	3.6	At the junction with a tarmac road, turn right and then left down a gravel path, the old Roman Road	Towards the wind farm	S	136
24A1.006	6500	10.0	At intersection with the road continue straight ahead on the track	D54, wind-farm on left	S	159
24A1.007	1900	11.9	At the intersection with the road turn right on the road	D79 towards Fontaine-sur-Coole	SW	147
24A1.008	1700	13.6	At the junction in the village of Fontaine-sur-Coole (LXVIII) turn left	Direction Coole	SE	127
24A1.009	1700	15.3	Fork left. Note:- 1km can be saved by remaining on the D4 to the crossroads in Coole	Direction Faux-Coole, D281	SE	129

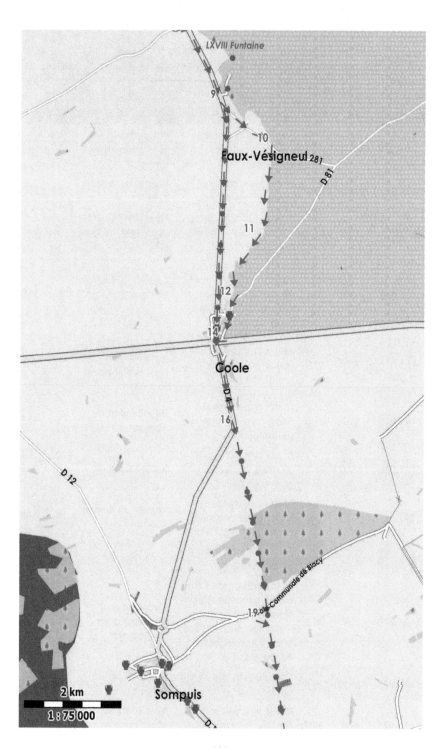

LXVIII Funtaine

9

10

Faux-Vésigneul 281

D 81

11

12

14

Coole

D 4

16

D 12

19 ou Communale de Blacy

2 km

Sompuis

1:75 000

D

Waypoint	Distance between waypoints	Total km	Directions	Verification Point	Compass	Altitude m
24A1.010	1400	16.7	After passing through Faux turn right onto gravel track	Proceed with line of trees and river on right	S	140
24A1.011	1900	18.6	At junction, continue ahead on main track	Keep river to the right	S	150
24A1.012	1400	20.0	At road junction, turn right and bear left on the road	Trees on the right, open fields on the left	S	154
24A1.013	400	20.4	On the crown of the bend to the right, turn left and immediately right onto ruelle Mont Beau	VF sign	S	153
24A1.014	500	20.9	At the junction with the major road turn right beside the N4	Les Routiers restaurant on right, water tower to the left	W	156
24A1.015	140	21.0	At the crossroads in Coole turn left onto rue de Sompuis	D4, direction Sompuis	S	153
24A1.016	1800	22.8	At the bend in the D4, go straight ahead on the gravel track	Roman Road	S	172
24A1.017	3700	26.5	At the crossroads with the tarmac road, continue straight ahead	Remain on Roman Road	S	169
24A1.018	220	26.7	Fork right after a slight bend in the track		SW	165
24A1.019	160	26.9	At the crossroads in the tracks, continue straight ahead to the following T-junction, turn left and bear right to rejoin the Roman Road	Hedge on your left, large open field on right	S	172
24A1.020	2800	29.6	Continue straight ahead on the road	Water tower to the left	S	158
24A1.021	600	30.2	At the junction with the D12, bear left into Humbauville	Voie Romaine, stone cross on right	S	138

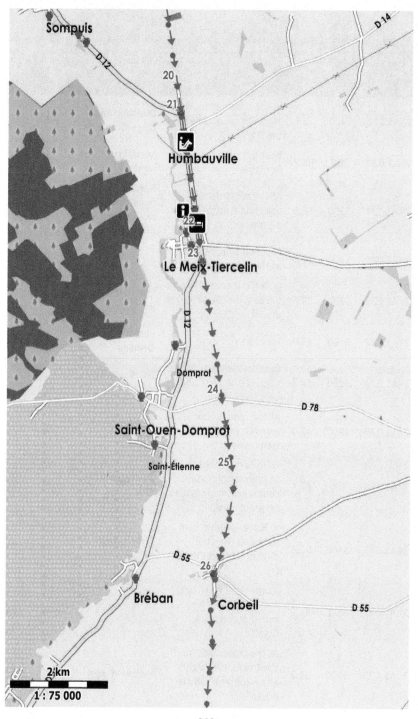

Sompuis

D 12

D 14

20

21

Humbauville

22

23

Le Meix-Tiercelin

D 12

Domprot

24

D 78

Saint-Ouen-Domprot

Saint-Étienne

25

D 55

26

Bréban

Corbeil

D 55

2 km

1 : 75 000

Waypoint	Distance between waypoints	Total km	Directions	Verification Point	Compass	Altitude m
24A1.022	2400	32.6	In the centre of le-Meix-Tiercelin continue on the D12	Direction Saint-Ouen-Domprot	S	136
24A1.023	700	33.2	Bear left onto the Voie Romaine	Metal crucifix on right	S	139
24A1.024	2800	36.0	At the crossroads, continue straight ahead on the track	Between farm buildings and towards the brow of the hill	S	140
24A1.025	1500	37.5	Proceed straight ahead at the crossroads		S	143
24A1.026	2200	39.6	At the crossroads in Corbeil, proceed straight ahead	Rue Haute des Romains	S	121
24A1.027	3400	43.0	Fork left	Pass the farm - les Ormées	S	161
24A1.028	1200	44.2	Continue straight ahead through the farm and over the hill	Small wood on right	S	147
24A1.029	2800	47.0	At the road junction, turn left onto rue de Dampierre	Part-timbered house	SE	107
24A1.030	400	47.4	At the crossroads in Donnement (LXVII), continue straight ahead on rue de Braux	Direction Braux, D24	SE	107
24A1.031	3400	50.8	In Braux-le-Petit, turn right and then left, direction Braux Centre, D5	Over a small bridge	SE	109
24A1.032	400	51.2	As the road turns left, fork right onto the broad gravel track, uphill		S	109
24A1.033	3100	54.2	At the crossroads in the tracks, turn right and rejoin the"Official Route"	Yellow VF sign		162

Accommodation & Facilities for Alternate Route via Coole, Humbauville and Le-Miex-Tiercelin

🛏️ Chambres d'Hôtes - Régine & Patrick Picard,6 rue du Moulin,51240 Nuisement-sur-Coole,Marne,France; Tel:+33(0)3 26 67 62 14; Email:pat.picard@wanadoo.fr; Web-site:chambres.voila.net; Price:B

ℹ️ Mairie,1 rue Grande,51240 Cernon,Marne,France; Tel:+33(0)3 26 70 47 21

👥 Mme Monique Songy,Rue de Châlons,51320 Coole,Marne,France; Tel:+33(0)3 26 74 05 67; +33(0)6 08 58 33 41

👥 Marc Yverneau,51320 Humbauville,Marne,France; Tel:+33(0)3 26 74 60 10; +33(0)6 17 85 00 79

👥 Esat les Antes,Rue du Four,51320 Le-Meix-Tiercelin,Marne,France; Tel:+33(0)3 26 72 41 20; +33(0)3 26 72 00 59; Web-site:cat-lesanteswanadoo.fr; Price:C; Note:Normally only a bed for one pilgrim. Meals can be provided for more,

🛏️ B&B - Collombar,7 Grande rue,51320 Le-Meix-Tiercelin,Marne,France; Tel:+33(0)3 26 72 40 37; Price:B

🖼️ Canivet Martial,36 Grande rue,51320 Humbauville,Marne,France; Tel:+33(0)3 26 72 42 77

ℹ️ Mairie,9 rue Chanterelle,51320 Le-Meix-Tiercelin,Marne,France; Tel:+33(0)3 26 72 73 42

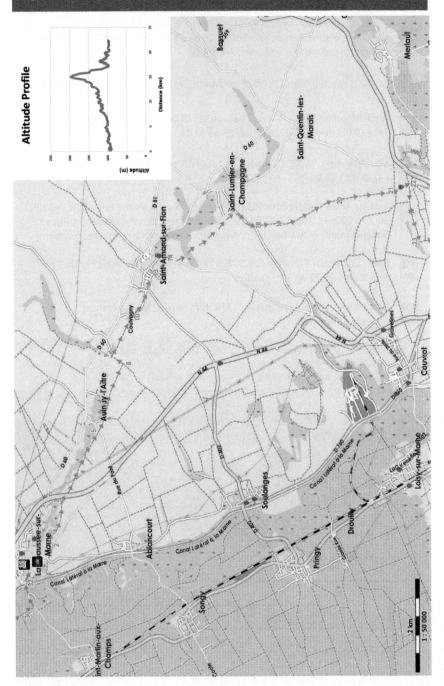

Altitude Profile

Stage Summary: the route continues beside the river Fion before taking to the rolling hills through the vast cereal fields of the region. Vitry-le-François offers a full range of facilities.

Distance from Canterbury: 529km   Distance to Besançon: 381km
Stage Ascent: 260m   Stage Descent: 258m

Waypoint	Distance between waypoints	Total km	Directions	Verification Point	Compass	Altitude m
25.001	0	0.0	From the junction beside the Hôtel du Midi in La-Chaussée-sur-Marne centre, continue with the line of trees on your left and then turn right at the Stop sign and proceed with care beside the busy road	GR sign	SE	95
25.002	800	0.8	As the road bears right, take the left fork on the track	Vitry-le-François 22km, yellow VF sign	E	94
25.003	1000	1.8	At the crossroads in the tracks, continue straight ahead between the trees	Motorway ahead, GR sign	SE	97
25.004	800	2.5	At the junction in the tracks, continue straight ahead	Pass a plantation of beech trees on your left , GR sign	SE	97
25.005	1000	3.6	At the crossroads with the D81, continue straight ahead on the gravel track	GR sign	E	96
25.006	300	3.8	At the crossroads with the small tarmac road, continue straight ahead on the stony track	Trees on the left of the track, GR sign	E	98
25.007	400	4.2	Take the right fork, between the fields	Parallel to the valley bottom	E	100
25.008	900	5.1	At the T-junction in the tracks, turn left on the gravel track	GR sign	NE	102
25.009	290	5.4	At the junction in the tracks, turn right towards the village	Saint-Amand-sur-Fion 2km, yellow VF sign	SE	99

Waypoint	Distance between waypoints	Total km	Directions	Verification Point	Compass	Altitude m
25.010	900	6.3	At the crossroads with the tarmac road, continue straight ahead on rue de la Liberté towards the village	Timber framed house on the right, GR sign	SE	102
25.011	900	7.2	At the T-junction, turn right and then immediately left	GR sign	SE	105
25.012	400	7.6	At the T-junction at the end of rue des Ruelles, turn right and immediately left	Pass timber framed house n° 8 on right, GR sign	S	110
25.013	210	7.8	At the T-junction at the end of rue des hauts Prés, turn left	Towards the trees	E	111
25.014	300	8.1	At the T-junction with the D260, turn right, uphill beside the main road	GR sign	S	117
25.015	260	8.4	Fork left on the stony track	Saint-Lumier-en-Champagne 2km, yellow VF sign	SE	117
25.016	1500	9.9	At the T-junction with a tarmac road, turn right and then bear left	Sports field on your right, GR sign	SE	123
25.017	290	10.2	At the T-junction with a tarmac road, turn right	GR sign	SW	118
25.018	500	10.7	Immediately after passing the metal barn on your left, bear left on the gravel track	GR sign	S	123
25.019	700	11.4	At the crossroads in the tracks, continue straight ahead	Pass a copse of trees on your left, GR sign	SE	123
25.020	1200	12.6	At the crossroads in the tracks, continue straight ahead, uphill on the gravel track	Between large fields	S	127
25.021	1500	14.1	At a junction in the tracks, continue straight ahead	Hedgerow on your right, GR sign	SE	155

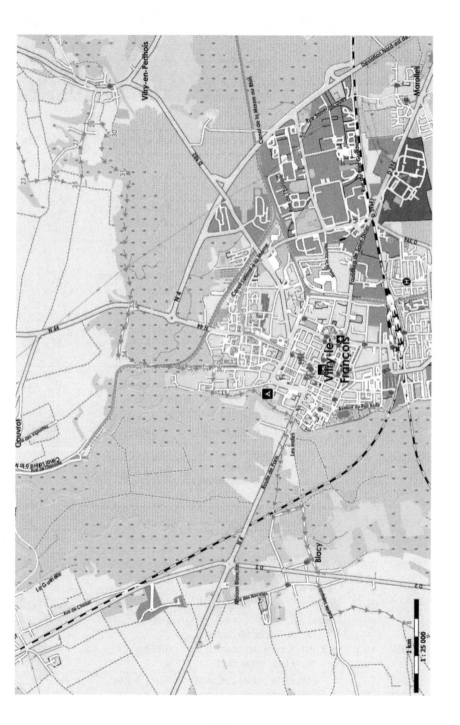

Waypoint	Distance between waypoints	Total km	Directions	Verification Point	Compass	Altitude m
25.022	300	14.4	At the crossroads, turn right on the gravel track, uphill. Note:- the GR14 continues straight ahead, while the GR145 turns right	Yellow VF sign	W	158
25.023	1300	15.7	At the junction in the tracks, turn left and continue downhill between the vines, towards the large silos	Vitry-en-Perthois 2km, GR sign	S	177
25.024	260	15.9	At the crossroads at the foot of the hill, continue straight ahead on the broad gravel track	Between the open fields	S	148
25.025	400	16.3	At the crossroads in the tracks, turn left and quickly fork right, downhill on the narrow track	Pass chapelle Sainte Geneviève on your right	E	145
25.026	300	16.6	Continue straight ahead beside the tarmac road	Pass house n° 4 on your left	E	115
25.027	130	16.7	At the road junction, continue straight ahead	Chemin de la Chapelle!GR sign	E	111
25.028	220	16.9	Beside house n°35, fork right down the steep concrete pathway and then turn right	Yellow GR654 sign	S	105
25.029	160	17.1	Bear right on the track	GR sign	SW	98
25.030	130	17.2	At the junction in tracks, turn right	Pass between the fence and the trees, GR sign	SW	96
25.031	700	17.9	Continue straight ahead into the woods	Avoid the path on the left, GR sign	W	106
25.032	1500	19.3	At the T-junction in the track, turn left towards the very busy main road	GR sign	S	99
25.033	50	19.4	Cross the main road with great care and then turn right on the tarmac road	GR sign	W	96

Waypoint	Distance between waypoints	Total km	Directions	Verification Point	Compass	Altitude m
25.034	600	20.0	At the junction, turn left, pass the metal barrier and continue between the metal fencing	GR sign	SW	103
25.035	400	20.4	Turn right over the bridge and then turn left, keep the lock on your left. Note: -the path beside the lock is not passable by horses. Riders should remain with the canal on their right to the second and quieter highway bridge and cross this to find the centre of Vitry-en-François and then rejoin the "Official Route" by the Marne river bridge on the N4	GR sign	S	95
25.036	500	20.8	Keep to the track beside the right hand branch of the canal		S	98
25.037	300	21.1	Turn right down a steep narrow track	GR sign	SW	97
25.038	20	21.1	At the junction with the road, turn right	Between walled gardens, GR sign	W	97
25.039	220	21.3	At the mini-roundabout, continue straight ahead on the small path and then bear left	River on your right, GR sign	S	96
25.040	1000	22.4	Arrive at Vitry-le-François. Note:- the town centre is to the left	Beside the Marne river bridge		98

Hôtel de la Cloche,34 rue Aristide Briand,51300 Vitry-le-François,Marne,France; Tel:+33(0)3 26 74 03 84; Email:chef.sautetepicerie@wanadoo.fr; Web-site:www.hotel-de-la-cloche.com; Price:B

Hotel - le Saint Eloi,5 rue Châlons,10230 Mailly-le-Camp,Aube,France; Tel:+33(0)3 25 37 30 04; Price:B

Hôtel Restaurant du Centre,64 rue Gén de Gaulle,10230 Mailly-le-Camp,Aube,France; Tel:+33(0)3 25 37 30 08; Price:B

Camping Camp Municipal la Peupleraie,6 Esplanade de Tauberbischofsheim,51300 Vitry-le-François,Marne,France; Tel:+33(0)3 26 74 20 47; Price:C

Centre Hospitalier,2 rue Charles Simon,51300 Vitry-le-François,Marne,France; Tel:+33(0)3 26 73 60 60; Web-site:www.ch-vitrylefrancois.fr

Cab Docteurs Carlier Hutasse Mergen,18 Boulevard Carnot,51300 Vitry-le-François,Marne,France; Tel:+33(0)3 26 72 66 66

Reaux Sylvie,1 rue des Pères,51300 Vitry-le-François,Marne,France; Tel:+33(0)6 58 10 02 04

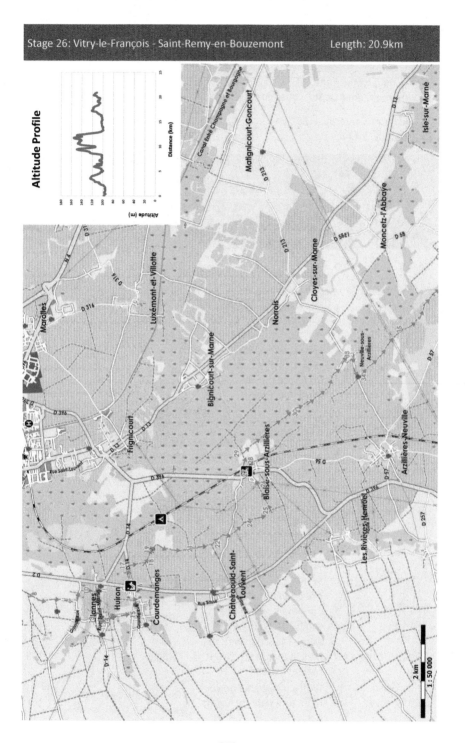

Stage Summary: the route quickly leaves the busy roads surrounding Vitry and continues to follow the chemin de St Jacques on good farm tracks broadly parallel to la Marne river.

Distance from Canterbury: 552km   Distance to Besançon: 358km
Stage Ascent: 241m   Stage Descent: 227m

Waypoint	Distance between waypoints	Total km	Directions	Verification Point	Compass	Altitude m
26.001	0	0.0	With great care follow the main road across the bridge	River Marne	W	97
26.002	300	0.3	Just after passing the car sales lot, carefully cross the road and turn left on Vieille Route	Direction Blacy, yellow VF sign	W	96
26.003	800	1.1	After passing under the railway bridge, take the first turning to the left on the gravel track	GR sign	S	94
26.004	400	1.4	At the T-junction in the tracks, turn right	Trees on your right, field on your left, GR sign	W	96
26.005	400	1.8	With a river ford on your right, continue straight ahead over the bridge	Towards the church in Blacy, GR sign	W	95
26.006	400	2.2	At the crossroads with the D2, continue straight ahead	Rue de Sompuis	W	98
26.007	500	2.7	On the edge of the village, turn left on the gravel track, uphill	Pass radio tower, yellow VF sign	S	107
26.008	900	3.5	At the junction in the tracks, with the radio tower on your immediate right, continue straight ahead	Towards the prominent church in Glannes, GR sign	S	123
26.009	1100	4.7	At the T-junction with the road in Glannes, turn left beside the road	GR sign	E	104
26.010	270	4.9	With a picnic area on your right, turn right on a grass track	Towards the trees! GR sign	S	101

Waypoint	Distance between waypoints	Total km	Directions	Verification Point	Compass	Altitude m
26.011	400	5.3	At the crossroads in the tracks, turn right on the gravel track	Pass the rear of the houses on your left, GR sign	W	102
26.012	500	5.8	Cross to the far corner of the gravel area in Huiron	Yellow VF sign	W	109
26.013	110	5.9	At the crossroads, turn left to follow the road uphill	Towards the water tower, yellow VF sign	S	113
26.014	100	6.0	At the crossroads at the foot of the water tower, continue straight ahead on the D602	Rue Saint Claude, GR sign	S	116
26.015	1300	7.2	At the T-junction in front of the Mairie in Courdemanges, turn left	GR sign	E	106
26.016	600	7.8	At the crossroads with the D2, continue straight ahead on the D14e	Direction Frignicourt, GR sign	E	101
26.017	500	8.3	Turn right on the gravel track, uphill	Direction Monument Militaire de Mont-Môret, yellow VF sign	S	101
26.018	400	8.7	At the junction at the top of the initial climb, bear left	Pass oil-well on your right	SE	123
26.019	300	9.1	Continue straight ahead on the track	Pass the monument on your left	S	129
26.020	900	10.0	At the crossroads in the tracks, continue straight ahead, towards the lone tree	Camping a la Ferme to the left	S	113
26.021	140	10.1	At the next crossroads in the tracks, again continue straight ahead on the grass track, uphill	GR sign	S	117
26.022	400	10.5	At the junction in the tracks near the top of the hill, continue straight ahead	Oil-well on the right	SE	144
26.023	500	11.0	At the crossroads with a tarmac road, continue straight ahead on the gravel track	Blaise-sous-Arzillières 2km, yellow VF sign	SE	144

Waypoint	Distance between waypoints	Total km	Directions	Verification Point	Compass	Altitude m
26.024	400	11.4	At the junction in the track, continue straight ahead, uphill	Oil storage tank on the left, GR sign	SE	141
26.025	700	12.1	At the foot of the hill, turn left on the grass track	Yellow VF sign	NE	139
26.026	700	12.7	At the junction with the tarmac road, continue straight ahead, downhill	Chemin des hauts Traversins, GR sign	NE	121
26.027	270	13.0	At the crossroads with the D396 in Blaise-sous-Arzillières, continue straight ahead, on rue Basse	Pass the bar on your right	NE	105
26.028	400	13.3	At the junction in the tracks, bear left	Avoid the track to the right, GR sign	E	99
26.029	160	13.5	At the junction in the tracks, turn right towards the bridge	Neuville-sous-Arzillières 3.5km, yellow VF sign	SE	100
26.030	1400	14.9	Continue straight ahead on the path	Continue between the trees	SE	103
26.031	500	15.4	At the end of the plantation, turn right and then left on the gravel track	GR sign	SE	101
26.032	1400	16.8	In place Napoléon in Neuville-sous-Arzillières, continue straight ahead	Church on the left, GR sign	SE	110
26.033	110	16.9	Bear right on the road towards Arzillières	GR sign	W	110
26.034	500	17.4	Beside the picnic table and calvaire, turn left on the gravel track	Saint-Rémy-en-Bouzemont 3.5km, yellow VF sign	SE	119
26.035	1500	18.9	At the crossroads in the tracks, continue straight ahead on the gravel track, uphill	GR sign	SE	106
26.036	1500	20.4	At the T-junction with the main road, turn left	Saint-Rémy-en-Bouzemont 0.5km, yellow VF sign	SE	117
26.037	600	20.9	Arrive at Saint-Remy-en-Bouzemont	Mairie on your right		111

Marc Yverneau,51320 Humbauville,Marne,France; Tel:+33(0)3 26 74 60 10; +33(0)6 17 85 00 79

Esat les Antes,Rue du Four,51320 Le-Meix-Tiercelin,Marne,France; Tel:+33(0)3 26 72 41 20; +33(0)3 26 72 00 59; Web-site:cat-lesanteswanadoo.fr; Price:C; Note:Normally only a bed for one pilgrim. Meals can be provided for more,

Café de la place,2 rue Pont de la Noue,51300 Blaise-Sous-Arzillières,Marne,France; Tel:+33(0)3 26 72 80 01; +33(0)6 63 86 89 57; Email:heitzmannfr@wanadoo.fr; Price:C; Note:Pilgrim friendly,

B&B - Collombar,7 Grande rue,51320 Le-Meix-Tiercelin,Marne,France; Tel:+33(0)3 26 72 40 37; Price:B

Au Brochet du Lac,15 Grande rue,51290 Saint-Rémy-en-Bouzemont,Marne,France; Tel:+33(0)3 26 72 51 06; Web-site:www.au-brochet-du-lac.com; Price:B

Camping,Ferme du Mont Morêt,51300 Courdemanges,Marne,France; Tel:+33(0)3 26 72 09 97; Email:info@ferme-mont-moret.com; Web-site:www.ferme-mont-moret.com; Price:C; Note:Gîte and chambre d'hôte also available,

Droulez Bornier Christine,2 rue Frignicourt,51300 Courdemanges,Marne,France; Tel:+33(0)3 26 62 25 98

Canivet Martial,36 Grande rue,51320 Humbauville,Marne,France; Tel:+33(0)3 26 72 42 77

Mairie,9 rue Chanterelle,51320 Le-Meix-Tiercelin,Marne,France; Tel:+33(0)3 26 72 73 42

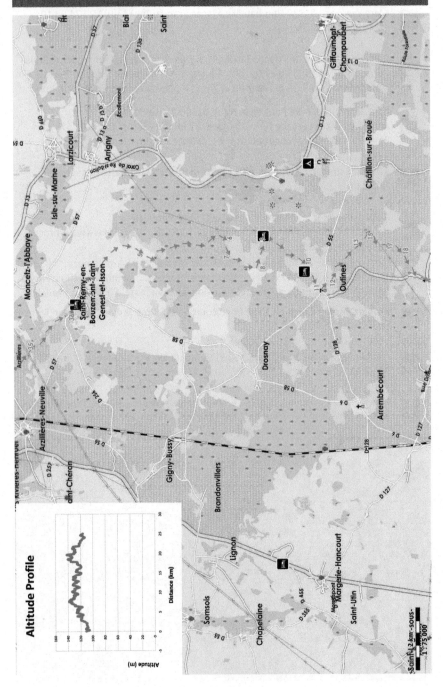

Altitude Profile

Stage Summary: the "Official Route" - GR145, continues to share the path with the chemin de St Jacques – GR654. This is an extremely exposed section with long distances between villages. You will pass the hamlet of "Au Milieu de Nulle Part" - "the middle of nowhere" which probably says it all. The tracks are generally broad and of good quality in dry weather. However a number of signposts have fallen victim to agricultural machinery and so it is best to keep careful track of your progress in the guide book.

Distance from Canterbury: 573km   Distance to Besançon: 337km
Stage Ascent: 206m   Stage Descent: 200m

Waypoint	Distance between waypoints	Total km	Directions	Verification Point	Compass	Altitude m
27.001	0	0.0	From the junction in Saint-Remy-en-Bouzemont with the Mairie on your right, continue straight ahead on the D58	Towards Drosnay, GR sign	SE	111
27.002	500	0.5	Just before the factory, turn left on the road	Route des Landres, yellow VF sign	NE	109
27.003	240	0.7	At the mini-roundabout, continue straight ahead	Route des Landres, GR sign	SE	110
27.004	400	1.1	Continue straight ahead on the broad gravel track	Speed bump, GR sign	S	107
27.005	2500	3.6	At the junction in the tracks, continue straight ahead on the main track	Lakes on the left and right, GR sign	S	118
27.006	3000	6.5	At the junction immediately before the timber framed farmhouse, turn right	Lake below on your right, GR sign	SW	129
27.007	700	7.2	At the junction in the tracks, continue straight ahead	Woods on your right, fence on the left, GR sign	S	135
27.008	1000	8.2	At the crossroads in the tracks, follow the gravel track to the left	Pass woods on your right, GR sign	E	134
27.009	1000	9.2	At the crossroads in the tracks, beside the hamlet of la Pierre, turn right towards Outines	Gîte Au Milieu de Nulle Part on the left at the junction	SW	131

Waypoint	Distance between waypoints	Total km	Directions	Verification Point	Compass	Altitude m
27.010	1400	10.6	At the T-junction with a road, turn right and then take the first turning to the left	Water tower on the left, yellow VF sign	SW	129
27.011	1300	11.9	At the crossroads in Outines, turn left on the D55	Beautiful timbered church on the right, GR sign	SE	132
27.012	220	12.2	Take the right fork on the small road. Note:- the route ahead has some navigation challenges. There are few signs and landmarks and often follow the less obvious tracks. Carefully follow the instructions and the distances between the waypoints	Rue du Moulin Neuf, GR sign	SE	130
27.013	1800	14.0	At the crossroads in the tracks, with a copse of trees on your left, continue straight ahead on the gravel track	GR sign on the ground	SE	131
27.014	400	14.3	At the T-junction in the tracks, turn right on the grass track. Note:- the GR145 and GR14B separate at this point with the GR14B continuing on the more definite track to the left	Pass under power lines	S	127
27.015	280	14.6	At the foot of the hill, turn right towards the copse of trees and then bear left between the trees and the stream	Line of white stones	W	120
27.016	270	14.9	Cross the metal footbridge and at the crossroads in the tracks, continue straight ahead on the grass track, uphill	GR654 sign	S	120

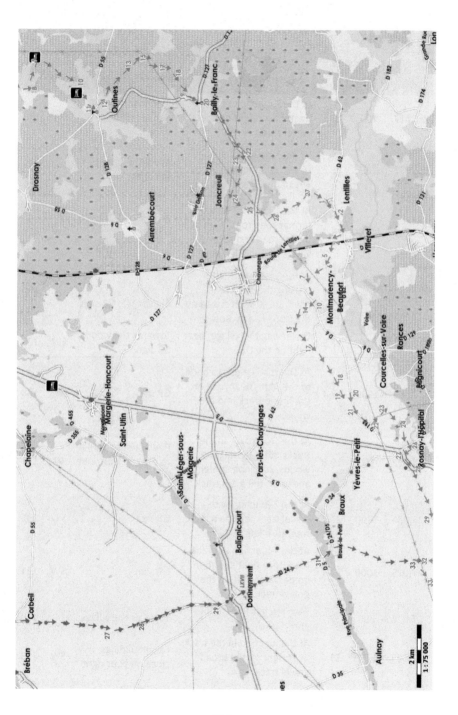

Waypoint	Distance between waypoints	Total km	Directions	Verification Point	Compass	Altitude m
27.017	700	15.5	At the T-junction in the tracks, turn right on the gravel track	Towards the slender church spire	SW	125
27.018	230	15.7	At the junction in the tracks, continue straight ahead on the gravel track	Avoid the track to the right	SW	126
27.019	1000	16.7	At the T-junction with the tarmac road road, turn left on the road and enter the village of Bailly-le-Franc	GR sign	SW	119
27.020	500	17.1	At the crossroads, after passing the church, continue straight ahead on the D56 - rue du Bois	Towards Chavanges, GR sign	S	125
27.021	400	17.5	On leaving the village, bear right on the D56	Towards the woods, GR sign	SW	125
27.022	1900	19.4	As the road begins to bend to the right, bear right on the broad track into the woods	GR sign	W	138
27.023	300	19.8	At the crossroads in the tracks, after leaving the woods, continue straight ahead on the grass track	Power lines parallel to the track on your right	W	131
27.024	1300	21.1	At the T-junction with a gravel track, beside a lone tree, turn left	GR sign	SW	132
27.025	1000	22.1	At the T-junction with the road, turn right and then immediately left on the gravel track	GR sign	SW	121
27.026	600	22.7	Take the left fork on the gravel track	Towards the village	SE	120
27.027	1700	24.4	At the junction in the tracks bear right on the broad gravel track	Farm buildings close on your right	SW	119
27.028	600	25.0	Arrive at Lentilles	Beside the timbered church		116

Gîte,Au Milieu de Nulle Part,51290 Outines,Marne,France; +33(0)6 67 36 74 93; Email:lacabane@aumilieudenullepart.fr; Price:A

Chambres d'Hôtes - Ferme de Hancourt,(Michelle & Denis Geoffrey),16 rue de Hancourt,51290 Margerie-Hancourt,Marne,France; Tel:+33(0)3 26 72 48 47; +33(0)6 28 29 21 44; Email:denis.geoffrey@wanadoo.fr; Price:B

Gîte Chatelot,(Mme Chatelot),29 rue des Echalas,51290 Outines,Marne,France; Tel:+33(0)3 26 72 58 82; +33(0)6 83 13 01 45; Price:B

Le Clos du Vieux Moulin,33 rue Lac,51290 Châtillon-sur-Broué,Marne,France; Tel:+33(0)3 26 41 30 43; Web-site:www.leclosduvieuxmoulin.fr; Price:C

Maignier Michel,35 rue Grande Inglee,52220 Montier-en-Der,Haute Marne,France; Tel:+33(0)3 25 04 61 82

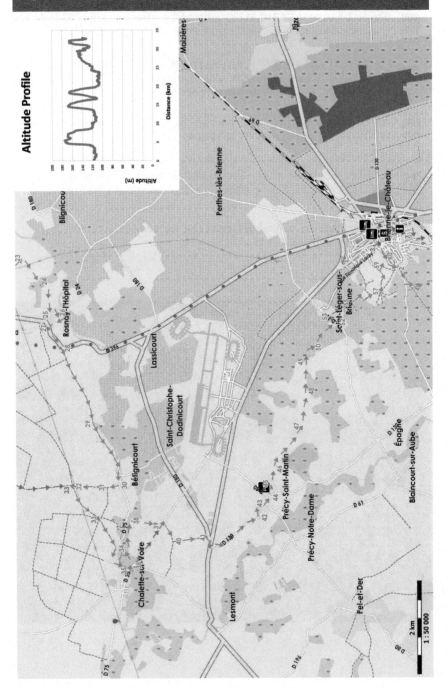

Stage Summary: this long section continues through the open cereal fields and woodland, still sharing the chemin de St Jacques. There are number of steep climbs to be tackled which will be difficult for cyclists with loaded bikes. There are few intermediate facilities, ensure that you have enough food and water for a long day.

Distance from Canterbury: 598km   Distance to Besançon: 312km
Stage Ascent: 382m   Stage Descent: 359m

Waypoint	Distance between waypoints	Total km	Directions	Verification Point	Compass	Altitude m
28.001	0	0.0	From the junction beside the part timbered church in Lentilles, keep right D62	Direction Villeret	SW	117
28.002	400	0.4	Take the right fork - D2	Direction Villeret	W	117
28.003	900	1.2	After crossing the bridge and with a railway crossing visible ahead, turn right on a gravel track	Pass a line of trees on your right	NW	112
28.004	600	1.8	Cross the railway and continue straight ahead on the grass track	Between the fields	W	114
28.005	400	2.2	At the T-junction with the gravel track, turn right and then keep straight ahead at the next junction	Towards the woods, GR sign	NW	118
28.006	400	2.6	At the junction in the tracks with the woods immediately on your left, continue straight ahead	Power lines parallel on the right	NW	117
28.007	700	3.3	At the T-junction in the tracks, turn left on the gravel track towards the village	GR sign	W	115
28.008	700	4.0	At the T-junction with the D6 in Montmorency-Beaufort, turn left	Yellow VF sign	SW	125

Waypoint	Distance between waypoints	Total km	Directions	Verification Point	Compass	Altitude m
28.009	250	4.2	In the centre of Montmorency-Beaufort, after passing house n°8, turn right on the small road uphill	Rue Haute, yellow VF sign	W	127
28.010	100	4.3	At the top of the rise turn sharp right, steeply uphill on the grass track into the trees	Pass a conifer hedge on your left, GR sign	N	135
28.011	130	4.4	At the T-junction after the steep climb, turn right and continue straight ahead on the broad track at the next crossroads	GR sign	N	158
28.012	160	4.6	At the T-junction with a gravel track, turn left	GR sign	W	169
28.013	230	4.8	Take the indistinct right turn on a grass track over the brow of the hill	GR sign on the ground	N	170
28.014	180	5.0	At the junction in the tracks, turn left between the fields	Towards an isolated tree on the horizon	W	173
28.015	700	5.7	At the crossroads in the tracks, beside the tree, turn left on the gravel track	GR sign	SW	169
28.016	400	6.1	At the crossroads in the tracks, continue straight ahead, uphill on the gravel track	Grass track to the right	SW	164
28.017	500	6.5	At the crossroads with a tarmac road, continue straight ahead on the gravel track	Track ahead bears left, GR sign	SW	169
28.018	1200	7.7	At the crossroads in the tracks, continue straight ahead	Large silo to the right	SW	156
28.019	700	8.4	At the T-junction after a long descent, turn left	Towards the road, GR sign	SE	127
28.020	240	8.7	At the T-junction with the main road, turn right	GR sign	W	121

Waypoint	Distance between waypoints	Total km	Directions	Verification Point	Compass	Altitude m
28.021	700	9.3	Continue straight ahead beside the main road	Avoid the turning to the left to les Presles	SW	120
28.022	700	9.9	With a copse of trees in the field to your right, turn left on the gravel track	Pass under the power lines	SE	121
28.023	800	10.8	At the junction in the middle of the fields, turn right	Towards the woods	SW	112
28.024	600	11.4	At the crossroads in the tracks, continue straight ahead into the woods on the broad gravel track	GR sign	W	113
28.025	900	12.3	At the Stop sign in the centre of Rosnay-l'Hôpital, turn left	Rue Dulong, yellow VF sign	S	117
28.026	150	12.4	Turn right on rue Saint George	Towards the church, GR sign	NW	115
28.027	700	13.1	At the T-junction with the main road, cross over, turn left and continue with care beside the road	GR sign	SW	118
28.028	500	13.6	As the main road turns to the left, take the right fork on the small road	Chemin de Betignicourt, GR sign	SW	121
28.029	1800	15.4	At the crossroads in the tracks, continue straight ahead and remain on this track to the village of Betignicourt	Avoid the track on the left downhill into the woods	SW	157
28.030	1500	16.9	Shortly before leaving Betignicourt, turn right uphill on the gravel track	Immediately after house n°14, GR sign	N	116
28.031	260	17.2	At the junction in the tracks, continue straight ahead up the hill	Avoid the turning to the left, GR sign	N	126

Waypoint	Distance between waypoints	Total km	Directions	Verification Point	Compass	Altitude m
28.032	800	18.0	At the crossroads at the top of the hill, turn left on the broad gravel track. Note:- the Alternate Route via le-Meix-Tiercelin joins from the track ahead	Parallel to the power lines, yellow VF sign	SW	162
28.033	1000	18.9	At the crossroads in the tracks, continue straight ahead on the main track	Water tower ahead, GR sign	SW	151
28.034	800	19.7	At the T-junction with the D75, turn right and follow the road as it bears left	Pass old wooden farm building on your left	SW	116
28.035	700	20.4	At the T-junction at the end of rue du Marais in Chalette-sur-Voire, turn left	Direction Lesmont, yellow VF sign	SE	107
28.036	140	20.5	After crossing 2 bridges, take the left fork beside the calvaire	Direction les Fontaines, GR sign	SE	106
28.037	220	20.7	Turn left on the gravel track and skirt the field on your right. Note:- 1 km may be saved by remaining on the road until the track returns from the left	Pass a large barn on your left, GR sign	E	106
28.038	1100	21.8	Follow the track as it turns right, away from the river	Towards a wooden cabin at the foot of the trees	S	109
28.039	700	22.5	At the T-junction with the road, turn left and then immediately right on the gravel track	Pass lakes on your left, GR sign	SW	105
28.040	500	23.0	Take the left fork, towards the main road	Lakes on your left, GR sign	S	105
28.041	800	23.8	At the T-junction with a tarmac road, turn right and with care follow the main road towards Troyes. Then take the first road on the left	Direction Précy-Saint-Martin, GR sign	S	107

Waypoint	Distance between waypoints	Total km	Directions	Verification Point	Compass	Altitude m
28.042	1600	25.4	At the T-junction, after passing a house with an aeroplane in the garden, bear left into the village of Précy-Saint-Martin	Yellow VF sign	SE	123
28.043	400	25.8	At the junction in the village, keep straight ahead on the D80	Direction Epagne, GR sign	SE	125
28.044	170	26.0	Take the left fork - rue des Marronniers	Pass the Mairie on your right, GR sign	E	130
28.045	300	26.3	At the crossroads, continue straight ahead	Towards the garden centre, GR sign	E	134
28.046	300	26.6	Take the right fork, beside the water tower	GR sign	SE	138
28.047	1200	27.8	At the junction in the tracks, bear left on track	Between the fields	E	146
28.048	800	28.5	At the junction beside the woods, continue straight ahead	Avoid the 2 tracks on your right, GR sign	E	148
28.049	700	29.2	At the junction in the tracks, continue straight ahead, towards the woods	Avoid the track on your left, GR sign	SE	149
28.050	400	29.6	At the junction in the tracks, continue straight ahead on the main track	Parallel to the main road, GR sign	SE	136
28.051	700	30.2	Join a tarmac road then bear right, downhill at the junction	Pass fruit trees on your left, GR sign	SE	131
28.052	140	30.4	At the end of Voie de Précy in Saint-Léger-sour-Brienne, turn left	Towards the church, GR sign	NE	126
28.053	210	30.6	Immediately after passing the church, turn right into place de la Mairie	Pass close to the churchyard walls, GR sign	SE	126
28.054	140	30.7	At the crossroads, turn right on voie des Vonnes and then take the first left	GR sign	SE	125

Waypoint	Distance between waypoints	Total km	Directions	Verification Point	Compass	Altitude m
28.055	500	31.2	At the junction just before the top of the hill, continue straight ahead on the gravel track	Towards the trees, GR sign	S	152
28.056	600	31.7	At the junction in the tracks, continue straight ahead	Pass the telephone tower on your left, GR sign	S	162
28.057	250	32.0	At the crossroads in the tracks, turn left on the main track and then take the left fork	Pass a calvaire on your left, yellow VF sign	E	163
28.058	500	32.5	At the junction in the tracks, turn right on the smaller track into the trees	GR sign	SE	137
28.059	140	32.6	At the T-junction with a gravel track, turn left and then immediately right on the small track, slightly uphill	Pass through the trees, GR sign	E	133
28.060	210	32.8	Arrive at Brienne-le-Château at a T-junction with a tarmac road Note:- the town centre is down the hill to your left. The Alternate Route for the next section will lead you to the centre and offer a more direct exit from the town	Château directly ahead		140

Château de Pougy - Chambres d'Hôtes,28 Grande rue,10240 Pougy,Aube,France; Tel:+33(0)3 25 37 09 41; Email:antoine.morlet@wanadoo.fr ; Web-site:www.chateau-de-pougy.com; Price:B

Chambres d'Hotes - la Grenouillère,6 rue de la Louvière,10500 Précy-Saint-Martin,Aube,France; Tel:+33(0)3 25 27 16 60; +33(0)9 77 79 77 13; Email:ppourrier@wanadoo.fr; Web-site:www.chambresdhotes-lagrenouillere.com; Price:B

Hôtel des Voyageurs,30 avenue Pasteur,10500 Brienne-le-Château,Aube,France; Tel:+33(0)3 25 92 83 61; Email:jl_garnier@orange.fr; Web-site:hotel-restaurant-traiteur-soiree-etape-pension.hotelrestaurant-voyageurs.com; Price:B

Hôtel de la Croix Blanche,7 avenue Pasteur,10500 Brienne-le-Château,Aube,France; Tel:+33(0)3 25 92 80 27; Email:hr.lacroixblanche@wanadoo.fr; Web-site:www.hotel-restaurant-croix-blanche.fr; Price:B

Centre Equestre - Brienne la Vieille,Chemin de Milbert,10500 Brienne-la-Vieille,Aube,France; Tel:+33(0)3 25 92 62 76; Web-site:www.annuaire-equestre.com/annuaire/France

Office du Tourisme,34 rue de l'Ecole Militaire,10500 Brienne-le-Château,Aube,France; Tel:+33(0)3 25 92 82 41; Web-site:www.tourisme.barsuraube.org

Crédit Mutuel,90 rue Ecole Militaire,10500 Brienne-le-Château,Aube,France; Tel:+33(0)8 20 09 30 16

Caisse d'Epargne,78 rue Ecole Militaire,10500 Brienne-le-Château,Aube,France; Tel:+33(0)8 21 01 05 19

Cazet Christophe,41 rue Grande rue,60460 Blaincourt-les-Precy,Oise,France; Tel:+33(0)3 44 56 05 27

Taxi Arcis,38 rue de Troyes,10700 Arcis-sur-Aube,Aube,France; Tel:+33(0)3 25 37 81 50

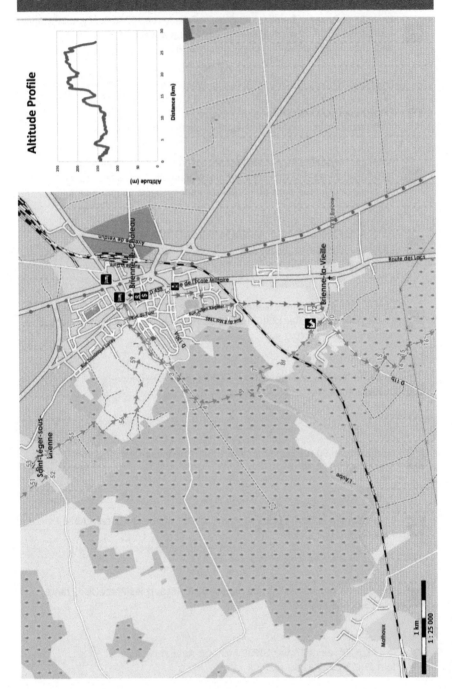

Stage Summary: the route begins in woodland following the valley of the Aube river, but again bypassing the Sigeric location of Brienne-la-Vielle (LXVI) before making another wide loop over the rolling hills of open cereal fields. The via Francigena (GR145) and chemin de St Jacques (GR654) finally separate in the village of Amance. The route can be considerably reduced by taking the Alternate Route via Jessains. Dolancourt is dominated by the Nigloland theme park and as a result accommodation can be both expensive and fully booked in the high season.

Distance from Canterbury: 631km   Distance to Besançon: 279km
Stage Ascent: 334m   Stage Descent: 322m

Waypoint	Distance between waypoints	Total km	Directions	Verification Point	Compass	Altitude m
29.001	0	0.0	From the T-junction beside the château, proceed with the stone wall on your left	Woods on your right	SW	141
29.002	400	0.4	At the crossroads, turn left on the road and then immediately turn right on the gravel track, pass the house with the deer sculptures on your left	Château on the hill to your left, GR sign	SW	142
29.003	180	0.6	After crossing the small stone bridge, bear right and follow the grass track parallel to the gravel road and rejoin the road at the end of the avenue of trees. Note:- although the "Official Route" makes its way through the trees on the right, you may find the conditions better on the road	GR sign	SW	143
29.004	500	1.1	At the crossroads, turn left on the pathway	Into the woods	S	146
29.005	600	1.6	At the T-junction, turn right on the grass track	Pass between 2 concrete pillars, GR sign	SW	137

Waypoint	Distance between waypoints	Total km	Directions	Verification Point	Compass	Altitude m
29.006	110	1.8	Turn left on the small track	Metal cover on the ground, GR sign	E	133
29.007	300	2.1	After crossing the gully, take the right fork	GR sign	S	134
29.008	210	2.3	At the junction in the tracks between the fields, continue straight ahead on the broader track	GR sign	SE	126
29.009	170	2.4	Cross the railway track and continue straight ahead on the gravel track	Woods on your right, GR sign	SE	127
29.010	600	3.0	At the T-junction with the road, after passing the Eco-Musée, turn right on the D11B. Note:- the Alternate Route via the town centre joins from the left	Cross the river bridge, yellow VF sign	SW	122
29.011	180	3.2	Continue straight ahead beside the road	Information panel on the right, GR sign	SW	126
29.012	700	3.9	At the top of the hill with a view of the lake ahead, turn left onto the track	Enter woods, yellow VF sign	SE	153
29.013	160	4.0	At the junction in the tracks, with apple trees on your left, turn right on the small track	Proceed between trees, GR sign	SW	158
29.014	160	4.2	Briefly emerge from the woods with a view of the lake again ahead, turn left on the broad track	Re-enter the woods, GR sign	SE	153
29.015	200	4.4	Take the left fork on the smaller track	GR sign	SE	153
29.016	220	4.6	Emerge from the woods and continue straight ahead	Trees on left, field on the right	SE	148
29.017	600	5.2	Continue straight ahead on the track, skirting the woods	Avoid the turning to the left, GR sign	S	142
29.018	1000	6.1	At the junction with a gravel track, continue straight ahead	House n° 36 on your left, GR sign	E	134

Waypoint	Distance between waypoints	Total km	Directions	Verification Point	Compass	Altitude m
29.019	250	6.4	At the end of Ruelle aux Crapauds, turn right	Towards part timbered buildings, GR sign	S	127
29.020	400	6.8	At the T-junction with the road, turn left	Cross the bridge over the river, GR sign	NE	127
29.021	110	6.9	Take the right fork on the D11	Pass the church on your left, GR sign	SE	126
29.022	500	7.3	Take the right fork on the small road, beside the walls of the château gardens	Rue du Moulin, yellow VF sign	SE	130
29.023	500	7.8	After passing the flour mill, continue straight ahead and then bear right on the gravel track	Straight track between fields, GR sign	S	129
29.024	1000	8.8	At the crossroads in the tracks, just before reaching the woods, turn left	Skirt the woods on your right	E	131
29.025	230	9.0	Take the right fork on the grass track	Towards lone tree, GR sign	SE	131
29.026	1000	10.0	At the T-junction with the tarmac road, turn right	GR sign	SW	136
29.027	600	10.6	At the road junction, keep right on the D46. Note:- to reduce your journey by 7km, turn left on the Alternate Route via Jessains	Towards Unienville, GR sign	W	130
29.028	280	10.9	At the road junction beside the church in Unienville, turn right	Grand Rue	NW	133
29.029	170	11.0	Beside the Gîte d'Etape, turn left and then continue straight ahead on the road	Rue de la Croix, Gr sign	SW	131

Waypoint	Distance between waypoints	Total km	Directions	Verification Point	Compass	Altitude m
29.030	260	11.3	As the road turns sharply to the right, turn left on the gravel track. Note:- at the time of writing there were badly placed yellow VF signs at the junction	Pass metal barn on your right	SE	137
29.031	190	11.5	Take the right fork towards the woods	GR sign	SW	139
29.032	800	12.3	After crossing the canal d'amenée take the right fork	GR sign	SW	141
29.033	1000	13.3	At the crossroads in the tracks in the woods, continue straight ahead on the broad track	GR sign	SW	178
29.034	900	14.2	At the junction with a gravel track, continue straight ahead	GR sign	SW	184
29.035	900	15.1	At the T-junction with the main road, turn left	Gîte d'Etape ahead, GR sign	S	155
29.036	250	15.3	At the junction in the centre of Amance continue straight ahead. Note:- the GR 654 chemin de St Jacques separates and leaves to the right	Direction Vauchonvilliers, yellow VF sign	S	157
29.037	500	15.8	Beside the calvaire, as you begin to leave Amance, turn left and leave the main road	Pass the agricultural equipment store on your left, GR sign	SE	165
29.038	280	16.0	At the junction in the tracks, continue straight ahead	Towards the woods, GR sign	S	168
29.039	2200	18.3	Take the right fork, towards the houses	GR sign	SW	224
29.040	400	18.7	At the T-junction with the D112, turn left	Stone bench to the right of the junction, yellow VF sign	SE	221

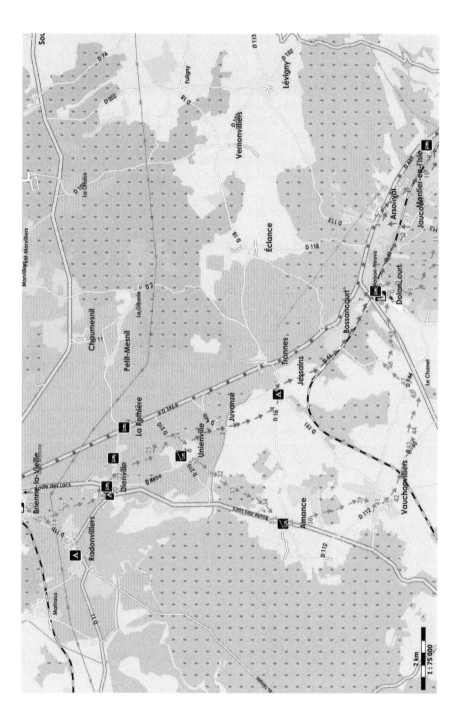

Waypoint	Distance between waypoints	Total km	Directions	Verification Point	Compass	Altitude m
29.041	400	19.1	At the crossroads in the centre of Vauchonvilliers, continue straight ahead	Rue de l'Eglise, GR sign	S	218
29.042	290	19.4	On the edge of the village take the left fork, D183	Direction Maison des Champs, GR sign	SE	212
29.043	2000	21.3	Just before D183 kilometre sign n°2, turn left on the track	Towards wind generators, GR sign on the ground	NE	214
29.044	500	21.8	Fork right on the grassy track	Towards the woods	E	217
29.045	1300	23.1	At the crossroads in the tracks, just after passing under the power lines, turn left	Towards the farm buildings, GR sign	NE	227
29.046	400	23.5	At junction with the road in the hamlet of la Chanet, continue straight ahead	Rue Principale, GR sign	E	222
29.047	220	23.7	Turn left on the D146	Direction Bossancourt, GR sign	NE	225
29.048	1000	24.7	After passing the D186 kilometre sign n°1, turn right on the grassy track	Towards woods, GR sign	E	227
29.049	1300	26.0	At the T-junction with the busy D619, turn left and follow the grass track parallel to the road	GR sign	NE	219
29.050	500	26.4	Turn right, carefully cross the road and take the D44A	Direction Dolancourt, GR sign	E	201
29.051	800	27.2	At the T-junction, turn left on the D44	Towards Dolancourt centre, GR sign	NE	159
29.052	260	27.4	At the war memorial, bear right. Note:- the Alternate Route rejoins from the road ahead	Pass the church on your left, GR sign	NE	153
29.053	40	27.5	Arrive at Dolancourt	Beside the church of Saint Léger		153

Alternate Route #29.A1   Length: 3.2km

Stage Summary: via Brienne-le-Château centre and Brienne-la-Vielle (LXVI)

Stage Ascent: 16m   **Stage Descent: 34m**

Waypoint	Distance between waypoints	Total km	Directions	Verification Point	Compass	Altitude m
29A1.001	0	0.0	Turn left on the road and continue downhill	Château on your right	NE	140
29A1.002	270	0.3	At the T-junction at the foot of the hill, turn right	Towards the bridge	S	122
29A1.003	60	0.3	Take the first turning to the left	Rue Blanchot	NE	125
29A1.004	160	0.5	At the T-junction, turn right and continue straight ahead at the crossroads	Towards the church	S	123
29A1.005	600	1.1	At the crossroads between rue de l'Ecole Militaire and rue Maréchal Valée (D130), take the D130 direction Epagne	Low-rise apartment building on the right	W	124
29A1.006	100	1.2	Turn left on rue Louis Chavance	No Through Road	S	123
29A1.007	300	1.5	Take the third road on the right	Rue Léo Lagrange	W	126
29A1.008	180	1.7	At the T-junction, turn left onto rue Julian Régnier	Sports ground to the right at the junction	S	125
29A1.009	400	2.0	Continue straight ahead	Over railway crossing	SE	125
29A1.010	60	2.1	Turn right onto a gravel track immediately after the level crossing	Red and white barrier	S	124
29A1.011	800	2.9	At the junction, continue straight ahead	Second red and white barrier	S	126
29A1.012	160	3.0	At the T-junction turn right on rue du Vieux Moulin in Brienne-la-Vieille (LXVI). Note:- town centre to the left	Furniture maker, n° 22	W	125

Waypoint	Distance between waypoints	Total km	Directions	Verification Point	Compass	Altitude m
29A1.013	140	3.2	At the road junction with the Eco-Musée on your right, continue straight ahead and rejoin the "Official Route"	Towards the river bridge		122

Alternate Route #29.A2 **Length: 9.7km**

Stage Summary: more direct route to Dolancourt using minor roads and farm tracks and passing through Jessains - saving 7 km.Stage Ascent: 101m **Stage Descent: 78m**

Waypoint	Distance between waypoints	Total km	Directions	Verification Point	Compass	Altitude m
29A2.001	0	0.0	Turn left direction Jessains, D46	Pass through the hamlet of l'Autre Monde	S	130
29A2.002	1600	1.6	Immediately after descending from the highway bridge, turn right on the gravel track	Initially parallel to the road	SE	144
29A2.003	1900	3.5	At the crossroads with a tarmac road, turn left	Former railway cottage on your left	E	154
29A2.004	400	3.9	Bear left at the junction	Towards the village of Jessains	NE	147
29A2.005	180	4.1	At the T-junction in Jessains, turn right rue de Puise	Direction Dolancourt, D46	SE	146
29A2.006	230	4.3	In Jessains centre, bear right	Direction Dolancourt, D46, Grand Rue	SE	146
29A2.007	4500	8.8	At the T-junction turn right with care, direction Troyes	Very busy N19	SW	154
29A2.008	280	9.0	Cross main road and turn left, direction Dolancourt, D44	Rue de la Vallée du Landon	SE	167
29A2.009	600	9.7	Arrive in Dolancourt, turn left onto rue de Vannage and rejoin the "Official Route" at the end of the section	Direction Jaucourt		153

Gite d'Etape - Communal,(Mme Danielle Milley),6 rue Saint-Antoine,10140 Unienville,Aube,France; Tel:+33(0)3 25 92 71 39; +33(0)3 25 92 72 62; Price:C

Gîte d'Etape,19 Grande rue,10140 Amance,Aube,France; Tel:+33(0)3 25 41 37 36; Email:commune-amance@wanadoo.fr; Web-site:www.amancevilleaubois.fr; Price:C; Note:Contact the Mairie,

Chambre d'Hote - le Colombier,8 avenue Jean Lanez,10500 Dienville,Aube,France; Tel:+33(0)3 25 92 23 47; Email:lecolombier10500@wanadoo.fr; Price:B

Chambres d'Hôtes - Blouquin,(Serge Blouquin),58 avenue Paul Girard,10500 Dienville,Aube,France; Tel:+33(0)3 25 92 23 23; Price:B

Auberge de la Plaine,15 route Plaine,10500 La-Rothière,Aube,France; Tel:+33(0)3 25 92 21 79; Email:contact@auberge-plaine.com ; Web-site:www.auberge-plaine.com; Price:B

Hotel le Moulin du Landion,5 rue Saint Léger,10200 Dolancourt,Aube,France; Tel:+33(0)3 25 27 92 17; Email:contact@moulindulandion.com; Web-site:moulindulandion.com; Price:A

Camping le Garillon,10 rue des Anciens Combattants,10500 Radonvilliers,Aube,France; Tel:+33(0)3 25 92 21 46; Web-site:www.campinglegarillon.fr; Price:C

Camping le Colombier,8 avenue Jean Lanez,10500 Dienville,Aube,France; Tel:+33(0)3 25 92 23 47; Web-site:lecolombier10500.com; Price:C

Camping du Tertre,Rue Fontaine du Mont,10500 Dienville,Aube,France; Tel:+33(0)3 25 92 26 50; Email:campingdutertre@wanadoo.fr; Web-site:www.campingdutertre.fr; Price:C

Camping Municipal,Route de Vauchonvilliers,10140 Jessains,Aube,France; Tel:+33(0)3 25 92 72 06; Email:mairie.jessains@wanadoo.fr; Price:C

Gelis Veronique Francine,27 rue Vallée du Landion,10200 Dolancourt,Aube,France; Tel:+33(0)3 25 27 90 55

Taxi Sebastien,7 rue de Brienne,10140 Vendeuvre-sur-Barse,Aube,France; Tel:+33(0)3 25 41 08 39

Taxi Dienvillois Sarl,20 rue de la Pellière,10500 Dienville,Aube,France; Tel:+33(0)3 25 92 22 49

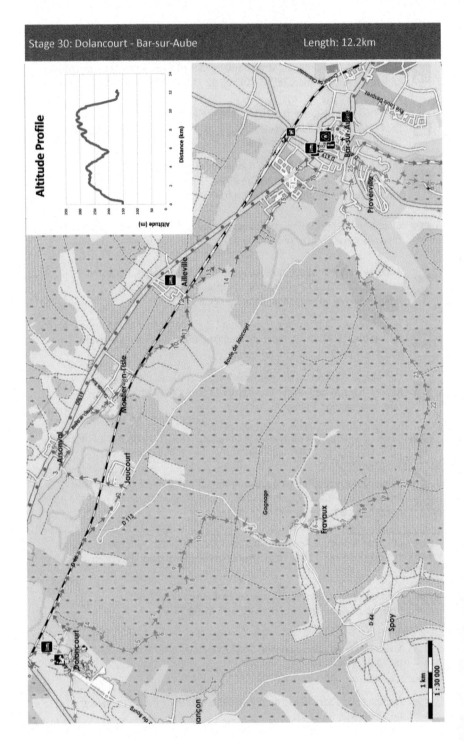

Stage Summary: this is a short but strenuous stage climbing 200m through woods and farmland before returning to the Aube valley. A shorter Alternate Route remains in the river valley.

Distance from Canterbury: 658km   Distance to Besançon: 252km
Stage Ascent: 314m   Stage Descent: 297m

Waypoint	Distance between waypoints	Total km	Directions	Verification Point	Compass	Altitude m
30.001	0	0.0	From the church in Dolancourt, take the D46	Pass the church on your left	E	152
30.002	80	0.1	Bear right on rue de Vannage	Weir on your right, GR sign	SE	151
30.003	240	0.3	At the exit from Dolancourt, turn right - direction Nigloland livraison - and immediately bear left on the forest track. Note:- the track ahead is both narrow and very steep and is not recommended for cyclists or horse riders. To follow the easier and more direct Alternate Route, bear left on the road	GR sign	SE	154
30.004	260	0.6	At the T-junction, at the top of the very steep climb, turn right	GR sign	S	196
30.005	1100	1.6	At the junction in the tracks, continue straight ahead on the well defined track	GR sign	SE	248
30.006	190	1.8	At the junction in the track, where the main track turns right, take the first turning on the left and continue straight ahead at the next junction	Avoid the propriété privée, GR sign	E	252
30.007	280	2.1	At crossroads in the tracks, continue straight ahead	Propriété privée on your right, GR sign	SE	266

Waypoint	Distance between waypoints	Total km	Directions	Verification Point	Compass	Altitude m
30.008	600	2.7	Emerge from the forest and bear left on the track	Open fields on your right, GR sign	NE	269
30.009	180	2.9	Bear right on the track between the field and the forest	Towards the farmhouse	SE	265
30.010	500	3.4	Take the right fork, uphill towards the farmhouse and the radio mast	GR signs on the left which can be misleading	SE	262
30.011	400	3.7	Bear right on the main track	Pass the farm buildings on your right, GR sign	S	276
30.012	400	4.2	At the T-junction in the track, turn left and then immediately right on the tarmac	GR sign	S	270
30.013	210	4.4	Turn right on the grass track, steeply downhill	GR sign	W	262
30.014	130	4.5	At the T-junction with the road, turn right and follow the road downhill		S	258
30.015	1100	5.6	At the entry to Fravaux, turn left	Rue de la Fontaine, GR sign	SW	202
30.016	140	5.7	At the end of the tarmac, continue straight ahead on the gravel track	Woods on your right, GR sign	S	205
30.017	600	6.3	As the main track turns left into the vines, continue straight ahead	Vines on your left, woods on your right	SE	244
30.018	180	6.5	In the woods, take the right fork	GR sign	S	256
30.019	500	7.0	At the T-junction, as you leave the woods, turn left on the broad track	Towards the concrete tower, GR sign	NE	279
30.020	140	7.1	Beside the tower, bear right on the stony track	GR sign	S	281
30.021	400	7.5	At the crossroads in the tracks, take the second left	Downhill, between the woods, yellow VF sign	E	293

Waypoint	Distance between waypoints	Total km	Directions	Verification Point	Compass	Altitude m
30.022	1100	8.5	At the junction in the tracks, continue straight ahead	Avoid the track to the right, GR sign	E	296
30.023	400	9.0	At the junction in the tracks, continue straight ahead in the trees, begin to descend	GR sign	NE	309
30.024	2400	11.3	At the Stop sign, turn right on Grand Rue	GR sign	E	172
30.025	800	12.1	At the T-junction, turn left	Yellow VF sign	E	171
30.026	100	12.2	Arrive at Bar-sur-Aube (LXV). Note:- the town centre is over the river bridge on the left	Junction between rue Romagon and rue Pierre Brossolette		169

Alternate Route #30.A1   **Length: 10.2km**

Stage Summary: more direct route via Jaucourt and Montier-en-l'Isle. The route follows minor roads and tracks close by the l'Aube river.

Stage Ascent: 123m   **Stage Descent: 112m**

Waypoint	Distance between waypoints	Total km	Directions	Verification Point	Compass	Altitude m
30A1.001	0	0.0	Bear left and remain on the D46	Woodland to the right	SE	157
30A1.002	2200	2.2	In Jaucourt, turn left towards Arsonval, D113	Grande Rue, cross the railway	N	163
30A1.003	900	3.1	Turn right onto rue du Désert	After crossing the second river bridge	SE	153
30A1.004	260	3.4	Bear left on the road	Uphill towards main road	NE	154
30A1.005	170	3.5	At the T-junction, turn sharp right direction Bar-sur-Aube. Take the minor road to the right of the D619	Exit Arsonville sign	SE	163
30A1.006	600	4.1	Turn right on the small road	Rue de l'Abreuvoir	S	160
30A1.007	400	4.5	In the centre of Montier-en-l'Isle, continue straight ahead on rue de l'Isle	Church on your right	SE	156

Waypoint	Distance between waypoints	Total km	Directions	Verification Point	Compass	Altitude m
30A1.008	500	4.9	At the end of the street turn right on rue du Prieuré	Cross the railway	S	156
30A1.009	60	5.0	Immediately after crossing the railway, turn left on the gravel track	Pass an orchard on the right	SE	156
30A1.010	900	5.8	Fork left into an open field	Towards a line of trees	SE	154
30A1.011	210	6.0	Bear left on the track	Keep the river to your right	E	156
30A1.012	400	6.4	Turn left onto larger gravel track and then right before the railway-crossing	Parallel and close to the railway	SE	158
30A1.013	600	7.0	Fork right into trees away from open field	Railway behind	SW	158
30A1.014	270	7.3	Turn left	After crossing concrete bridge	SE	158
30A1.015	1300	8.6	Continue straight ahead direction Centre Ville	Through a housing estate	SE	162
30A1.016	500	9.1	Turn left down an avenue of trees, rue du Jars	Salle de Spectacle on your right	NE	164
30A1.017	210	9.3	At the T-junction turn right	Avenue du Général de Léclerc	SE	162
30A1.018	400	9.7	In Bar-sur-Aube (LXV) centre, turn right on rue d'Aube	Beside the Mairie and tourist office	SW	169
30A1.019	300	10.0	At the crossroads beside the river, continue straight ahead over the bridge	Direction Proverville	SW	165
30A1.020	110	10.2	At the junction beside the car park, continue straight ahead	Rue Pierre Brossolette	SW	166
30A1.021	50	10.2	Rejoin the the "Official Route" at the end of the section from Brienne-le-Château	Junction with rue Romagon		168

Presbytère,4Bis rue Saint-Pierre,10200 Bar-sur-Aube,Aube,France; Tel:+33(0)3 25 27 06 34; Price:D

Gîte Rural - Hubail,(Patrice Hubail),4 rue Saint Nicolas,10200 Ailleville,Aube,France; Tel:+33(0)9 66 81 35 20

Logis le Saint Nicolas,2 rue du Général de Gaulle,10200 Bar-sur-Aube,Aube,France; Tel:+33(0)3 25 27 08 65; Email:lesaintnicolas2@wanadoo.fr; Web-site:www.lesaintnicolas.com; Price:A

Hôtel de la Pomme d'Or,79 Faubourg Belfort,10200 Bar-sur-Aube,Aube,France; Tel:+33(0)3 25 27 09 93; Email:hotel.pommedor@neuf.fr; Web-site:hotel-chambre-bar-cafe-hebergement.hoteldelapommedor.com; Price:B

Office du Tourisme,3 rue du Théatre,10200 Bar-sur-Aube,Aube,France; Tel:+33(0)3 25 92 42 68

Banque Populaire,3 place Carnot,10200 Bar-sur-Aube,Aube,France; Tel:+33(0)8 90 90 90 90

LCL,141 rue Nationale,10200 Bar-sur-Aube,Aube,France; Tel:+33(0)3 25 27 54 81

Credit Agricole,36 rue Thiers,10200 Bar-sur-Aube,Aube,France; Tel:+33(0)3 25 27 66 37

Centre Médico Social,8 rue Saint Pierre,10200 Bar-sur-Aube,Aube,France; Tel:+33(0)3 25 27 44 34

Molderez Etienne,43 rue Gén de Gaulle,10200 Bar-sur-Aube,Aube,France; Tel:+33(0)3 25 27 46 64

Chagrot Philippe,2 rue Saint Vincent Beauvoir,10340 Bragelogne-Beauvoir,Aube,France; Tel:+33(0)3 25 29 11 29

Altitude Profile

Stage Summary: the majority of this section is off-road, but using good tracks through vineyards and through the Clairvaux forest. There is, however, a very steep climb into the forest on the outskirts of Bar-sur-Aube which bike riders and walkers with heavy packs will find a challenge. For those that make the climb the reward is a beautiful view over the valley of the Aube. Over the sections between Clairvaux and Langres the accommodation options are again limited with substantial distances between them. Walkers are advised to secure accommodation in good time and carefully plan their route with due regard to their fitness and the distances involved.

Distance from Canterbury: 670km   Distance to Besançon: 240km
Stage Ascent: 383m   Stage Descent: 366m

Waypoint	Distance between waypoints	Total km	Directions	Verification Point	Compass	Altitude m
31.001	0	0.0	From the junction between rue Romagon and rue Pierre Brossolette, take the small road up the hill. Note:- to avoid the very steep climb ahead, turn towards the town centre and take the first turning to the right and follow the Alternate Route	No Entry and GR signs	SW	171
31.002	60	0.1	As the road again turns right, continue straight ahead on the gravel track	Via Francigena panel on your left	SW	177
31.003	210	0.3	Take the left fork	GR sign	SW	201
31.004	120	0.4	At the road junction, continue straight ahead	Lycée on your left	SW	214
31.005	150	0.5	At the fork in the track continue straight ahead	Uphill	S	228
31.006	130	0.7	At the entrance to the woods, turn left on the unmade track	Keep the metal fencing on your left	E	247
31.007	120	0.8	At the junction at the end of the metal fencing, turn right	Uphill	S	246

Waypoint	Distance between waypoints	Total km	Directions	Verification Point	Compass	Altitude m
31.008	400	1.1	On reaching an open grass area beside a timber framed house, bear left across the grass	Keep the metal fence on your left	S	306
31.009	270	1.4	At the end of the grassed area turn right	Pass between the wooden barriers, keeping the woods to your left	W	311
31.010	140	1.6	At the T-junction with the tarmac road, turn left	Farmhouse and radio tower to your right at the junction	S	309
31.011	800	2.3	As the road bends sharply to the right, bear left onto the left-most gravel track	Signpost Bergéres	S	325
31.012	600	2.9	Shortly after entering the woods take the left fork	GR sign ahead	SE	342
31.013	80	3.0	Continue straight ahead	GR sign	S	340
31.014	800	3.8	At the crossroads in the tracks, continue straight ahead	GR sign	S	349
31.015	240	4.0	At the junction in the tracks, continue straight ahead	Avoid the broad track to your right	S	345
31.016	500	4.5	At the crossroads in the tracks turn left	VF sign, Baroville 1.5km	E	336
31.017	900	5.5	At the junction with a broad track continue straight ahead	Downhill, between vines	E	281
31.018	100	5.6	At the crossroads in the tracks, turn right on the tarmac	Towards the village of Baroville	SE	275
31.019	400	6.0	At the crossroads, continue straight ahead on rue de Couvignon	Towards the church	SE	231
31.020	90	6.1	At the next crossroads, turn left	Pass metal barn on your left	E	224
31.021	170	6.2	At the crossroads, turn right. The Alternate Route rejoins from the left	Towards the Mairie	S	219

Waypoint	Distance between waypoints	Total km	Directions	Verification Point	Compass	Altitude m
31.022	60	6.3	At the fork in the road in Baroville, bear left onto rue des Pressoirs	Direction Bayel	SE	218
31.023	180	6.5	At the crossroads, continue ahead uphill on rue de la Côte Sandrey	Coat of arms on building ahead	SE	226
31.024	180	6.7	At the edge of the village, continue straight ahead on a stony track between the vines	Towards the brow of hill	SE	235
31.025	230	6.9	At the crossroads with the tarmac road proceed straight ahead	Wooden crucifix on the left	S	261
31.026	240	7.1	Fork left off the concrete road onto the broad unmade road	Continue briefly between vines	SE	249
31.027	500	7.6	Continue straight ahead avoiding the track to the right	Towards the wooded ridge	SE	246
31.028	130	7.7	At the crossroads in the tracks, continue straight ahead		SE	243
31.029	170	7.9	Fork left on the smaller track	Towards the gap in the woods	SE	243
31.030	1000	8.9	At the junction with the broad track in the woods continue straight ahead on the forest road	Sign Sommière des Moines	SE	267
31.031	1800	10.8	At the crossroads with a very broad track, continue straight ahead	GR signed to the right, ignore	SE	286
31.032	300	11.1	At a crossroads in the grassy track, continue straight ahead	Climb short steep hill	SE	270
31.033	500	11.6	At the junction with a broad gravel track, fork right	Pass sign Sommière de la Culbute on your left	S	268
31.034	1100	12.7	At the T-junction with the road, turn left on the road, downhill	VF sign Clairvaux 1.5km	E	217

Waypoint	Distance between waypoints	Total km	Directions	Verification Point	Compass	Altitude m
31.035	1500	14.2	At the T-junction beside the abbey entrance, turn left keeping the abbey wall on you left	VF sign, bar to the right of the junction	E	196
31.036	500	14.6	Arrive at Clairvaux at the crossroads with D396	Abbey grounds on the left, hotel on the right		188

Alternate Route #31.A1   **Length: 5.2km**

Stage Summary: route for cyclists and for those wishing to avoid the steep climb of les Côtes d'Aube. The Alternate Route generally follows very minor roads in the river valley and reduces total distance by 1.2km.

Stage Ascent: 152m   **Stage Descent: 100m**

Waypoint	Distance between waypoints	Total km	Directions	Verification Point	Compass	Altitude m
31A1.001	0	0.0	Turn right onto rue Gaston Bachelard	Direction Cité Scolaire G. Bachelard	S	167
31A1.002	2100	2.1	Fork right on impasse Buffery, the road becomes a track after leaving the houses	Junction after distinctive house with sloping roof on the right	S	178
31A1.003	300	2.4	Turn left on the track	Downhill	E	200
31A1.004	140	2.6	At the junction, turn right and then bear left	Pass a tennis court on your left	SE	185
31A1.005	110	2.7	At the junction with the tarmac road, turn left and then take the right fork	Pass modern bungalows on your right	E	183
31A1.006	400	3.0	At the next fork in the road, bear right on rue Saint Antoine	Confier hedge on your right	SE	180
31A1.007	270	3.3	Continue straight ahead and bear gently to the right on road	Ignoring blue and white sign to the right	SE	207
31A1.008	160	3.4	Shortly after passing a metal crucifix on your left, take the left fork	Narrower track between trees	S	211

Waypoint	Distance between waypoints	Total km	Directions	Verification Point	Compass	Altitude m
31A1.009	270	3.7	At the junction, continue straight ahead on the tarmac	Towards woods	S	203
31A1.010	1400	5.2	At the crossroads in Baroville, continue straight ahead to rejoin the "Official Route"	Towards the church		220

Accommodation & Facilities .... Bar-sur-Aube - Clairvaux

Fraternité Saint Bernard,14 rue Abbaye Clairvaux,10310 Clairvaux-sur-Aube,Aube,France; Tel:+33(0)3 25 27 86 48; Price:C

Gîte d'Etape - la Largeotte,(Michel Urbain),Rue de la Côte Sandrey,10200 Baroville,Aube,France; Tel:+33(0)3 25 27 00 36; Email:champagne.urbain@wanadoo.fr; Price:C; Note:Open all year except for the grape picking season,

Gîte Chez Jo,10 rue Piverotte,10310 Longchamp-sur-Aujon,Aube,France; Tel:+33(0)3 25 27 34 65; +33(0)6 28 37 93 66; Email:georges.mauger@cegetel.net; Web-site:www.gitechezjo.com; Price:B

Hôtel de l'Abbaye,19 route de Dijon,10310 Clairvaux-sur-Aube,Aube,France; Tel:+33(0)3 25 27 80 12; Price:B

Ferme Auberge - Saint Malachie,(Mr & Mme François Guenin),15 Grande rue Outre-Aube,10310 Longchamp-sur-Aujon,Aube,France; Tel:+33(0)3 25 27 80 26

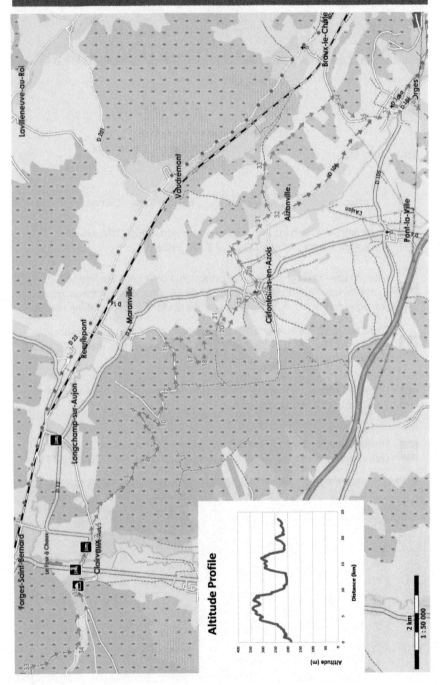

Altitude Profile

2 km   1 : 50 000

Stage Summary: the generally off-road route initially zig-zags in woodland on the hills above the Aujon valley and temporarily shares the path of the GR703 – Sentier Historique de Jeanne d'Arc. The route then crosses the valley to climb the parallel ridge top before descending to the small town of Châteauvillain. The "Official Route" bypasses Blessonville (LXIV). Alternate Routes reduce climbing and overall distance and also visit Blessonville.

Distance from Canterbury: 685km   Distance to Besançon: 225km
Stage Ascent: 475m   Stage Descent: 427m

Waypoint	Distance between waypoints	Total km	Directions	Verification Point	Compass	Altitude m
32.001	0	0.0	From the crossroads beside the Hôtel de l'Abbaye in Clairvaux take the D12	Direction Longchamp-sur-Aujon	E	189
32.002	800	0.7	After leaving Outre Aube, where the road turns sharp left, continue straight ahead on the gravel track	Pass lone birch tree on your left	E	198
32.003	100	0.8	Continue straight ahead up the hill, avoiding the turning to the right	VF sign	E	206
32.004	140	1.0	Slightly before the top of the hill turn right on the smaller track. Note:- pay special attention as this turning is easily missed. Bikers and others wishing to avoid the possibly muddy forest tracks ahead can remain on the track to Longchamp-sur-Aujon where they should turn right and follow the D12 to Cirfontaines-en-Azois	Between fields towards the wooded valley	SE	216
32.005	1500	2.4	Towards the end of the meadow, bear left on the track	Line of trees and the end of the meadow on your right	SE	217
32.006	500	2.9	At the crossroads in the track continue straight ahead	Red and white cross on the left	SE	231

Waypoint	Distance between waypoints	Total km	Directions	Verification Point	Compass	Altitude m
32.007	500	3.4	At the crossroads in the track with a small foot bridge on your right, turn left	Pass a sign for the Sentier Historique de Jeanne d'Arc on your right	NE	239
32.008	900	4.3	Turn right to leave the main track and follow the path up a small bank. Note:- this path may be easily overlooked	GR sign, just before the turning	SE	310
32.009	50	4.4	At the top of the bank, turn right	Back tracking on the main track	SW	312
32.010	500	4.8	In the clearing, turn sharp left and follow the broad gravel road	GR sign	E	300
32.011	130	5.0	In the next clearing, bear right	Avoid the stony track on the left	E	303
32.012	600	5.6	Remain on the broad track as it bends to the right		S	330
32.013	400	5.9	Bear left remaining on the broad gravel track		E	326
32.014	900	6.8	Continue on the broad track to the left	Avoid the wooded pathway on your right	NE	335
32.015	60	6.9	Bear right down the hill on the broad track	Ignore the track on the left	NE	334
32.016	110	7.0	Shortly after joining the tarmac, turn sharp right onto a wooded track	VF sign on your left	SW	326
32.017	900	7.8	Continue straight ahead	Avoid track on the right	SW	325
32.018	130	8.0	Take the right fork	GR sign	SE	333
32.019	1000	8.9	At the crossroads in the track, continue straight ahead on the stony track	GR sign	SE	324
32.020	110	9.0	Continue straight ahead	Circuit des Lavoirs sign, Cirfontaine 1.5km	E	306

Waypoint	Distance between waypoints	Total km	Directions	Verification Point	Compass	Altitude m
32.021	300	9.3	At the crossroads, turn right on the track, keep the open field to your left	Metal barn ahead at the junction	SW	264
32.022	290	9.6	At the T-junction at the foot of the hill turn left on the grassy track	GR sign	SE	258
32.023	700	10.3	At the crossroads beside the farm building, continue straight ahead	Keep the farm buildings on your left	SE	216
32.024	170	10.5	At the bus stop, bear right	Pass the lavoir and Mairie on your left	SE	214
32.025	80	10.6	At the T-junction with the main road, turn right	Towards the church	SE	212
32.026	190	10.8	After passing the church in Cirfontaines-en-Azois turn left on rue de la Fontaine aux Chênes	GR sign	E	217
32.027	220	11.0	At the crossroads, continue straight ahead	Keep the Lavoir close on your right	NE	212
32.028	400	11.4	At the junction at the edge of the village bear right	GR sign	NE	205
32.029	400	11.8	After crossing the river, continue straight ahead beside the watermill	Sign Sainte Libère on the building on your left	NE	205
32.030	230	12.0	At the T-junction, turn right	Circuit des Lavoirs, Aizanville 1km	SE	204
32.031	1000	13.0	At the crossroads in Aizanville, continue straight ahead on rue de l'Eglise	VF Sign – Orges 5km	SE	209
32.032	200	13.2	Turn left up the hill on the gravel track. Note:- the more direct Alternate Route continues straight ahead on the road	Orchard on your left, GR sign	E	207
32.033	1100	14.3	At the top of the hill turn right onto the grassy track between the woods and the open field	VF sign - Orges 4.5km	SE	291

Waypoint	Distance between waypoints	Total km	Directions	Verification Point	Compass	Altitude m
32.034	2200	16.5	At the crossroads with the tarmac road, briefly continue straight ahead on the unmade road then turn right into the woods	VF sign	SW	289
32.035	1000	17.5	At the T-junction with the road, turn left. Note:- the Alternate Route rejoins from the right	Pass the cemetery on your right	S	222
32.036	400	17.9	At the T-junction in Orges turn left	Rue de la Forge	SE	212
32.037	210	18.1	Turn right on the D106, rue des Pressoirs. Note:- to visit Blessonville(LXIV), continue straight ahead on the Alternate Route	Direction Châteauvillain	S	215
32.038	160	18.2	Continue straight ahead	Cross the river bridge	S	213
32.039	50	18.3	At the T-junction immediately after the bridge, turn left	Direction Châteauvillain	SE	213
32.040	300	18.6	Turn right on chemin Paillot	VF sign - Châteauvillain 5.5km	SW	213
32.041	2400	21.0	Bear right	Pass under the autoroute bridge	S	221
32.042	1200	22.1	At the junction bear right on the broken tarmac road	Pass stone crucifix	S	223
32.043	150	22.3	At the T-junction with the tarmac road, turn left in the direction of "Pêche à la Truite"	Lavoir on the right of the junction	S	225
32.044	1100	23.4	Cross over railway tracks and continue straight ahead	Towards the walled gardens	S	232
32.045	230	23.6	Arrive at Châteauvillain at the T-junction with the D65. Note:- for the centre of Châteauvillain bear right on rue de Penthievre	Cemetery wall wall ahead at the junction		237

Stage Summary: route for cyclists and for those wishing to avoid the steep climb of les Côtes d'Aube. The Alternate Route generally follows very minor roads in the river valley and reduces total distance by 1.2km.

Stage Ascent: 22m Stage Descent: 12m

Waypoint	Distance between waypoints	Total km	Directions	Verification Point	Compass	Altitude m
32A1.001	0	0.0	Continue straight ahead on the road	Between the farm buildings	SE	208
32A1.002	3200	3.2	Continue straight ahead on the road towards the village of Orges. The "Official Route" joins from the left	Pass the cemetery on your right		218

Stage Summary: road route from Orges bypassing Châteauvillain but passing through Blessonville (LXIV).

Stage Ascent: 157m Stage Descent: 32m

Waypoint	Distance between waypoints	Total km	Directions	Verification Point	Compass	Altitude m
32A2.001	0	0.0	Continue straight ahead remaining on rue de la Forge	Direction Bricon	E	216
32A2.002	2900	2.9	At the T-junction, turn left and proceed with care beside the D65	Direction Bricon	E	246
32A2.003	1600	4.5	At the crossroads in Bricon turn right onto the D102, direction Blessonville	Bar on the right just before the junction	SE	261
32A2.004	3100	7.6	In Blessonville (LXIV) continue straight ahead on D102	Pass a church on the right, towards the motorway and the forest	SE	301
32A2.005	4500	12.1	Continue straight ahead on the road. Note:- the "Official Route" joins from the track on the right	Pass the edge of the forest on your right		341

Chambres d'Hotes - la Maison du Milieu À Châteauvillain,(Maggie & Steve Tait),13 rue de Penthièvre,52120 Châteauvillain,Haute Marne,France; Tel:+33(0)3 25 32 08 45; +33(0)6 66 85 08 45; Email:steve@sjtait.fsnet.co.uk; Price:B

Poney Club Centre Equestre Parc,Porte Bonshommes,52120 Châteauvillain,Haute Marne,France; Tel:+33(0)3 25 32 91 90

Syndicat d'Intiative,14 rue de Penthièvre,52120 Châteauvillain,Haute Marne,France; Tel:+33(0)3 25 32 99 22; Email:syndicat-dinitiative-canton-chateauvillain@wanadoo.fr

Caisse d'Epargne,9 rue Penthièvre,52120 Châteauvillain,Haute Marne,France; Tel:+33(0)8 21 01 05 77

Credit Agricole,2 rue Penthièvre,52120 Châteauvillain,Haute Marne,France; Tel:+33(0)3 25 31 44 94

Cabinet Fortier Haquin Pagel,4 rue Maladière,52120 Châteauvillain,Haute Marne,France; Tel:+33(0)9 63 08 81 34

Guyot Jean-Claude,12 route Chatillon,52120 Châteauvillain,Haute Marne,France; Tel:+33(0)3 25 32 94 74

Stage Summary: the GR145 "Official Route" continues on minor roads and isolated forest tracks over generally level ground. The woods are a popular with hunters and home to deer and wild boar. Hunting may take place on any day. It is advisable not to deviate from the tracks and if possible wear something bright.

Distance from Canterbury: 709km   Distance to Besançon: 201km
Stage Ascent: 317m   Stage Descent: 175m

Waypoint	Distance between waypoints	Total km	Directions	Verification Point	Compass	Altitude m
33.001	0	0.0	Cross the main road and take the smaller road with the cemetery on your right. Note:- cyclists and others that may wish to avoid the forest tracks and reduce their distance by 3km, can turn right at this point towards the centre of Châteauvillain and then turn left on the D107 to rejoin the "Official Route" in Richebourgh. The D107 is normally a very quiet road	VF sign Richebourg 13.5km	E	237
33.002	1500	1.5	At the crossroads with the track, continue straight ahead	Pass farm buildings across the field on your right	E	258
33.003	1100	2.6	At the T-junction, turn right on the grassy track	Woodland on your left as you proceed	S	270
33.004	600	3.2	At the T-junction, turn left on the grassy track towards the woods	GR sign on a stone	E	275
33.005	500	3.7	At the crossroads with the tarmac road, turn left on the gravel track into the woods	VF sign Richebourg 9.5km	NE	286
33.006	180	3.9	Continue straight ahead	Red and white metal barriers	NE	294

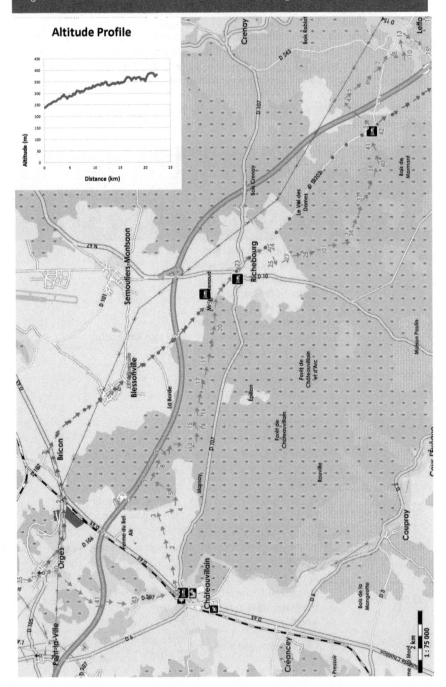

Altitude Profile

Waypoint	Distance between waypoints	Total km	Directions	Verification Point	Compass	Altitude m
33.007	800	4.7	At top of the rise turn sharp right	GR sign	SE	279
33.008	600	5.2	At the crossroads in the forest continue straight ahead	GR sign	SE	286
33.009	500	5.7	At the T-junction in the woods, with the sound of the autoroute to your left, turn right	GR sign	SW	297
33.010	260	6.0	At a crossroads in the forest briefly continue straight ahead and then turn left	GR sign	E	294
33.011	500	6.4	At the crossroads in the track, turn right	Keep the metal deer fencing on your right	S	310
33.012	300	6.7	In the clearing at the end of the fencing, continue straight ahead on the partially gravelled track		S	309
33.013	600	7.3	At the junction with the broader track, turn left		E	308
33.014	700	7.9	At the T-junction, turn left on the main track	GR sign	N	312
33.015	90	8.0	Bear right on the main track	Pass the sign "Route Foestière François d'Orléans"	E	315
33.016	500	8.5	At the junction in the tracks, continue straight ahead	Avoid the turning to the left	E	320
33.017	1000	9.5	At the crossroads in the tracks, continue straight ahead	GR sign in the trees ahead	E	326
33.018	400	9.9	Continue straight ahead on the track	GR sign on a tree on the left	E	327
33.019	400	10.3	At the junction, continue straight ahead	GR sign	E	333

Waypoint	Distance between waypoints	Total km	Directions	Verification Point	Compass	Altitude m
33.020	1100	11.3	At the junction in the tracks at the end of the long straight track, bear slightly left	Avoid the broad track signed "Route Forestière de la Maison Renaud" and the wooded track to the left	E	340
33.021	1100	12.4	Emerge from the forest at the T-junction with a minor road, turn right. Note:- the Alternate Route via Blessonville joins from the left	VF sign Richebourg 1km, chambre d'hôtes ahead on the left	SE	342
33.022	1000	13.4	At crossroads with D10 in Richebourg continue on the D102, direction Leffonds	Rue de la Levée de César	SE	340
33.023	400	13.8	At the crossroads at the exit from Richebourg, continue straight ahead	D102, direction Leffonds	SE	341
33.024	1000	14.8	Turn right onto the small tarmac track. Note:- to reduce the distance by 2km and avoid further forest tracks, remain on the road to the end of the section beside the hamlet of Mormant	VF sign Mormant 8km	SW	343
33.025	700	15.5	At the junction in the middle of the fields with the Richebourg church visible to the right, turn left on the grass track towards the forest	Wooden post with GR sign	S	345
33.026	600	16.0	At the T-junction immediately before entering the woods turn left and immediately right. Note:- at the time of writing there is an electrified fence at the entry to the woods, with an insulated wire gate - proceed with care	GR sign inside the woods	E	357

Waypoint	Distance between waypoints	Total km	Directions	Verification Point	Compass	Altitude m
33.027	90	16.1	After entering the forest turn left and then right on the well defined track	GR signs	S	361
33.028	280	16.4	At a crossroads with a broad track, continue straight ahead and then slightly to the right on the narrower track	GR sign	S	369
33.029	400	16.8	At a T-Junction with a broad track in a grassy area, turn left	GR sign	E	367
33.030	50	16.9	At the end of the grassy area, turn right on the narrow track	GR sign	S	366
33.031	600	17.5	At the T-junction in the tracks, turn left	GR sign	E	362
33.032	50	17.5	Turn right on the track	GR sign	S	363
33.033	700	18.2	At a T-Junction with a gravelled road, turn left on the road	GR sign	E	360
33.034	300	18.5	Turn right	Route Forestière du Long-Boyau	S	367
33.035	160	18.6	At the junction in the track, turn left on the broad track	GR sign	SE	368
33.036	1300	19.9	As the main track bends to the right (Route Forestière de Champ Corot) continue straight ahead on the grassy track	GR sign	E	360
33.037	80	19.9	At the junction in the tracks, continue straight ahead on the small grass track	Downhill	SE	357
33.038	700	20.7	Continue straight ahead at crossroads in the tracks	GR sign	SE	383
33.039	300	21.0	At the crossroads in the track, continue straight ahead	GR sign ahead	E	386

Waypoint	Distance between waypoints	Total km	Directions	Verification Point	Compass	Altitude m
33.040	150	21.1	At the junction with a broad gravel track, continue straight ahead	GR sign	E	387
33.041	700	21.8	On emerging from the woods, continue straight ahead towards the hamlet	Large open field on left	E	381
33.042	500	22.3	Continue straight ahead on the tarmac road into the hamlet of Mormant and the remaining abbey buildings	VF sign - Leffonds 4.5km	NE	379
33.043	80	22.3	Arrive at Mormant	Beside ancient Abbaye de Mormant		379

Accommodation & Facilities .... Châteauvillain - Mormant

Chambres d'Hôtes - la Maison Renaud,(Patrick & Thérèse Devilliers),3 Domaine Orchamps,52120 Richebourg,Haute Marne,France; Tel:+33(0)3 25 31 05 46; +33(0)6 75 94 40 49; Email:contact@lamaisonrenaud.com; Web-site:www.lamaisonrenaud.com; Price:B

Gîte - Barret,(Alain Barret),1 Impasse Grand Cour,52120 Richebourg,Haute Marne,France; Tel:+33(0)3 25 31 03 74; Price:B

Meuble de Tourisme - l'Abbaye,(Mme Annick Michelot),12 rue de l'Abbaye,52210 Leffonds,Haute Marne,France; Tel:+33(0)3 25 31 21 41; +33(0)6 79 01 33 53; Email:annick.michelot@laposte.net; Web-site:www.meubles-tourisme-abbaye.com; Price:B

Hotel du Parc,1 place Moreau,52210 Arc-en-Barrois,Haute Marne,France; Tel:+33(0)3 25 02 53 07; Price:B

Gîte - Domaine Val Bruant,Route Giey,52210 Arc-en-Barrois,Haute Marne,France; Tel:+33(0)3 25 01 57 71; Email:contact@val-bruant.com; Web-site:www.val-bruant.com; Price:B

Office du Tourisme,2 place Moreau,52210 Arc-en-Barrois,Haute Marne,France; Tel:+33(0)3 25 02 52 17

Centre Hospitalier de la Haute-Marne,4 rue Val Barizien,52000 Chaumont,Haute Marne,France; Tel:+33(0)3 25 32 28 21

Arc Taxi,9 rue des Eleux,52210 Arc-en-Barrois,Haute Marne,France; Tel:+33(0)3 25 03 18 78

Hep Taxi,11 Bis rue Pierre Simon,52000 Chaumont,Haute Marne,France; Tel:+33(0)3 25 31 22 06

Altitude Profile

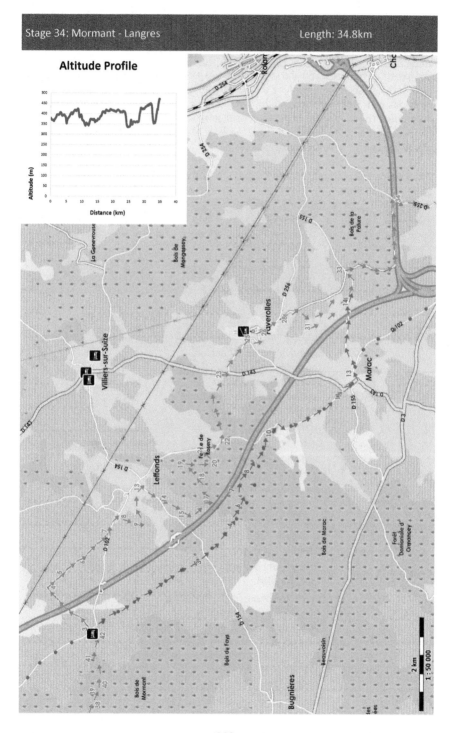

Stage Summary: this very long section of the "Official Route" weaves through farmland and forests on remote tracks and small roads. We prefer a more direct route avoiding the most tortuous sections, beginning on the flat and well made old Roman road followed by woodland tracks that can be muddy before taking the route départementale over the Autoroute. The shorter Alternate Routes will save 6.5km. The routes join to pass beside the Réservoir de la Mouche and make the long climb to the historic town of Langres where you can find a full range of facilities.

Distance from Canterbury: 731km   Distance to Besançon: 179km
Stage Ascent: 640m   Stage Descent: 548m

Waypoint	Distance between waypoints	Total km	Directions	Verification Point	Compass	Altitude m
34.001	0	0.0	Go straight ahead on rue de l'Abbaye	Pass the arched stone building on your right	N	379
34.002	90	0.1	At the T-junction, turn right	D102	NE	377
34.003	60	0.2	Continue straight ahead on the gravel track. Note:- the shorter Alternate Route initially follows the road to the right	VF sign	NE	375
34.004	1300	1.5	At the T-junction, turn right on the main track	GR sign, towards the radio tower	SE	377
34.005	500	2.0	At the junction in the tracks, continue straight ahead on the main track	Towards the radio tower	SE	394
34.006	400	2.3	Avoid the track to your left and remain on the main track as it passes the radio tower	GR sign	SE	394
34.007	1100	3.4	At the T-junction with the road, turn left	Sign Leffonds Cente – 2km	SE	399
34.008	400	3.8	Shortly after passing the sign for the entry to Leffonds, turn right on a gravel track. Note:- unfortunately Leffonds does not offer either shops or eating places	"Circuit des Templiers", pass an orchard on your left	S	390
34.009	600	4.4	At the T-junction with the small tarmac road, turn left	GR sign	E	393

Waypoint	Distance between waypoints	Total km	Directions	Verification Point	Compass	Altitude m
34.010	160	4.5	At the T-junction with a tarmac road, turn left	"Circuit des Templiers"	NE	387
34.011	200	4.7	With house n° 22 on your left, turn right onto the gravel track	GR sign	E	386
34.012	260	5.0	At the T-junction with the small tarmac road, turn right towards the church	GR sign	SE	354
34.013	290	5.3	At the T-junction at the top of the hill, beside the church, turn right	"Circuit des Templiers"	SW	371
34.014	500	5.7	Shortly after passing a stone crucifix on your left, leave the tarmac road and bear left on the gravel track	Etang de Chênot – 6.5km	SW	383
34.015	700	6.5	At the junction in the tracks, continue straight ahead	GR sign, towards the autoroute	SE	403
34.016	700	7.1	At the crossroads in the woods, continue straight ahead on the narrow track	GR sign	E	405
34.017	90	7.2	At the T-junction with a broader track, turn left	GR sign ahead on the left	NE	409
34.018	600	7.8	At the crossroads in the tracks, continue straight ahead	GR sign	NE	417
34.019	400	8.2	Turn sharp right	"Etang de Chênot", GR sign	S	413
34.020	600	8.7	At the T-junction in the track turn left and keep left at the next junction	GR sign	E	424
34.021	300	9.0	At the T-junction with a tarmac road, turn right	GR sign	SE	388
34.022	400	9.4	Turn left and leave the tarmac road	"Circuit de Mausolée", direction Faverolles	E	391

Waypoint	Distance between waypoints	Total km	Directions	Verification Point	Compass	Altitude m
34.023	1600	11.0	At the T-junction with the tarmac road, turn right and then immediately left	Direction Faverolles	SE	342
34.024	1000	12.0	At the road junction, continue straight ahead towards Faverolles. Note:- unfortunately there are no shops or eating places in Faverolles	"Mausolée Gallo-Romain"	SE	344
34.025	110	12.1	After crossing the river bridge, bear right on the road	GR signs	SE	348
34.026	400	12.5	Immediately in front of the Mairie in Faverolles, bear right on the road. Note:- continue straight ahead for the gîte	Direction Beauchemin	SE	366
34.027	140	12.6	At the road junction, bear right	Towards Beauchemin - 7km	SE	373
34.028	400	13.1	Take the right fork on chemin de Beauchemin	GR sign	SE	372
34.029	500	13.5	Turn right off the tarmac road onto the farm track. Note:- to reduce distance by approximately 1.5km and avoid more woodland tracks, you can continue straight ahead on the small road to rejoin the "Official Route" at the crossroads	GR sign	SW	370
34.030	400	13.9	Take the left fork, downhill, into a glade and between trees	GR sign	SW	373
34.031	190	14.1	At the T-junction in the tracks with a field ahead, turn left and remain in the woods	GR sign on the left	SE	362

Waypoint	Distance between waypoints	Total km	Directions	Verification Point	Compass	Altitude m
34.032	1400	15.4	At the T-junction with the road, turn left on the road. Note:- the Alternate Route joins from the right	Beside rock outcrop	E	374
34.033	700	16.1	At the crossroads, turn right	Direction Beauchemin, GR sign	SE	389
34.034	2700	18.8	At the T-junction, turn right and cross the bridge over the autoroute, direction Beachemin	VF sign Beauchemin - 2km	S	413
34.035	1900	20.6	Beside the war memorial in Beauchemin, take the right fork	Direction Beauchemin Centre	S	412
34.036	180	20.8	Take the left fork towards the main road	Pass garage door on your right	S	411
34.037	70	20.9	At the T-junction, turn left and continue with care beside the D3. Note:- the Alternate Route follows the minor road to theright leading directly to the Réservoir de la Mouche	Direction Humes	E	410
34.038	1100	21.9	Turn right onto a stone and grass track, towards the silos and water tower. Note:- to pass beside Humes (LXIII) remain on the road and follow the Alternate Route	VF Sign St Martin lès Langres - 2km	S	415
34.039	1900	23.8	At the T-junction in St Martin lès Langres, turn left	"Circuit du Val de Mouche"	SE	404
34.040	110	23.9	Just after passing the church, turn sharp right down the hill	Magnificent view of the barrage, GR sign	S	398
34.041	160	24.1	At the T-junction with a road, beside the stone crucifix, turn left and then immediately right	GR signs, towards the barrage	SE	382

Waypoint	Distance between waypoints	Total km	Directions	Verification Point	Compass	Altitude m
34.042	210	24.3	At the T-junction with the road, turn right down the hill	GR signs	S	350
34.043	400	24.7	At the bottom of the hill, after passing through Moulin de St Martin, turn right on the gravel track	GR signs	W	336
34.044	600	25.3	At the T-junction with the small road, turn right	Cross over the bridge	W	339
34.045	300	25.6	At the T-junction turn left, towards the Auberge de Lac. Note:- the Alternate Route joins from the right	Running water opposite the junction	S	367
34.046	130	25.7	Just before reaching the Auberge, turn left downhill on the small road	Large stone at the entrance to the road, GR sign	SE	366
34.047	50	25.8	At the T-junction with the road at the foot of the hill, turn left	Cross the barrage, GR sign	E	360
34.048	400	26.2	At the end of the barrage, turn right on the path beside the road	D286, direction Langres	S	355
34.049	1300	27.5	Bear right away from the road on the gravel path beside the lake. Note:- there is a narrow entry in a metal barrier ahead. To avoid this, horse-riders should remain on the road and then take the left fork to rejoin the "Official Route" beside the church in Perrancey	Toilet block ahead	S	363
34.050	600	28.1	At the T-junction in the tracks, turn left	GR sign, metal barrier	NE	362
34.051	40	28.2	At the crossroads with the main road, continue straight ahead up the hill	Pass No Entry sign, VF sign Perrancey 0.5 km	E	365

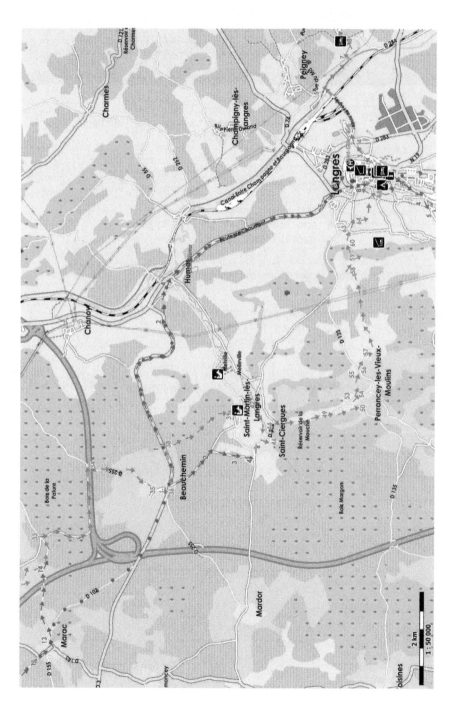

Waypoint	Distance between waypoints	Total km	Directions	Verification Point	Compass	Altitude m
34.052	220	28.4	At the T-junction in the centre of Perrancey, turn right and immediately left on the small road up the hill	GR signs, pass church on your right	NE	392
34.053	170	28.6	Shortly after joining a grassy track, turn sharp right	Between a stone wall and the rear of the house, GR sign	SE	406
34.054	90	28.6	At the end of the grassy area, bear left on the grass track up the hill	GR sign	E	411
34.055	500	29.1	At the T-junction in the tracks, turn right towards the road	GR sign	E	424
34.056	110	29.2	At the junction with road, cross over and continue straight ahead on the gravel track	GR7 sign	SE	423
34.057	500	29.7	At the junction with the tarmac road, turn left and continue on the gravel track	GR sign	E	426
34.058	2000	31.7	At the T-junction with a gravel track, turn right	"Circuit de la Croisée de Voie Romain"	SE	445
34.059	400	32.1	Turn left onto the grass track	GR sign, Langres - 2km	NE	448
34.060	500	32.5	Take the right fork downhill between the trees	GR sign	E	390
34.061	40	32.5	At the junction in the tracks, turn right	Downhill	E	384
34.062	210	32.8	At the T-junction with the road, turn left	"Circuit de la Croisée de Voie Romain"	E	360
34.063	60	32.8	Beside the church in Brevoines, bear right on the road	Rue du Chanoine Roussel	SE	357
34.064	200	33.0	Turn right on chemin du Murot	GR sign	SE	358

Waypoint	Distance between waypoints	Total km	Directions	Verification Point	Compass	Altitude m
34.065	800	33.8	Turn left and pass through the tunnel under the disused railway. Note:- horse-riders can continue straight ahead to join the railway and turn left and then right to find the track at the exit from the tunnel	GR sign	NE	401
34.066	40	33.8	At the T-junction in the track, turn right up the grassy slope	GR sign, Langres Centre 1.1km	E	403
34.067	90	33.9	At the T-junction on the grass track, turn right	GR sign	S	415
34.068	30	34.0	At the T-junction with the tarmac road, turn left up the hill	GR sign	E	417
34.069	60	34.0	Turn left	GR sign Brevoines	N	424
34.070	280	34.3	At the T-junction, turn right	GR sign	SE	435
34.071	70	34.4	At the T-junction with rue Louis Massotte, cross over and take the uphill path with the metal handrails	GR sign	S	447
34.072	80	34.4	At the T-junction with a tarmac path, turn left towards the main road	GR sign	NE	453
34.073	20	34.5	At the T-junction with the main road, turn initially left and take the pedestrian crossing, then turn right and left to enter the town through the archway - Porte Neuve	GR signs	SE	456
34.074	100	34.6	Continue straight ahead on rue Boulière. Note:- the GR145 will turn right to climb the steps and follow the walls around the town	Pass house n° 21 on your right	E	463
34.075	120	34.7	Take the right fork on rue Jean Roussat	Pass Hôtel de la Poste on your right	SE	472
34.076	130	34.8	Arrive at Langres centre	Place Diderot		471

Alternate Route #34.A1				Length: 10.7km		
Stage Summary: more direct route via Marac						
Stage Ascent: 151m				**Stage Descent: 151m**		

Waypoint	Distance between waypoints	Total km	Directions	Verification Point	Compass	Altitude m
34A1.001	0	0.0	Bear right on the road	D102	SE	376
34A1.002	140	0.1	As the road bends to the left, continue straight ahead on the Circuit de Templier, direction Bugniéres. Note:- a woodland section ahead may be difficult for cyclists in wet conditions. The section can be avoided by remaining on the D102	VF sign	SE	377
34A1.003	2900	3.0	At the crossroads continue straight ahead on the Ancienne Voie Romaine	Remain parallel to motorway	SE	425
34A1.004	1100	4.1	At the T-junction, turn left and bear right	Into the wood	E	410
34A1.005	160	4.3	Turn right and then left	Onto a grassy track	SE	413
34A1.006	300	4.6	Take the left fork		E	427
34A1.007	400	5.0	At the T-junction in the track, turn right	Straight track, parallel to the Autoroute	SE	432
34A1.008	500	5.5	At the crossroads, continue straight ahead		SE	433
34A1.009	210	5.7	At the T-junction, bear left onto a gravel track		SE	420
34A1.010	800	6.5	At the T-junction turn right onto a minor road. Note:- cyclist taking the D102 rejoin from left	Autoroute visible to the left at the junction	SE	383
34A1.011	1900	8.4	At the road junction, continue straight ahead	Enter Marac, D102	SE	364
34A1.012	400	8.8	At the T-junction in Marac turn left on rue des Charmes	Direction Langres, D102	E	355

Waypoint	Distance between waypoints	Total km	Directions	Verification Point	Compass	Altitude m
34A1.013	300	9.1	Take the left fork	D155, direction Rolampont	E	365
34A1.014	1600	10.7	As the road passes through the woods, after crossing the autoroute bridge, continue straight ahead on the road. Note:- the "Official Route" rejoins from the left	Rock outcrop in the woods to the left		374

Alternate Route #34.A2   **Length: 2.7km**

Stage Summary: direct route using a minor road to the Réservoir de la Mouche saving 2km

Stage Ascent: 12m   **Stage Descent: 54m**

Waypoint	Distance between waypoints	Total km	Directions	Verification Point	Compass	Altitude m
34A2.001	0	0.0	Turn immediately right	Direction Saint Ciergues	SE	411
34A2.002	1300	1.2	At the fork in the road bear right	Towards Saint Ciergues	S	413
34A2.003	700	1.9	Continue straight ahead	Grain store on left	S	413
34A2.004	400	2.3	At a 5 way junction take the third right	Direction la Mouche, D286	SE	405
34A2.005	300	2.6	Take the left fork	Direction la Mouche, D286	SE	379
34A2.006	70	2.7	Bear right towards the Auberge du Lac on Rue du Lac. Note:- the "Official Route" joins from the left	Water trough on the right		371

Alternate Route #34.A3   **Length: 9.8km**

Stage Summary: from Beauchemin to Langres via Humes (LXIII) and the very busy N19.

Stage Ascent: 164m   **Stage Descent: 123m**

Waypoint	Distance between waypoints	Total km	Directions	Verification Point	Compass	Altitude m
34A3.001	0	0.0	Continue straight ahead on the long straight road		E	415
34A3.002	3500	3.5	At the fork in the road, bear right leaving the D3	Direction Humes	E	346

Waypoint	Distance between waypoints	Total km	Directions	Verification Point	Compass	Altitude m
34A3.003	900	4.4	In Humes (LXIII) at the T-junction at the end of Grande Rue turn left	Rue de la Fontaine Saint Vinebaut	NE	319
34A3.004	30	4.4	At the intersection with the main road turn right	Cross river bridge, N19	SE	319
34A3.005	4100	8.4	At the roundabout continue uphill on the N19	Avenue de la Collinière, pass the cemetery on left	SE	388
34A3.006	600	9.0	Bear right to briefly leave the main road	Chemin des Lingons	SE	417
34A3.007	130	9.1	Return to the main road and turn right	Keep the town walls on your left	SW	429
34A3.008	700	9.8	Turn left through the archway and rejoin the "Official Route"			457

Accommodation & Facilities .... Mormant - Langres

L'Abri du Pèlerin,1 rue Aubert,52200 Langres,Haute Marne,France; Tel:+33(0)3 25 87 11 48; Email:paroissedelangres@orange.fr; Web-site:www.catholique-hautemarne.cef.fr; Price:C; Note:2 beds, open 17.00 to 19.00,

Gîte d'Etape - le Passage,1 Chemin de Chirey,52260 Faverolles,Haute Marne,France; Tel:+33(0)3 25 84 55 69; +33(0)6 73 73 79 54; Email:lepassage@hotmail.fr; Price:B

Gite d'Etape - Sainte Anne,(Agnès),Ferme Saint-Anne,52200 Langres,Haute Marne,France; Tel:+33(0)3 25 90 76 51; +33(0)6 26 14 08 93; Email:association-sainteanne@orange.fr; Web-site:gitesainteanne.site.voila.fr; Price:C

Auberge de la Fontaine,2 place de la Fontaine,52210 Villiers-sur-Suize,Haute Marne,France; Tel:+33(0)3 25 31 22 22; Email:auberge-de-la-fontaine@wanadoo.fr; Web-site:www.aubergedelafontaine.fr; Price:B

Gîte de la Vallée de la Suize,1 rue du Pont de la Côte,52210 Villiers-sur-Suize,Haute Marne,France; Tel:+33(0)3 25 31 22 22; Price:B

Chambres d'Hôtes - Ferme du Bas Bois,(Eric and Roselyne Gruot),15 rue Théodore Régnier,52210 Villiers-sur-Suize,Haute Marne,France; Tel:+33(0)3 25 31 11 80; +33(0)6 80 30 16 11; Email:fermebasbois@wanadoo.fr; Price:B

Hôtel des Voiliers,Lac de la Liez,52200 Langres,Haute Marne,France; Tel:+33(0)3 25 87 05 74; +33(0)9 70 61 19 61; Email:auberge.voiliers@wanadoo.fr; Web-site:www.hotel-voiliers.com ; Price:B

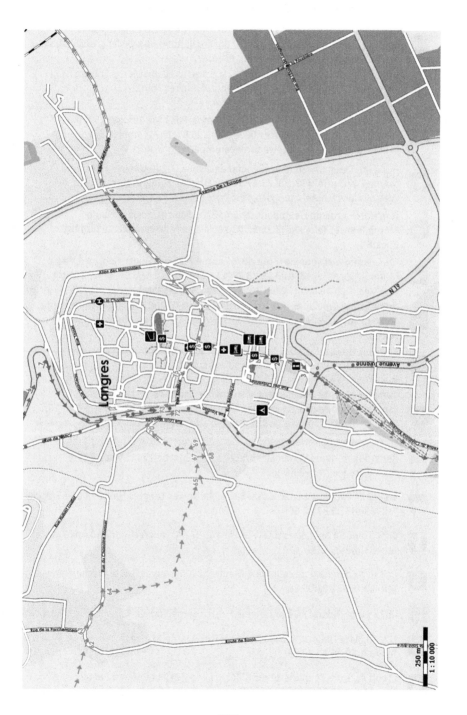

Grand Hôtel de l'Europe Langres,25 rue Diderot,52200 Langres,Haute Marne,France; Tel:+33(0)3 25 87 10 88; Email:hotel-europe.langres@wanadoo.fr; Web-site:www.logishotels.com; Price:A

Hôtel le Cheval Blanc,4 rue Estre,52200 Langres,Haute Marne,France; Tel:+33(0)3 25 87 07 00; Email:info@hotel-langres.com; Web-site:ww.hotel-langres.com; Price:A

Chambres d'Hôtes - le Belvedere des Remparts,33 rue Lombard,52200 Langres,Haute Marne,France; Tel:+33(0)3 25 87 09 71; Email:lorenelliott@yahoo.com; Web-site:lebelvederedesremparts.com; Price:A

Hotel Inn Design,Avenue du Général de Gaulle,52200 Langres,Haute Marne,France; Tel:+33(0)3 25 87 57 57; Email:hid.langres@gmail.com; Web-site:www.hotel-inn.fr/langres; Price:B

Jum'Hotel,2 rue du Lieutenant Didier,52200 Saints-Geosmes,Haute Marne,France; Tel:+33(0)3 25 87 03 36; Web-site:www.auberge3jumeaux.fr; Price:B

Les Chambres d'Eponine,4 rue de la Fontaine,52200 Saints-Geosmes,Haute Marne,France; Tel:+33(0)3 25 88 23 40; +33(0)6 02 24 66 94; Email:petitot.christelle@gmail.com; Web-site:www.langres-leschambresdeponine.fr; Price:B

Auberge des Trois Jumeaux,2 route d'Auberive,52200 Saints-Geosmes,Haute Marne,France; Tel:+33(0)3 25 87 03 36; Web-site:www.auberge3jumeaux.fr; Price:B

Camping du Lac de la Liez,Peigney,52200 Langres,Haute Marne,France; Tel:+33(0)3 25 90 27 79; Email:campingliez@free.fr; Web-site:www.campingliez.com; Price:C

Camping Navarre,9 Boulevard Maréchal de Lattre de Tassigny,52200 Langres,Haute Marne,France; Tel:+33(0)3 25 87 37 92; +33(0)6 10 74 10 16; Email:contact@campingnavarre.fr; Web-site:www.camping-navarre-langres.fr; Price:C

Renard Jean,Hameau Melleville,52200 Saint-Martin-Lès-Langres,Haute Marne,France; Tel:+33(0)3 25 87 39 93

Voillemin Paul,Rue Lavoir,52200 Saint-Martin-Lès-Langres,Haute Marne,France; Tel:+33(0)3 25 87 12 66

Office du Tourisme,Square Olivier Lahalle,52200 Langres,Haute Marne,France; Tel:+33(0)3 25 87 67 67

Caisse d'Epargne,4 place Jeanne Mance,52200 Langres,Haute Marne,France; Tel:+33(0)8 21 01 05 68

CIC,2 place Diderot,52200 Langres,Haute Marne,France; Tel:+33(0)3 25 30 48 80

LCL,10 place Diderot,52200 Langres,Haute Marne,France; Tel:+33(0)8 20 82 30 43

Credit Agricole,24 place Diderot,52200 Langres,Haute Marne,France; Tel:+33(0)3 25 90 96 86

$ Credit Agricole,24 place Diderot,52200 Langres,Haute Marne,France;
Tel:+33(0)3 25 90 96 86

$ Société Générale,28 rue Diderot,52200 Langres,Haute Marne,France;
Tel:+33(0)3 25 87 07 11

$ Banque Populaire,48 rue Diderot,52200 Langres,Haute Marne,France;
Tel:+33(0)8 90 90 90 90

$ Banque Populaire,48 rue Diderot,52200 Langres,Haute Marne,France;
Tel:+33(0)8 90 90 90 90

$ Crédit Mutuel,70 rue Diderot,52200 Langres,Haute Marne,France; Tel:+33(0)8
20 08 60 05

$ Crédit Mutuel,70 rue Diderot,52200 Langres,Haute Marne,France; Tel:+33(0)8
20 08 60 05

H Centre Hospitalier,10 rue de la Charité,52200 Langres,Haute Marne,France;
Tel:+33(0)3 25 87 88 88

+ Canet Claude,23 rue Barbier d'Aucourt,52200 Langres,Haute Marne,France;
Tel:+33(0)3 25 87 35 77

+ Gillet David,12 rue Diderot,52200 Langres,Haute Marne,France; Tel:+33(0)3 25
90 19 42

Altitude Profile

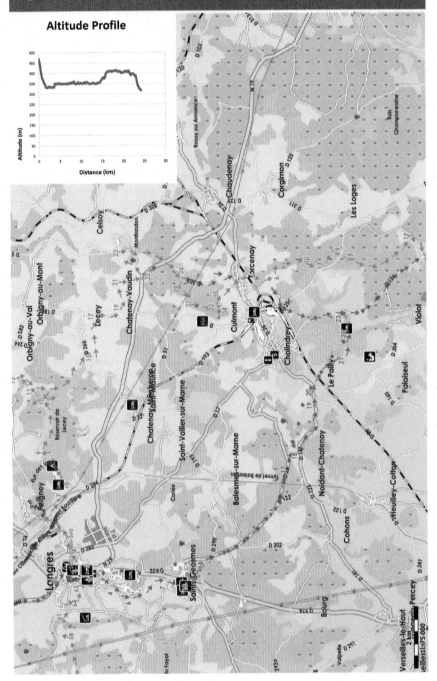

Stage Summary: after leaving Langres the"Official Route" follows pleasant canal and lakeside paths (shared with a tributary of the Chemin de St Jacques) before meandering through farmland and woods. However, it is very long, has very limited accommodation options and beyond Torcenay the woodland tracks include a difficult water crossing. The Alternate Route is substantially shorter, but follows more, although generally minor, roads. There is no accommodation available in Torcenay – the centre of Chalindrey is 2km "off-piste".

Distance from Canterbury: 766km   Distance to Besançon: 144km
Stage Ascent: 279m   Stage Descent: 432m

Waypoint	Distance between waypoints	Total km	Directions	Verification Point	Compass	Altitude m
35.001	0	0.0	From Place Diderot take the small street downhill	Rue du Grand Cloitre	E	471
35.002	180	0.2	Continue straight ahead downhill on the road	Pass through archway in the town walls	NE	458
35.003	230	0.4	At the crossroads, after passing through the second archway, continue straight ahead	VF sign	NE	426
35.004	400	0.8	At the crossroads, after passing under the road bridge, continue straight ahead	Route de Peigney	NE	375
35.005	1500	2.3	Immediately after crossing the bridge over the canal, turn right on the track close beside the canal	Lac de la Lieze - 3km	SE	337
35.006	900	3.2	Just before the canal bridge, turn left onto the gravel track	GR and cockle shell signs	E	334
35.007	80	3.3	At the T-junction in the track turn left on the gravel track	Pass a clump of trees on your right	E	334
35.008	500	3.8	At the crossroads beside the end of the barrage, continue straight ahead into the parking area and remain on the path beside the lake	Pass the hotel on your left, VF sign	NE	351

Waypoint	Distance between waypoints	Total km	Directions	Verification Point	Compass	Altitude m
35.009	1300	5.1	At the metal barrier, continue straight ahead	GR sign	E	349
35.010	3200	8.3	At the crossroads, following the barrier, continue straight ahead	GR cross on the left	E	361
35.011	400	8.7	At the junction in the tracks, bear left	Keep field on the left	NE	348
35.012	400	9.1	As the main track turns left, continue straight ahead into the trees	GR sign, Lecey - 4km	NE	354
35.013	400	9.5	At the junction in the tracks, bear right keeping the trees on your right	Cockle shell sign, church steeple ahead at the junction	S	350
35.014	3300	12.7	At the crossroads with a tarmac road, turn right	Direction Chatenay-Vaudin	SW	353
35.015	400	13.1	After passing a copse of trees on your left, turn left onto a broad gravel track	Chatenay-Vaudin - 2km	E	350
35.016	1100	14.1	At the fork in the track, take the right fork onto the smaller track	Towards metal gates	E	355
35.017	400	14.5	At the T-junction with the road, turn right	Chatenay-Vaudin - 0.5km	S	358
35.018	700	15.2	Shortly after passing the church in the centre of Chatenay-Vaudin, take the left fork	Impasse des Vignes, GR sign	SE	380
35.019	300	15.5	Keep straight ahead uphill on the tarmac	Pass orchard on your left	E	377
35.020	700	16.2	At the junction in the tracks, continue straight ahead on the grass track	Avoid gravel track to the left, GR sign	E	406
35.021	230	16.4	In an open field, bear right around the edge of the field	Keep the barbed-wire fence on your left	S	408

Waypoint	Distance between waypoints	Total km	Directions	Verification Point	Compass	Altitude m
35.022	800	17.2	At the T-junction with the road, turn left. Note:- it is possible save 2km, by turning right and then left proceeding with care for 900m beside the busy N19 to the next crossroads	VF sign, Montlandon	NE	409
35.023	1100	18.3	At the junction beside the war memorial in Montlandon, take the right fork and then immediately turn right	Rue du Tennis	S	415
35.024	1700	19.9	At the crossroads with the N19, continue straight ahead, direction Torcenay, on the D307	VF sign	SW	405
35.025	500	20.4	Turn right on the track into the woods. Note:- a further 2km can be saved by remaining on the road to the junction beside the war memorial and then turning right to rejoin the GR145 beside the grocery store in Torcenay. At the time of writing there were numerous fallen trees on the very muddy and sometimes overgrown path through the woods	VF sign, Torcenay - 4km	NW	409
35.026	80	20.5	Shortly after entering the woods take the left fork	GR sign	W	411
35.027	160	20.6	Take the left fork	GR sign	W	409
35.028	400	21.0	At the crossroads in the tracks continue straight ahead	GR sign	W	408
35.029	240	21.3	Take the right fork	GR sign	SW	413
35.030	500	21.7	Emerge into an open field, and follow the path around the edge of the field	Keep woods on your right	SW	395

Waypoint	Distance between waypoints	Total km	Directions	Verification Point	Compass	Altitude m
35.031	230	21.9	At the corner of the field, turn right into the woods	GR sign	S	396
35.032	500	22.4	At the crossroads in the tracks, continue straight ahead	GR sign	SW	397
35.033	500	22.9	In the clearing, continue briefly ahead on the tarmac and then turn sharp left onto a track	VF sign, Torcenay - 1.5 km	SE	386
35.034	130	23.0	At the crossroads in the track, continue straight ahead and then immediately take the left fork	GR sign	E	390
35.035	600	23.6	At the T-junction in the track, turn right	GR sign	SE	337
35.036	700	24.2	Arrive at Torcenay at the T-junction with the D26. Note:- the facilities of Culmont and Chalindrey are to the right	"Circuit Le Diable du Foultot"		318

Alternate Route #35.A1		Length: 20.0km				

Stage Summary: this more direct route leaves Langres through parkland on the famous promenade de Blanchefontaine before joining the footpath (Voie Verte) on the disused railway track to Saint-Geosmes. The route continues on generally minor roads passing beside the les Archots and the isolated B&B that has been popular with many modern day pilgrims.

Stage Ascent: 223m			Stage Descent: 336m			
35A1.001	0	0.0	From place Diderot take the main street south between shops	Small road downhill	S	471
35A1.002	400	0.4	At the crossroads continue straight ahead. Note:- The GR145 crosses the Main Route from right to left and then continues to follow the town walls	Towards archway	S	468

Waypoint	Distance between waypoints	Total km	Directions	Verification Point	Compass	Altitude m
35A1.003	130	0.5	After leaving the main gate of Langres, take the pedestrian crossing keeping the roundabout on your left	Pass through the large metal gates and continue on the avenue between trees	SW	467
35A1.004	900	1.4	Continue straight ahead downhill on the tarmac	Pass under the road bridge	SW	441
35A1.005	400	1.8	At the crossroads, with the disused railway track, turn left	Voie Verte	S	415
35A1.006	400	2.1	At the crossroads, continue straight ahead on the Voie Verte	Water trough on the left	SE	420
35A1.007	1400	3.5	At the crossroads, shortly after passing under a road bridge, continue straight ahead on the road opposite, rue Belle Vue	Towards the church in the distance	S	439
35A1.008	180	3.7	At the road junction, continue straight ahead on the tarmac path and bear right	Follow Voie Verte signs	S	442
35A1.009	200	3.9	After passing the sports hall on your left, join the road and continue straight ahead	Pass red and white barrier	SW	443
35A1.010	130	4.0	At the crossroads, turn left and leave the Voie Verte	Towards to the church	SE	446
35A1.011	70	4.1	At the mini-roundabout, continue straight ahead	Pass the cemetery on your left and church on your right	E	448
35A1.012	70	4.2	At the junction with the main road, take the pedestrian crossing and turn right	Tree lined pathway with commercial building on your left	S	448
35A1.013	220	4.4	At the road junction, turn left on the D290	Pass the hotel on the right	SE	450
35A1.014	1000	5.4	At the T-junction, turn right on the D122	Towards Chalindrey	S	464

Waypoint	Distance between waypoints	Total km	Directions	Verification Point	Compass	Altitude m
35A1.015	220	5.6	Continue straight ahead	D122, direction Noidant-Chatenoy	SE	465
35A1.016	2800	8.4	At the fork in the road, keep left	Direction Chalindrey, D51	E	460
35A1.017	1400	9.8	Fork right	Direction Noidant-Chatenoy, D141	SE	456
35A1.018	1200	11.0	At the T-junction turn left	Direction le Pailly, D141	E	420
35A1.019	1900	12.9	At the road junction following the entrance to le Pailly, continue straight ahead	Direction Chalindrey	E	327
35A1.020	500	13.4	In front of the church, turn left and then right	Direction Les-Archots, rue des Moulins	SE	322
35A1.021	1700	15.0	Fork left	Direction Les-Archots	E	313
35A1.022	1000	15.9	From the bridge, continue uphill on the road	Keep the B&B on your right	E	294
35A1.023	600	16.5	At the crossroads, turn right	D136 (Voie Romain)	SE	318
35A1.024	3400	19.9	Continue straight ahead on the D136. Note:- The GR145 joins the road from the left	Towards the Ferme de la Grosse Sauve		358

Accommodation & Facilities   ....   Langres - Torcenay

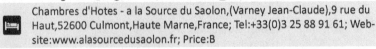

Chambres d'Hôtes - les Coquelicots,11 rue Auguste Laurent,52200 Saint-Maurice,Haute Marne,France; Tel:+33(0)3 25 84 93 41; Email:gmarie@cegetel.net; Web-site:les_coquelicots.perso.sfr.fr; Price:A

Chambres d'Hotes - a la Source du Saolon,(Varney Jean-Claude),9 rue du Haut,52600 Culmont,Haute Marne,France; Tel:+33(0)3 25 88 91 61; Web-site:www.alasourcedusaolon.fr; Price:B

Auberge de la Gare,2 rue Gare,52600 Chalindrey,Haute Marne,France; Tel:+33(0)3 25 87 13 14; Web-site:www.auberge-gare-chalindrey.fr; Price:B

B&B -,(M Serge Francois),Les Archots,52600 Chalindrey,Haute Marne,France; Tel:+33(0)3 25 88 93 64; Price:B

Chanson Daniel Louis Henri,3 Hameau Caquerey,52600 Palaiseul,Haute Marne,France; Tel:+33(0)3 25 88 53 71

Mairie,47 rue de Langres,52600 Chalindrey,Haute Marne,France; Tel:+33(0)3 25 90 88 74

Caisse d'Epargne,8 rue Diderot,52600 Chalindrey,Haute Marne,France; Tel:+33(0)8 21 01 05 09

Intersport,Centre Commercial Léclerc,52200 Saint-Geosmes,Haute Marne,France; Tel:+33(0)3 25 84 86 75

Delahaye Maréchalerie,141 rue Neuve,88320 Isches,Vosges,France; Tel:+33(0)3 29 07 33 93

Pl Jacques Taxis Trans de Colis Locati,2 rue de Champagne,52600 Chalindrey,Haute Marne,France; Tel:+33(0)3 25 88 97 98

Eric Taxi,10 rue des Frayons,52360 Neuilly-l'Évêque,Haute Marne,France; Tel:+33(0)6 86 79 54 15

Altitude Profile

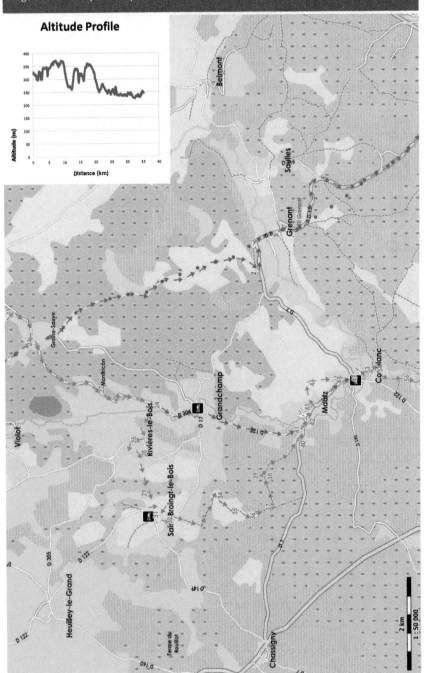

Stage Summary: this very long and tiring section of the "Official Route" continues on a meandering course on minor roads and often on muddy forest tracks with difficult water crossings and bypasses Grenant (LXII). Our Alternate Routes offer a more direct option, saving 6.5km and make for easier progress for all groups. If you wish to break the journey then accommodation is available in a number of intermediate villages.

Distance from Canterbury: 790km   Distance to Besançon: 120km
Stage Ascent: 662m   Stage Descent: 736m

Waypoint	Distance between waypoints	Total km	Directions	Verification Point	Compass	Altitude m
36.001	0	0.0	From the junction with the D26 in Torcenay, follow the main road towards the centre of the village	"Circuit Le Diable du Foultot"	NE	319
36.002	180	0.2	Turn right towards the grocery store	Direction Salle des Fetes	S	324
36.003	110	0.3	At the crossroads, continue straight ahead	Direction Salle des Fetes	S	326
36.004	400	0.7	Immediately after emerging from the tunnel, continue straight ahead on the tarmac road	Pass pond on your left	S	315
36.005	600	1.2	Continue straight ahead on the broad track, avoiding the small track to your left	Cross the bridge	S	304
36.006	260	1.5	At the T-junction with the tarmac road, turn left downhill into the hamlet of le Foultot. Note:- the GR145 ahead has a number of difficult obstacles including a steep sided river crossing and overgrown tracks. It is difficult for all groups, but should definitely be avoided by horse and bike riders. To bypass the difficulties, turn right on the road to the T-junction on the outskirts of Chalindrey, turn left and continue with the railway track on your right for 1200m to the T-junction with the D136. Then turn left and rejoin the "Official Route" in a further 5km beside la Ferme de la Grosse Sauve	Water trough on your left	SE	299

Waypoint	Distance between waypoints	Total km	Directions	Verification Point	Compass	Altitude m
36.007	200	1.7	At the end of the tarmac, bear right and then left over the concrete bridge	GR sign	SE	296
36.008	300	2.0	At the T-junction at the top of the rise, turn right	GR sign	S	327
36.009	700	2.7	At the T-junction at the bottom of the hill, turn left on the narrow track	Meadow on your right	SE	298
36.010	130	2.8	Continue straight ahead on the partially overgrown track	Ignore the broad track to your left	S	299
36.011	90	2.9	Turn right on the small track. With care, cross the steep sided river ford to the left of the collapsed bridge	GR sign	S	299
36.012	600	3.5	At the T-junction with the broad green fire-break, turn right on the track		SW	342
36.013	400	3.9	At the start of the tarmac, turn left on the forest track	GR sign	SE	340
36.014	500	4.4	Take the right fork	GR sign	S	345
36.015	90	4.5	At the junction in the tracks, continue straight ahead	Yellow stripe sign	SW	343
36.016	270	4.8	At the crossroads at the top of the rise, after crossing the stream, cross the tarmac road and continue straight ahead on the forest track uphill	Chalindrey - 7km	SW	312
36.017	80	4.8	At the crossroads in the track, continue straight ahead up the hill	Yellow signs	SW	322
36.018	70	4.9	At the T-junction with the tarmac road at the top of the hill, bear left and remain on the tarmac	GR sign	S	334
36.019	2800	7.7	At the T-junction in the road, turn right	GR sign	SW	362

Waypoint	Distance between waypoints	Total km	Directions	Verification Point	Compass	Altitude m
36.020	900	8.6	At the T-junction with the more major road, turn left towards Grenant on the Voie Romaine, D136. Note:- the Alternate Route joins from the right. Part of the 12th century pilgrim hospital of Grosse-Sauve can be seen on the left beyond the farm	VF sign	S	358
36.021	110	8.7	Turn right on the small tarmac road, direction Ferme de Montficon. Note:- to visit Grenant (LXII) continue straight ahead on the Alternate Route	VF sign, Rivières le Bois - 4km	SW	358
36.022	1900	10.6	Pass between the farm buildings and continue straight ahead on the gravel track		S	299
36.023	700	11.3	At the T-junction in the gravel tracks, turn right	GR sign	S	272
36.024	800	12.1	Continue straight ahead on the tarmac road. Note:- for the more direct Alternate Route, turn left	VF sign, Rivières le Bois - 1km	W	262
36.025	900	13.1	At the T-junction, turn right	Towards the church	N	325
36.026	210	13.3	At the crossroads, beside the bus stop, turn left	GR sign, "Circuit de Vallon de la Resaigne"	W	333
36.027	110	13.4	In front of house n° 6, turn left direction "Aire de Jeux et de Detente"	GR sign	SW	339
36.028	260	13.6	Bear right onto a farm track between fields	GR sign	W	334
36.029	900	14.5	Continue straight ahead	Over the bridge	W	287
36.030	300	14.9	At the top of the hill and behind the church, turn sharp left onto the grass track	Pass between the well and the disused lavoir	SW	322

Waypoint	Distance between waypoints	Total km	Directions	Verification Point	Compass	Altitude m
36.031	500	15.3	At the T-junction, turn left on rue Rente Gabrielle	GR sign, "Circuit de Vallon de la Resaigne", Maâtz - 6km	SW	321
36.032	140	15.5	Take the left fork, on the D122, direction Grandchamp	GR sign	S	319
36.033	250	15.7	Shortly after passing the stone crucifix, bear right on the gravel track	GR sign, "Circuit de Vallon de la Resaigne"	SE	311
36.034	1400	17.1	Take the right fork, uphill on the stony track	GR sign	SW	344
36.035	700	17.8	At the junction with the tarmac road, continue straight ahead on the tarmac	Barns on your right, GR sign	SW	352
36.036	200	18.0	Take the left fork. At the end of the tarmac, beside the stone building, follow the narrow grass track	GR sign	S	355
36.037	700	18.7	At the crossroads in the woods, turn left	Yellow sign	E	347
36.038	700	19.3	Turn left	GR and yellow signs	N	328
36.039	70	19.4	At the T-junction in the tracks, turn right, slightly downhill	GR sign	SE	325
36.040	1100	20.5	At the crossroads, with a tarmac road, turn left towards the centre of Maâtz	GR sign, Maâtz Centre - 0.5km	E	269
36.041	400	20.9	At the road junction, continue straight ahead. Note:- the Alternate Route joins from the left	Direction Coublanc	SE	256
36.042	200	21.1	Cross the river, la Resaigne, and turn left uphill towards the church	Pass a bus shelter on your right	E	248
36.043	130	21.2	Turn right, keeping the church on your left	VF sign, Coublanc - 1.5 km (in fact 2km)	S	256

Waypoint	Distance between waypoints	Total km	Directions	Verification Point	Compass	Altitude m
36.044	60	21.3	At the crossroads, continue straight ahead on the D7, towards Coublanc	GR sign	SE	256
36.045	240	21.5	Turn left on the farm track. Note:- the "Official Route" makes a dog-leg and returns to this road. You may wish to remain on the D7 to Coublanc and save 600m	VF sign, Coublanc - 2km	E	259
36.046	600	22.1	At the T-junction in the track, turn right towards the church in the valley	GR sign, open field on your right	S	280
36.047	900	23.0	Return to the D7 at the T-junction in Coublanc, turn left	VF sign, Haute Saône - 3km	S	259
36.048	210	23.2	At the crossroads in the centre of Coublanc, continue straight ahead	D122, direction Champlitte	SE	256
36.049	160	23.3	Bear left into place des Halles and cross the place	Pass the war memorial on your left	E	250
36.050	90	23.4	Turn right on rue de la Barre	Pass house n° 1 on your left	S	252
36.051	80	23.5	At the T-junction, turn left towards the No Throughroad	GR sign	SE	249
36.052	90	23.6	Bear right over the stone foot-bridge and at the end of the bridge bear left on the road	GR sign	S	244
36.053	120	23.7	At the T-junction, turn left	GR sign	SE	244
36.054	50	23.8	At the T-junction, turn right	Towards the farm	SW	244
36.055	160	23.9	At the end of the tarmac, continue straight ahead	Grass track between the fields and parallel to the D122	S	252
36.056	600	24.5	At the junction with the gravel track, continue straight ahead	Woodland to the left	S	251

Waypoint	Distance between waypoints	Total km	Directions	Verification Point	Compass	Altitude m
36.057	300	24.8	Continue straight ahead	Across the river	SE	239
36.058	700	25.5	At the T-junction, turn right on the broad track	Towards the wooded valley	S	259
36.059	1600	27.1	At the T-junction with the tarmac road, turn right, towards the church in Leffond. Note:- you have entered the région of Franche-Comté and the département of Haute-Saône. The GR and occasional VF signposts will be replaced by yellow hand painted signs in the direction of Rome and white signs towards Canterbury	Hand painted yellow VF sign, on the electricity pole	SW	239
36.060	90	27.2	Just before the river bridge, turn left on the road rue de Verdu	VF sign	E	235
36.061	500	27.6	Take the right fork with the stone cross on your left	Direction Montarlot - 4.1km	SE	239
36.062	2200	29.8	Bear left on the track, towards the woods	Pass Moulin de la Bataille on your right	SE	232
36.063	1400	31.2	At the T-junction with a tarmac road, turn right	A modern house directly ahead	E	245
36.064	600	31.7	Turn right towards the centre of Montarlot-lès-Champlitte	Cross the river bridge	S	229
36.065	160	31.9	At the crossroads, with the church to your left, continue straight ahead on the D222	Champlitte 3km, pilgrim sign	S	227
36.066	2600	34.4	Bear right on the road		S	237
36.067	400	34.8	At the T-junction with the main road, turn left	Towards the Château	SE	252
36.068	400	35.2	Arrive at Champlitte centre	Fountain below on the left		245

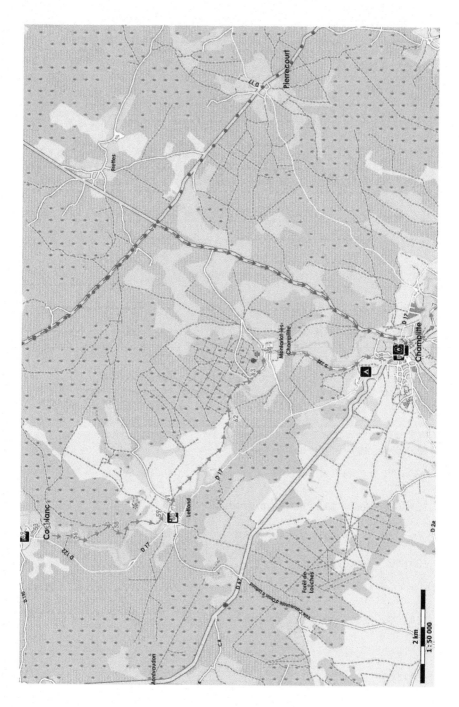

Alternate Route #36.A1   **Length: 20.0km**

Stage Summary: Alternate Route by road to Champlitte via Grenant (LXII).

Stage Ascent: 234m   **Stage Descent: 349m**

Waypoint	Distance between waypoints	Total km	Directions	Verification Point	Compass	Altitude m
36A1.001	0	0.0	Continue straight ahead on the D136	Pass the pilgrim hospital of Grosse-Sauve on your left	S	357
36A1.002	5800	5.8	At the T-junction, turn left	Direction Grenant, D7	SE	280
36A1.003	1200	7.0	Shortly after passing the church in Grenant (LXII), continue straight ahead on the small road	No Entry	S	260
36A1.004	230	7.2	At the T-junction with the route départmentale, bear right	Woods on the left, crash barrier on the right	S	289
36A1.005	400	7.5	Bear left on D17		SE	306
36A1.006	6000	13.5	At the crossroads, turn right	Direction Champlitte, D460	SW	272
36A1.007	6200	19.7	Bear right to proceed into the centre of Champlitte	Rue Pasteur, cross river bridge	SW	222
36A1.008	160	19.9	Bear right on rue du Bourg	Narrow street, uphill	W	229
36A1.009	140	20.0	Arrive in Champlitte centre at the end of the section	Beside the fountain		243

Alternate Route #36.A2				Length: 3.6km		
Stage Summary: our preferred more direct route to Maâtz						
Stage Ascent: 36m				**Stage Descent:** 42m		

Waypoint	Distance between waypoints	Total km	Directions	Verification Point	Compass	Altitude m
36A2.001	0	0.0	Turn left on the tarmac road		S	262
36A2.002	1000	0.9	At the Stop sign at the entry to Grandchamp, continue straight ahead down the hill	Pass metal railings on the right	SE	265
36A2.003	170	1.1	Turn right over the bridge	River la Resaigne	SW	259
36A2.004	40	1.2	After crossing the bridge, turn right	Towards the church	W	259
36A2.005	60	1.2	Take the left fork, direction Champlitte	Church on the right	SW	261
36A2.006	600	1.8	Keep left	Uphill	S	257
36A2.007	1800	3.6	At the T-junction in Maâtz, turn left. Note:- the GR145 joins from the right	Direction Coublanc, towards church		255

Presbytère,14 rue de l'Église,70600 Champlitte,Saône,France;
Tel:+33(0)3 84 67 61 56

Chambre d'Hôtes - Claude & Ghislaine Pelotte,2 rue Rente Gabrielle,52190
Saint-Broingt-le-Bois,Haute Marne,France; Tel:+33(0)3 25 90 85 03; Price:B

Chambres d'Hôtes - la Vallée Verte,8 rue du Cull de Sac,52600
Grandchamp,Haute Marne,France; Tel:+33(0)3 25 88 03 45;
Email:info@lavalleeverte.eu; Web-site:www.lavalleeverte.eu; Price:A

Chambres d'Hôtes - Chez Framboise,(Françoise Grandclerc,),7 Grande
rue,52500 Coublanc,Haute Marne,France; Tel:+33(0)3 25 90 07 32;
Tel:+33(0)3 25 88 91 61; Email:franclerchj@yahoo.fr; Price:B

Hotel le Donjon,46 rue de la République,70600 Champlitte,Saône,France;
Tel:+33(0)3 84 67 66 95; Email:hotel.du.donjon@wanadoo.fr;
Web-site:www.donjonchamplitte.com; Price:B

Henri Iv,15 rue Bourg,70600 Champlitte,Saône,France; Tel:+33(0)3 84 31 28 86;
Web-site:www.hotelrestauranthenri4.com; Price:B

Camping de Champlitte,Route de Leffond,70600 Champlitte,Saône,France;
+33(0)6 19 16 29 86; Email:camping-champlitte@hotmail.fr; Price:C

Drouhin Baulard Mireille,Place Eglise,70600 Leffond, Saône,France;
Tel:+33(0)3 84 64 80 09

Office de Tourisme,33Bis rue de la République,70600 Champlitte, Saône,France;
Tel:+33(0)3 84 67 67 19

Crédit Mutuel,Place Gargouille,70600 Champlitte,Saône,France;
Tel:+33(0)3 84 67 64 44

Garage Podubcik,101 route de Gray,70600 Champlitte,Saône,France;
Tel:+33(0)3 84 67 64 20

Altitude Profile

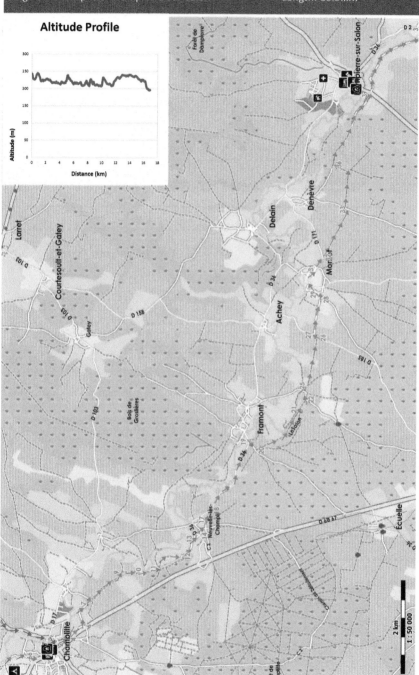

Stage Summary: the short and substantially off-road route follows the footpaths of the Sentier de la Vallée du Salon.

Distance from Canterbury: 825km   Distance to Besançon: 85km
Stage Ascent: 662m   Stage Descent: 736m

Waypoint	Distance between waypoints	Total km	Directions	Verification Point	Compass	Altitude m
37.001	0	0.0	From the fountain, take rue du Bourg, downhill	Pass Hôtel Henri IV on your left	E	244
37.002	160	0.2	At the crossroads, turn right on rue de la Brèche	VF sign	S	231
37.003	100	0.3	Continue straight ahead on rue de la Brèche. Note:- the VF signs turn left and make an unnecessary detour before returning to the road 200m ahead	Pass house n° 23 on your left	SE	228
37.004	230	0.5	Continue straight ahead on the road, uphill	VF sign	SE	228
37.005	90	0.6	Bear left between a wire fence and a house on the gravel path	VF sign	SE	233
37.006	400	0.9	At the T-junction, turn left down the hill	VF sign, pass commercial buildings on your right	E	243
37.007	600	1.5	Bear left on the road over the disused railway line	Pass railway building n° 22 on your right	E	226
37.008	90	1.6	At the T-junction, turn right	Sign Sentier de la Vallée du Salon	SE	221
37.009	1000	2.6	At the junction in the tracks, with a church visible on the ridge to your left, turn right on the grass track downhill	VF sign	S	225
37.010	260	2.9	Fork right through the narrower gap in the trees and proceed on the right-hand side of the small field	Red and yellow sign	S	217

Waypoint	Distance between waypoints	Total km	Directions	Verification Point	Compass	Altitude m
37.011	600	3.5	At the top of the small rise, beside the disused railway bridge, bear left on the grass track between the trees and the hedgerow	Red and yellow sign	SE	220
37.012	700	4.2	At the crossroads in the tracks, with another railway bridge on your right, continue straight ahead on the tarmac	Farm buildings behind the trees ahead	SE	215
37.013	500	4.7	Shortly after passing the farmhouse, continue straight ahead on the narrow road, slightly uphill into the village of Neuvelle Lès Champlitte	VF sign on your right	SE	217
37.014	120	4.8	At the Stop sign, cross over the more major road and continue on the small road, rue de la Fontaine	Pass the lavoir on your right	E	217
37.015	130	4.9	At the crossroads, turn right up hill	Stone garden wall on your left, VF sign	S	222
37.016	80	5.0	Take the left fork and then turn left	Keep the church close on your left	E	232
37.017	240	5.3	At the crossroads, at the exit from the village, continue straight ahead	Pass a cemetery on your right	E	231
37.018	300	5.6	At the T-junction with a more major road, turn right	Velo Route to Framont	SE	223
37.019	1800	7.3	As the road bends to the left, turn sharp right on the road, D36, direction Gray	VF sign	SW	209
37.020	230	7.6	Immediately after passing the garden centre, take the first turning to the left on the gravel track	Red and yellow sign	SE	213
37.021	1400	9.0	At the T-junction with a tarmac road, turn left	Pass large commercial building on your left	SE	212
37.022	260	9.2	At the T-junction with the road, turn left and then bear right	Pass green metal gates on your left	E	212

Waypoint	Distance between waypoints	Total km	Directions	Verification Point	Compass	Altitude m
37.023	140	9.4	At the T-junction at the bottom of a small hill, turn left on the road	Walled garden on the left	NE	210
37.024	110	9.5	Just before reaching the bridge over le Salon, turn right on the gravel track	Montot - 2.6km	SE	210
37.025	170	9.7	Take the left fork, uphill towards the trees	Red and yellow sign	E	209
37.026	1100	10.7	At the T-junction with the road, turn left on the road	Montot 1.4km	NE	215
37.027	100	10.8	Turn right on the tarmac road	Long straight road towards the village	E	214
37.028	800	11.6	As the road bears right, bear left on the partially gravelled track, towards the village of Montot	Conifers on your left	E	211
37.029	120	11.7	At the junction with the road, turn left	Enter Montot	NE	220
37.030	180	11.9	At the Stop sign, continue straight ahead on the D171	Direction Denèvre	E	224
37.031	600	12.4	At the junction at the exit from Montot, continue straight ahead on the D171	Pass a cemetery on your left	SE	232
37.032	270	12.7	As the D171, bends to the left, fork right on the small road	Pass a disused quarry on your left	SE	234
37.033	1200	13.9	At the T-junction with the road, turn left		NE	240
37.034	70	14.0	Turn right	Stone crucifix	E	240
37.035	800	14.8	At the junction, turn left on the track, slightly downhill	Between open fields	NE	237
37.036	400	15.1	At the T-junction, turn right	Towards the town	SE	231
37.037	1800	16.9	Arrive at Dampierre-sur-Salon. Note:- the town centre and facilities are to the left	Crossroads with the busy D70		197

Presbytère,70180 Dampierre-sur-Salon,Saône,France; Tel:+33(0)3 84 67 11 55

Chambres d'Hôtes - Tour Monies,4 rue de Fouvent,70180 Dampierre-sur-Salon,Saône,France; Tel:+33(0)3 84 67 16 37; +33(0)7 86 50 29 20; Email:stephanie.monney@orange.fr; Web-site:www.latourdesmoines.com; Price:B

Brit Hotel de la Tour,5 rue Alfred Dornier,70180 Dampierre-sur-Salon,Saône,France; Tel:+33(0)3 84 64 74 43; Email:hoteldelatour@brithotel.fr; Price:A

Laurent Aurelien,33 rue Carnot,70180 Dampierre-sur-Salon,Saône,France; Tel:+33(0)3 84 32 12 53

Office du Tourisme,2 Bis rue Jean Mourey,70180 Dampierre-sur-Salon,Saône,France; Tel:+33(0)3 84 67 16 94

Credit Agricole,1 rue Louis Dornier,70180 Dampierre-sur-Salon,Saône,France; Tel:+33(0)3 84 67 11 06

Groupe Médical Pasteur,20 avenue Bernard Louvot,70180 Dampierre-sur-Salon,Saône,France; Tel:+33(0)3 84 67 10 45

Groupe Vétérinaire,310 rue Stade,70180 Dampierre-sur-Salon,Saône,France; Tel:+33(0)3 84 67 12 04

Entreprise Bernard Konczewski,9 rue de Revaut,21490 Saint-Julien,Cote d'Or,France; Tel:+33(0)3 80 23 39 75

Graillot Brigitte,Rue Alfred Dornier,70180 Dampierre-sur-Salon,Saône,France; Tel:+33(0)3 84 67 17 14

Garage Podubcik,101 route de Gray,70600 Champlitte,Saône,France; Tel:+33(0)3 84 67 64 20

Altitude Profile

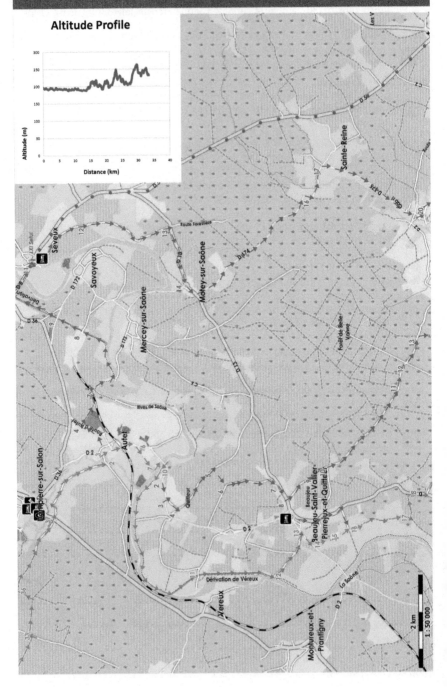

Stage Summary: the "Official Route" follows another long loop including a section beside the river Saône before following a series of minor roads and farm tracks. The "Official Route" bypasses Seveux (LXI) and again shares tracks with a tributary of the chemin de St Jacques. At the time of writing a section of the "Official Route" was overgrown requiring an additional detour. Alternate Routes are offered to visit Seveux or follow a direct route to Gy saving 8km.

Distance from Canterbury: 842km   Distance to Besançon: 68km
Stage Ascent: 381m   Stage Descent: 345m

Waypoint	Distance between waypoints	Total km	Directions	Verification Point	Compass	Altitude m
38.001	0	0.0	From the end of the previous section, take the small road, rue de Grande Ligne	VF sign	SE	197
38.002	1900	1.9	At the T-junction with the tarmac road, turn left	Towards the river bridge	E	192
38.003	200	2.1	At the T-junction with the more major road in the village of Autet, turn right	War memorial on the left at the junction	SE	195
38.004	30	2.1	Continue straight ahead on the road. Note:- the Alternate Route via Seveux (LXI) turns left on the pathway between the houses	Pass large house n° 4 on your right	SE	194
38.005	180	2.3	Bear right on the D40	Direction Quitteur	S	196
38.006	600	2.9	Just before the football field bear right on the small tarmac road	Pass the football field on your left	SW	194
38.007	700	3.6	At the T-junction, with the river directly ahead, turn left	Towards the river bridge	SE	192
38.008	140	3.7	Bear left on the ramp towards the main road and then turn right	Cross the river bridge	S	192
38.009	210	3.9	Immediately after the bridge, turn right onto the tarmac track beside the river Saône	"Rives de Saône"	NW	196
38.010	230	4.2	To reduce the total distance to Gy by 8.1km, turn left on the small road and follow the Alternate Route	Rue de la Barque	W	194

Waypoint	Distance between waypoints	Total km	Directions	Verification Point	Compass	Altitude m
38.011	3900	8.1	At the bridge over the lock, cross over the road and continue on the tarmac track beside the canal	Canal on your right	S	191
38.012	1700	9.8	Turn left on the tarmac road and continue straight ahead at the crossroads	"Rives de Saône" panel on your right at the junction	SE	191
38.013	1200	11.0	At the T-junction with the D2 on the outskirts of Beaujeu, turn right. Note:- at the time of writing, the track, 2 waypoints ahead, was totally blocked. To avoid this, turn left and immediately right on rue du Monument and then turn right on the D13 to the junction on the right immediately before the exit sign for Beaujeu. Turn right on the small road and rejoin the signed route by turning left at the first crossroads	VF sign	SW	195
38.014	300	11.3	Turn left onto a gravel track	Pass cattle fencing on your right	S	190
38.015	700	12.0	Continue straight ahead on the pathway. Note:- the pathway was totally overgrown at the time of writing	Between the hedgerows	SE	190
38.016	250	12.3	At the junction, take the middle track straight ahead		S	188
38.017	1500	13.7	At the junction with the tarmac road, turn left	Cross small bridge, towards the birch trees	E	188
38.018	600	14.3	At the T-junction with the D13, turn right	VF sign	S	199
38.019	400	14.7	Turn left on the C5	St Broing 3.5km	S	195
38.020	3600	18.3	On entering St Broing, bear left on the road	Rue de Grappigney	SE	203

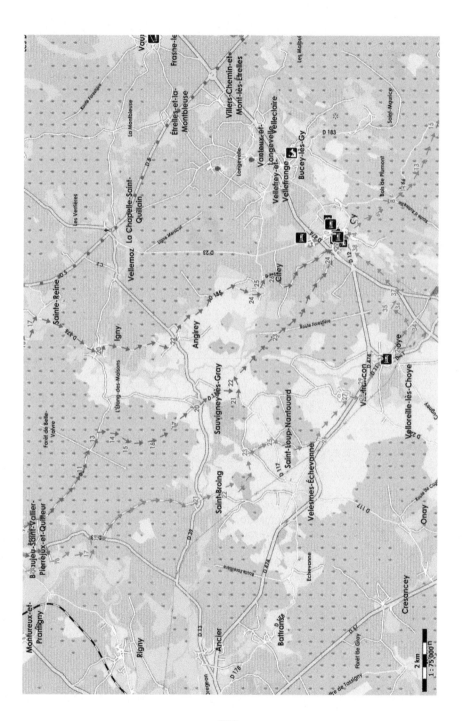

Waypoint	Distance between waypoints	Total km	Directions	Verification Point	Compass	Altitude m
38.021	270	18.6	At the Stop sign, turn right and then immediately left towards Velesmes	Church on your left and lavoir on your right	S	194
38.022	600	19.2	Following a bend to the right, take the second left turn	No Entry sign	SE	202
38.023	2300	21.5	At the crossroads, beside the hamlet of Nantouard, continue straight ahead on route de St Loup	Pass barns and farmhouse on your right	SE	204
38.024	900	22.4	At the crossroads in St Loup, turn right on route de Vellesmes	Church on your left at the junction	W	225
38.025	60	22.5	Take the first left	Rue de Bois	S	224
38.026	1600	24.1	Shortly before reaching the major road, turn sharp left on a dirt track and then bear right between the woods and the fields	VF and cockle shell signs	SE	228
38.027	1900	25.9	At the T-junction, beside Villefrancon, turn right	Chapel ahead at the junction	S	208
38.028	200	26.1	Shortly before the junction with the main road, turn left on the track parallel and close to the main road	Pass a stone crucifix on your right	SE	214
38.029	700	26.8	At the end of the track, carefully cross over the main road and take the minor road to the left. Note:- the signed VF route follows the main road to the next junction, but we feel that this is too dangerous	Towards the village of Choye	SE	205
38.030	1000	27.8	Immediately after passing the grassy area surrounding the war memorial, run left uphill towards the church	Grande Rue	SE	211
38.031	70	27.8	Continue straight ahead and rejoin the signed route	Keep church to your left	SE	214
38.032	240	28.1	Take the left fork on the more major road	Uphill	SE	223

Waypoint	Distance between waypoints	Total km	Directions	Verification Point	Compass	Altitude m
38.033	230	28.3	Take the right fork	Modern bungalow on your left at the junction	SE	237
38.034	800	29.1	Turn left on the small road	Towards the trees	NE	252
38.035	900	30.0	At the T-junction at the foot of the hill turn right on the narrow track	Cattle fencing on your left	SE	240
38.036	100	30.1	At the T-junction at the end of the cattle fencing, turn right and immediately left	Towards the main road	SE	238
38.037	500	30.6	At the T-junction with the main road, cross the road with great care and bear left into the parking area, cross the D29, turn left and take the right fork on the small road	Downhill, between the fields	NE	240
38.038	2300	32.9	At the T-junction with the D12, bear right	Towards Gy town centre	NE	240
38.039	400	33.3	Continue straight ahead. Note:- the Alternate Routes rejoin from the left	Grand Rue	NE	233
38.040	180	33.5	Arrive at Gy town centre	Tourist Office ahead on the right		233

Alternate Route #38.A1   **Length: 28.9km**

Stage Summary: route via Seveux (LXI). The route follows tracks and small roads on generally level ground.

Stage Ascent: 348m   **Stage Descent: 325m**

Waypoint	Distance between waypoints	Total km	Directions	Verification Point	Compass	Altitude m
38A1.001	0	0.0	Turn left on the pathway between the houses	Pass a walled garden on your right	E	194
38A1.002	130	0.1	At the crossroads, continue straight ahead on rue de l'Eglise	Towards the church	NE	203
38A1.003	600	0.7	At the T-junction with the more major road, turn left	Pass a large industrial building on your right	N	206

Waypoint	Distance between waypoints	Total km	Directions		Compass	Altitude m
38A1.004	110	0.9	Turn right on the track	Keep the car park close on your right	E	206
38A1.005	800	1.6	Continue straight ahead	Avoid the bridge to your right	NE	222
38A1.006	50	1.7	Bear right and then right again after passing under the railway	Towards the river	S	223
38A1.007	260	2.0	At the T-junction with the riverside track, turn left	Cycle track	E	205
38A1.008	1900	3.8	At the crossroads, continue straight ahead beside the canal	Canal enters a tunnel ahead	NE	203
38A1.009	700	4.4	At the crossroads, continue straight ahead on the small road into the woods	"Rives de Saône" sign	NE	228
38A1.010	1200	5.6	At the T-junction with the main road, beside the canal bridge, turn right on D5 towards Seveux	Towards the river bridge	SE	196
38A1.011	800	6.4	In Seveux (LXI) turn right on rue de Gatefer	Lavoir on the left at the junction	SE	197
38A1.012	1600	8.0	Continue straight ahead	Under the railway bridge	S	195
38A1.013	2100	10.1	At the T-junction with the main road in the woods, turn right	Towards Mercey-sur-Saône, D13	W	221
38A1.014	1300	11.4	At the junction in Motey, continue straight ahead on the road	Pass church on the right	SW	198
38A1.015	400	11.8	Turn left towards the woods	Direction Sainte-Reine, D174	SE	210
38A1.016	3600	15.3	After passing the farm, les Boutets, bear left on the road	Enter Sainte-Reine, D174	E	219
38A1.017	800	16.1	At the crossroads, turn right	Direction Igny, D175	SW	220
38A1.018	2400	18.4	At the crossroads in Igny, continue straight ahead	Pass the lavoir on the left	SW	206

Waypoint	Distance between waypoints	Total km	Directions	Verification Point	Compass	Altitude m
38A1.019	130	18.6	At the crossroads turn left, direction Angirey	Pass church on the left	SE	203
38A1.020	300	18.9	Bear right on the road	Cross the river bridge	S	204
38A1.021	2600	21.5	At the crossroads in Angirey, continue straight ahead	Towards church on the hill	SE	217
38A1.022	210	21.7	At the T-junction beside the church, turn left	Direction Citey, D185	E	228
38A1.023	180	21.9	Beside the crucifix, fork right	Direction Citey, D185	SE	235
38A1.024	3300	25.1	Facing the church in Citey, bear left on the road	Pass church on your right	E	207
38A1.025	700	25.8	Shortly after leaving Citey, fork right on the road	Pass stone built gateway on the right and cross bridge	S	201
38A1.026	500	26.3	Fork right	Smaller road	SW	199
38A1.027	700	27.0	Continue straight ahead		SE	206
38A1.028	1900	28.9	After passing between the farm buildings, continue straight ahead and join the direct Alternate Route to Gy	Cross highway bridge		217

Alternate Route #38.A2   **Length: 21.2km**

Stage Summary: direct route to Gy saving 8km. The route follows very small roads, woodland and farm tracks.

Stage Ascent: 271m   **Stage Descent: 233m**

Waypoint	Distance between waypoints	Total km	Directions	Verification Point	Compass	Altitude m
38A2.001	0	0.0	Turn left on the small road	Rue de la Barque	SW	194
38A2.002	150	0.1	At the T-junction with the main road, turn right	Open field on the right, conifers on the left	W	199
38A2.003	500	0.6	Shortly before the road bends to the left, turn left and then immediately right	Skirt the village of Quitteur on your right	SW	195
38A2.004	400	1.0	At the crossroads, turn left		SE	200

Waypoint	Distance between waypoints	Total km	Directions	Verification Point	Compass	Altitude m
38A2.005	1200	2.2	Take the first turning to the right	Between open fields	SW	224
38A2.006	500	2.6	At the T-junction with the road, turn left		S	227
38A2.007	1200	3.8	At the T-junction with the D13, turn right	Enter the village of Beaujeu	SW	218
38A2.008	400	4.2	At the roundabout in the centre of Beaujeu, turn left on rue Ste. Anne	Direction Igny	SE	212
38A2.009	800	5.0	Take the right fork		SE	230
38A2.010	400	5.4	At the crossroads, continue straight ahead		SE	211
38A2.011	2500	7.9	Continue straight ahead	Pass through the hamlet of Saint-Roch	E	254
38A2.012	500	8.4	At the crossroads, continue straight ahead		SE	245
38A2.013	700	9.0	At the junction, turn right		S	235
38A2.014	700	9.7	At the junction, bear right		SW	245
38A2.015	600	10.2	At the crossroads in the track, continue straight ahead		S	252
38A2.016	900	11.2	At the crossroads, continue straight ahead		SE	250
38A2.017	1000	12.2	At the junction, continue straight ahead	Leave the woods on your right	SE	211
38A2.018	700	12.9	At the junction in Sauvigney-lès-Gray bear right	Towards the church	S	201
38A2.019	50	12.9	Take the left fork and then turn left at the T-junction	Pass the hurch on your right	SE	201
38A2.020	280	13.2	Take the right fork, towards St-Loup-lès-Gray	Pass lavoir on your left	S	197
38A2.021	1400	14.6	Immediately after crossing the river bridge, turn sharp left on the track	Château de St Loup on the right	E	192
38A2.022	600	15.2	Bear right towards the woods	Long straight track	SE	193

Waypoint	Distance between waypoints	Total km	Directions	Verification Point	Compass	Altitude m
38A2.023	2100	17.3	At the crossroads, continue straight ahead		SE	212
38A2.024	3200	20.5	At the T-junction with the major road, D474, turn left on the small road parallel to the main road	Towards the bridge	NE	218
38A2.025	200	20.7	At the T-junction, turn right. Note:- the Alternate Route via Seveux joins from the left	Cross the road bridge	SE	218
38A2.026	140	20.8	At the crossroads, continue straight ahead on the small road	Pass a war memorial on your left	SE	220
38A2.027	400	21.2	At the T-junction, turn left and rejoin the "Official Route"	Grand Rue		232

Accommodation & Facilities .... Dampierre-sur-Salon - Gy

🛏️ Chambres d'Hôtes - le Tilleul,7 rue du Pâquis,70130 Seveux,Saône,France; Tel:+33(0)3 84 67 04 66; Price:B; Note:Reduced rate with credentials,

🛏️ Chambres d'Hôtes - le Domaine des Papillons,12 rue des Écoles,70100 Beaujeu-Saint-Vallier-Pierrejux-et-Quitteur,Saône,France; Tel:+33(0)3 84 67 32 84; +33(0)6 80 88 13 78; Web-site:www.domainedespapillons.fr; Price:B

🛏️ Gîte Rural - la Charmotte,2 route de la Chapelle-Saint-Quillain,70700 Gy,Saône,France; Tel:+33(0)3 84 32 95 25; +33(0)3 84 97 10 80; +33(0)6 47 69 35 20; Email:claudine.thorelle@wanadoo.fr; Web-site:www.gite-gy-la-charmotte.fr; Price:A

🛏️ Hotel Pinocchio,3 rue Beauregard,70700 Gy,Saône,France; Tel:+33(0)3 84 32 95 95; Web-site:www.hotel-pinocchio.fr; Price:B

🛏️ Gîte de la Fontaine,(Laurent Coutout & Solène Guillet),43 Grande rue,70700 Gy,Saône,France; Tel:+33(0)3 84 32 89 34; +33(0)6 64 32 21 10; Price:B

🏞️ Coursilly Noel Georges,Chemin Ecoliers,70700 Bucey-Lès-Gy,Saône,France; Tel:+33(0)3 84 32 80 30

ℹ️ Office du Tourisme,11 Grande rue,70700 Gy,Saône,France; Tel:+33(0)3 84 32 93 93

💲 Credit Agricole,2 rue Beauregard,70700 Gy,Saône,France; Tel:+33(0)3 84 32 83 40

Centre Hospitalier Val de Saône,5 rue Arsenal,70100 Gray,Saône,France;
Tel:+33(0)3 84 64 61 61; Web-site:www.ch-gray.fr

Charolle Michel,18 rue 10 Septembre,70700 Gy,Saône,France;
Tel:+33(0)3 84 32 92 06

Simonin François,Route Chapelle Saint Quillain,70700 Gy,Saône,France;
Tel:+33(0)3 84 32 86 55

Taxis Arcois,72 rue de Verdun,70100 Arc-Lès-Gray,Saône,France;
Tel:+33(0)3 84 64 96 96

Altitude Profile

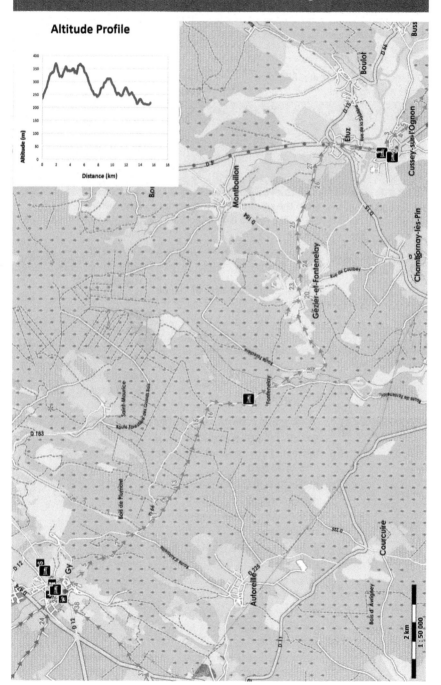

Stage Summary: this short section starts with a strenuous climb to the ridge top in the Grands Bois de Gy, on forest paths and then a gentle descent into the valley of l'Ognon along a minor road.

Distance from Canterbury: 876km   Distance to Besançon: 34km
Stage Ascent: 402m   Stage Descent: 418m

Waypoint	Distance between waypoints	Total km	Directions	Verification Point	Compass	Altitude m
39.001	0	0.0	From the crossroads in the centre of Gy take rue du Grand Mont up the hill	Pass the pharmacy on your right	SE	233
39.002	160	0.2	At the top of the hill, turn right on rue du Bourg	Cockle shell sign	SW	250
39.003	150	0.3	Turn left, then bear right on rue de l'Eglise	Pass the church on your left	S	259
39.004	120	0.4	At the crossroads continue straight ahead on the gravel track	Pass the château on your right	SE	267
39.005	600	1.0	At the junction in the tracks continue straight ahead	Ignore the turning to the right	SE	322
39.006	500	1.5	At T-junction in the tracks, turn right	VF sign	SE	335
39.007	500	2.0	Just after the crest of the hill where the main track turns left, bear right on a small track	Yellow arrow	SE	363
39.008	220	2.2	At the T-junction with the minor road, turn right	VF sign	S	337
39.009	160	2.4	At the road junction, continue straight ahead	Keep field on your right	SE	323
39.010	500	2.8	Bear right and take the broad forest track	Fontenay - 1hour15min	SE	319
39.011	270	3.1	At the crossroads in the tracks, turn left on the broadest track	Yellow pilgrim sign	SE	340
39.012	700	3.8	At the crossroads in the tracks, continue straight ahead slightly down the hill	Yellow arrow	E	343
39.013	140	3.9	At the crossroads in the tracks continue straight ahead	Yellow cross to the right	E	339

Waypoint	Distance between waypoints	Total km	Directions	Verification Point	Compass	Altitude m
39.014	1300	5.2	At the junction continue straight ahead on the smaller grass path, ignoring the left turn	VF sign, clearing ahead on your right	E	363
39.015	160	5.4	Ignore the broad path to the left and continue straight ahead on the narrow grass track		SE	368
39.016	180	5.5	At the T-junction with the road, turn right	Yellow arrow	S	362
39.017	2100	7.6	Take the left fork	Gezier - 3km	SE	248
39.018	600	8.2	Continue straight ahead on the road and ignore the turning on the forest road to the left	Yellow arrow ahead	E	262
39.019	2400	10.6	On the entry to Gézier bear left and then right	Pass lavoir on the left, D66	E	251
39.020	110	10.7	In the centre of Gézier pass the arched lavoir on your left, then turn left	Direction Montboillon, D184	E	252
39.021	50	10.8	Bear left on rue de la Corvée	Yellow arrow	NE	255
39.022	40	10.8	Continue straight ahead	Montboillon - 3km, yellow arrow	NE	256
39.023	100	10.9	Bear right on the road	Pass Calvaire on the left	E	254
39.024	500	11.5	Fork right on the smaller road	Towards the brow of the hill	E	249
39.025	900	12.3	At the crossroads, continue straight ahead		E	254
39.026	900	13.2	Continue straight ahead	Tarmac road	E	235
39.027	400	13.6	Bear right on the road	Enter Etuz	SE	216
39.028	600	14.3	At the T-junction with the main road, turn right on the D3	Towards Tabac	S	219
39.029	180	14.4	Keep left on the D3 in Ètuz towards the river bridge	Direction Cussey-sur-l'Ognon	S	213
39.030	1000	15.5	Arrive at Cussey-sur-l'Ognon (LX)	Beside Auberge		217

Association Saint Joseph,Rue Saint-Joseph,70700 Frasne-le-Château,Saône,France; Tel:+33(0)3 84 32 48 05; Email:fjt@st-joseph.asso.fr

Chambres d'Hôtes - Vieille Girardet,3 rue Montante,70700 Choye,Saône,France; Tel:+33(0)3 84 32 86 85; +33(0)6 30 86 32 54; Price:B; Note:Horses possible,

Gîte le Domainee de Fontenelay,Domaine de Fontenelay,70700 Gezier-et-Fontenelay,Saône,France; Tel:+33(0)3 81 50 39 88; Email:cris.alix@orange.fr; Price:B; Note:Price includes supper and breakfast,

Hôtel la Vieille Auberge,1 rue Grande,25870 Cussey-sur-l'Ognon,Doubs,France; Tel:+33(0)3 81 48 51 70; Email:lavielleauberge@wanadoo.fr; Web-site:www.la-vieille-auberge.fr; Price:B

Hôtel au Florida,10 Grande rue,25870 Cussey-sur-l'Ognon,Doubs,France; Tel:+33(0)3 81 57 78 32; Price:B

Mairie,1 rue Village,25870 Cussey-sur-l'Ognon,Doubs,France; Tel:+33(0)3 81 57 78 62

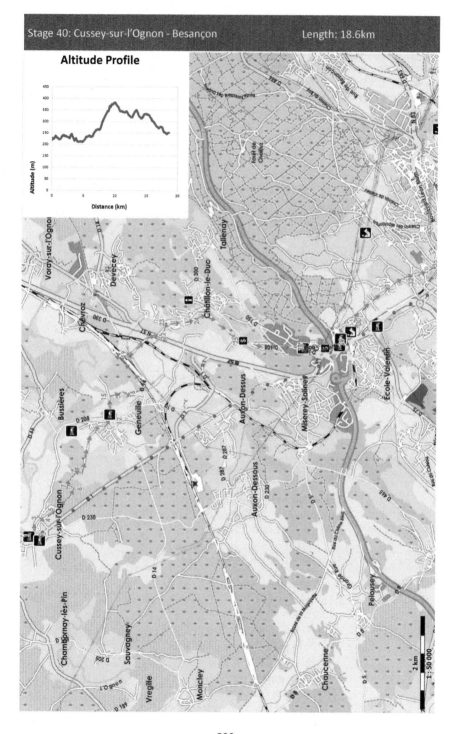

Altitude Profile

Stage Summary: this section begins on farm tracks but then continues substantially on road. The roads, before the outskirts of Besançon, are generally quiet although there are a number of difficult intersections to negotiate. The network of cycle tracks on the entry to Besançon provides some relief from the traffic, although most share the road with motor cars.

Distance from Canterbury: 891km   Distance to Besançon: 19km
Stage Ascent: 351m   Stage Descent: 318m

Waypoint	Distance between waypoints	Total km	Directions	Verification Point	Compass	Altitude m
40.001	0	0.0	At the junction beside the Auberge in Cussey-sur-l'Ognon (LX) bear left onto rue de Village	Climb the hill between the Mairie and Auberge	S	219
40.002	80	0.1	Turn left onto rue de Bussières	Yellow arrow	E	227
40.003	400	0.5	Turn right onto rue de Château	VF sign	SW	231
40.004	80	0.6	At the T-junction after the short rise, turn left	Rue des Ballottes	SE	237
40.005	400	1.0	At the mini roundabout continue straight ahead on the small road	No Entry "Sauf Ayants Doits"	SE	226
40.006	600	1.6	With a house on the right, bear left	Towards woodland	NE	234
40.007	130	1.7	Bear left in front of a shed onto a narrow track and follow the track to the right towards the woods	Between the fence and the edge of the field	SE	237
40.008	500	2.2	At the T-junction, turn left	Field ahead at the junction	E	236
40.009	120	2.3	At the T-junction, turn right and continue between the woods and the field	VF sign	E	233
40.010	1100	3.4	At the T-junction with a road in front of the metal gates, turn right down the hill into Geneuille	VF sign	S	229
40.011	160	3.5	At the bottom of the hill bear left on rue de la Gratotte, towards the church and then continue straight ahead	VF sign	SE	218

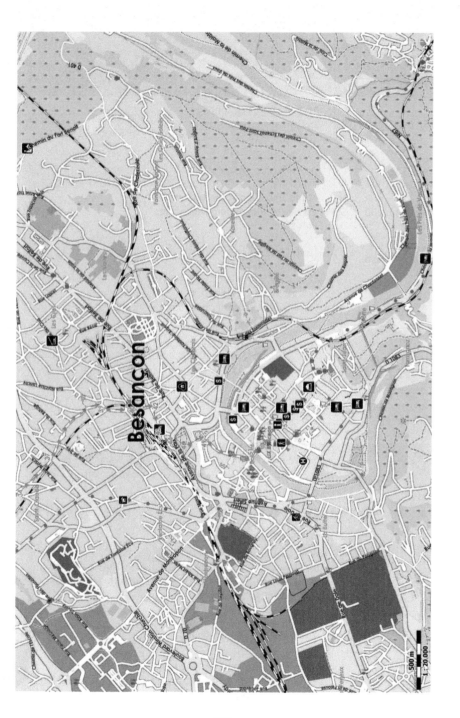

Besançon

Waypoint	Distance between waypoints	Total km	Directions	Verification Point	Compass	Altitude m
40.012	180	3.7	At the crossroads, continue straight ahead, direction Besançon, D14	Rue Lyautey, VF sign	SE	222
40.013	90	3.8	Turn left onto rue de l'Abrevoir	Pass bar	NE	226
40.014	130	3.9	At the T-junction at the bottom of the hill, turn right onto chemin des Prés Secs	Lavoir on your left	E	217
40.015	400	4.3	Turn right onto the pathway beside the lake	VF sign	S	213
40.016	400	4.8	Cross a broad gravelled area bearing right and exit close to the white metal gate	VF sign	S	211
40.017	400	5.1	Just before the crash barriers, turn left on the gravel track	Pass between the woods and the TGV line	NE	218
40.018	900	6.0	At the end of the gravel track turn right	Cross the railway bridge	S	234
40.019	280	6.3	At the crossroads continue straight ahead onto chemin du Marot	VF sign, pass large metal clad building on your right	SE	234
40.020	700	7.0	At the T-junction, turn right and proceed on the pathway on the right hand side of the very busy main road, N57	VF sign	S	264
40.021	260	7.3	Turn sharp right to take pedestrian subway under the main road and then turn left to backtrack to the first junction on the right	Sign "Passage Souterrain"	NE	267
40.022	260	7.6	Turn right on rue Léon Baud	Uphill towards Châtillon-le-Duc Village Centre	SE	265
40.023	400	8.0	At the crossroads turn right onto route de Devecey	Pass bus shelter on your right	S	295

Waypoint	Distance between waypoints	Total km	Directions	Verification Point	Compass	Altitude m
40.024	600	8.5	Beside the second bus shelter on the right, take the pedestrian crossing and continue straight ahead on the path on the left-hand side of the road. Note:- sections of the road ahead do not have pedestrian pathways and so proceed with care using the grass verges and pedestrian crossings as appropriate	Bus stop - Clos du Fort	S	328
40.025	1400	9.9	Continue straight ahead beside the road	Direction Besançon	S	381
40.026	1200	11.1	At the roundabout ignore the factory entrance on the right and take the 2nd road exit, route de Châtillon and continue down the hill	Pass a bicycle shop on the right	S	345
40.027	400	11.5	At the traffic lights, continue straight ahead	Cycle route to Besançon	S	341
40.028	700	12.2	At the roundabout take the 2nd exit on rue de la Combe du Puits	Pass Hotel Campanile on the right	SE	328
40.029	160	12.4	At the next roundabout take the 3rd exit down the hill	Pass the bar on your right	E	324
40.030	500	12.9	At the junction, bear right and continue uphill	Rue de la Combe du Puits	SE	331
40.031	1200	14.1	At the mini- roundabout, bear right and take the pathway on the left side of the road	Chemin de Valentin	S	315
40.032	290	14.4	Turn left onto chemin des Torcols, uphill and bear right at the top of the hill		SE	319
40.033	500	14.9	At the mini roundabout take the 2nd exit, on chemin des Torcols	Trees lining the right side of road	SE	333

Waypoint	Distance between waypoints	Total km	Directions	Verification Point	Compass	Altitude m
40.034	290	15.2	At the roundabout take the second exit. Note:- at this point the signed VF turns left and makes a circuitous route to the centre of Besançon. We prefer this more direct route	No Entry, rue Francis Clerc	SE	330
40.035	150	15.4	Take the left fork	Rounded apartment on the left	SE	328
40.036	180	15.5	At the crossroads continue straight ahead	Rue Francis Clerc, downhill	SE	322
40.037	140	15.7	At the crossroads with boulevard Léon Blum, continue straight ahead on rue Francis Clerc	Supermarket on the right before the junction	SE	316
40.038	700	16.4	At the T-junction, turn right on rue Nicolas Bruand	Cross the railway bridge	SW	290
40.039	70	16.4	Take the left fork	Rue Nicolas Bruand	S	287
40.040	170	16.6	At the T-junction turn left, pass under the railway, then bear right	Rue du Chasnot, one way	SE	279
40.041	200	16.8	Turn right on rue Jeanneney	Narrow road, towards trees	SW	275
40.042	130	16.9	At the T-junction, turn right on rue de la Viotte	Embankment on the right	SW	272
40.043	260	17.2	Turn right towards the entrance to the railway station	Pass mini roundabout on your left	W	277
40.044	90	17.3	In front of the railway station turn left on the pedestrian route through the car park	Towards the flight of steps	SE	278
40.045	40	17.3	At the top of the steps turn right, descend the ramp and take the underpass into the park – Jardin de la Gare		SW	278

Waypoint	Distance between waypoints	Total km	Directions	Verification Point	Compass	Altitude m
40.046	110	17.4	At the exit from the tunnel, continue straight ahead through the park		S	277
40.047	110	17.5	Bear left and cross the bridge over the highway and continue straight ahead through the second park	Pass Tour Carée on your left	SE	273
40.048	160	17.7	After passing the tower, bear right and leave the park, cross the road and bear left on rue Battant	Pass parking area on your right	SW	258
40.049	70	17.8	At the T-junction, bear left	Rue Battant	S	257
40.050	400	18.2	At the crossroads, turn left and cross the river bridge	Eglise de la Madeleine on your right at the junction	SE	248
40.051	90	18.3	At the end of the bridge continue straight ahead	Grande Rue	SE	246
40.052	300	18.6	Arrive at Besançon (LIX) centre, place du 8 Septembre	Beside the tourist office		252

Accommodation & Facilities .... Cussey-sur-l'Ognon - Besançon

Monastère Charité,131 Grande rue,25000 Besançon,Doubs,France; Tel:+33(0)3 81 82 00 89; Email:secretariatconseil.besancon@wanadoo.fr ; Web-site:www. suoredellacarita.org; Price:D; Note:Women only,

Franciscains de Besançon,Chemin de la Chapelle des Buis,25000 Besançon,Doubs,France; Tel:+33(0)3 81 81 33 25; Email:franciscains.besancon@ wanadoo.fr ; Web-site:www.chapelledesbuis.org; Price:D

Association Diocésaine Sacré Cœur,14 avenue Carnot,25000 Besançon,Doubs,France; Tel:+33(0)3 81 80 90 55

Mme Vieille Jeanne,51 Allée de la Fretille,25870 Châtillon-le-Duc,Doubs,France; Tel:+33(0)3 81 58 86 53

Fmjt les Oiseaux,48 rue des Cras,25000 Besançon,Doubs,France; Tel:+33(0)3 81 40 32 00; Email:accueil@fjtlesoiseaux.fr; Web-site:www.fjtlesoiseaux.fr/ auberge-de-jeunesse; Price:B

Hotel Formule 1 Besançon Ecole Valentin,Route de Châtillon le Duc, Zac Valentin Centre,25048 Besançon,Doubs,France; Tel:+33(0)8 91 70 51 82; Web-site:www. hotelf1.com; Price:C

Campanile Besançon Ecole Valentin,Rue de Châtillon,25048 Besançon,Doubs,France; Tel:+33(0)3 81 53 52 22; Email:besancon.valentin@ campanile.fr; Web-site:www.campanile.com; Price:B

Ibis Budget Hotel Besancon Nord,Rue de la Poste,25048 Besançon,Doubs,France; Tel:+33(0)8 92 70 12 88; Web-site:www.accorhotels.com; Price:B

Première Classe,RN 57, 7 route d'Epinal,25480 École-Valentin,Doubs,France; Tel:+33(0)1 73 21 98 00; Email:besancon@premiereclasse.fr; Web-site:www. premiereclasse.com; Price:B

Hôtel Logis Florel,6 rue Viotte,25000 Besançon,Doubs,France; Tel:+33(0)3 81 80 41 08; Email:contact@hotel-florel.fr; Web-site:www.hotel-florel.fr; Price:A

Hotel Mercure Besancon Parc Micaud,3 avenue Edouard Droz,25000 Besancon,Doubs,France; Tel:+33(0)3 81 40 34 34; Web-site:www.accorhotels. com; Price:A

Hotel Ibis Besançon Centre Ville,21 rue Gambetta,25000 Besancon,Doubs,France; Tel:+33(0)3 81 81 02 02; Web-site:www.accorhotels. com; Price:A

Chambres d'Hôtes - Vue des Alpes,(Mme Sylvie Pasteur),14 rue de la Vue des Alpes,25660 Montfaucon,Doubs,France; Tel:+33(0)3 81 81 25 31; Email:vuedesalpes@orange.fr; Price:B

Hôtel du Nord,8 rue Moncey,25000 Besançon,Doubs,France; Tel:+33(0)3 81 81 34 56; Email:contact@hotel-du-nord-besancon.com; Web-site:www.hotel-du-nord-besancon.com; Price:B

Chambre d'Hôtes - le Magasin de Sel,9 rue Chifflet,25000 Besançon,Doubs,France; +33(0)6 51 75 46 92; Email:magasindesel@gmail.com; Web-site:www.lemagasindesel.fr; Price:B; Note:Open April to November,

Hôtel Granvelle,13 rue Gén Lecourbe,25000 Besançon,Doubs,France; Tel:+33(0)3 81 81 33 92; Email:info@hotel-granvelle.fr; Web-site:www.hotel-granvelle.fr; Price:B

Hôtel Auberge de la Malate,10 Chemin Malâte,25000 Besançon,Doubs,France; Tel:+33(0)3 81 82 15 16; Web-site:www.lamalate.fr; Price:A

Chambre d'Hôtes - le Coin des Colverts,46 Chemin de Mazagran,25000 Besançon,Doubs,France; Tel:+33(0)3 81 52 34 78; +33(0)6 07 72 94 18; Email:lecoinddescolverts@orange.fr; Web-site:lecoindescolverts.free.fr; Price:B

Chambre d'Hôtes - le Jardin de Velotte,31 Chemin des Journaux,25000 Besançon,Doubs,France; Tel:+33(0)3 81 50 93 55; +33(0)6 87 14 20 75; Email:lejardindevelotte@orange.fr; Web-site:lejardindevelotte.free.fr; Price:B; Note:Reductions possible,

Etrier Bisontin,39 rue Combe du Puits,25480 École-Valentin,Doubs,France; Tel:+33(0)3 81 50 01 12

Ferme Equestre,Chemin des Bas de Chailluz,25000 Besançon,Doubs,France; Tel:+33(0)6 70 31 30 43

Ecuries de Saint-Paul les,48 Chemin Fort Benoit,25000 Besançon,Doubs,France; Tel:+33(0)3 81 88 32 41

Ecuries de Chateau Galland les,47 Chemin Chaille,25000 Besançon,Doubs,France; Tel:+33(0)3 81 50 00 11

Mairie,Place de la Mairie,25870 Châtillon-le-Duc,Doubs,France; Tel:+33(0)3 81 58 86 55

Office du Tourisme,2 place de la 1Ère Armée Française,25000 Besançon,Doubs,France; Tel:+33(0)3 81 80 92 55

Crédit Mutuel,Route Chatillon,25870 Châtillon-le-Duc,Doubs,France; Tel:+33(0)8 20 03 49 17

Caisse d'Epargne,4 rue Châtillon,25480 École-Valentin,Doubs,France; Tel:+33(0)8 20 33 22 11

Banque Populaire,1 place 1Ère Armée Française,25000 Besançon,Doubs,France; Tel:+33(0)8 20 33 75 00; Web-site:www.bpbfc.banquepopulaire.fr

Credit Agricole,11 avenue Elisée Cusenier,25000 Besançon,Doubs,France; Tel:+33(0)3 81 82 29 38

Credit Agricole,11 avenue Elisée Cusenier,25000 Besançon,Doubs,France; Tel:+33(0)3 81 82 29 38

CIC,54 Grande rue,25000 Besançon,Doubs,France; Tel:+33(0)8 20 36 04 31

Société Générale,68 Grande rue,25000 Besançon,Doubs,France; Tel:+33(0)3 81 83 50 78

LCL,86 Grande rue,25000 Besançon,Doubs,France; Tel:+33(0)8 20 82 47 50

BNP Paribas,1 rue de la Préfecture,25000 Besançon,Doubs,France; Tel:+33(0)8 20 82 00 01

Gare SNCF,1-7 avenue du Maréchal Foch,25000 Besançon,Doubs,France; Tel:+33(0)8 92 33 53 35; Web-site:www.sncf.fr

Centre Hospitalier Universitaire de Besançon,2 place Saint-Jacques,25030 Besançon,Doubs,France; Tel:+33(0)3 81 66 81 66

Médecins du Monde,7 rue Languedoc,25000 Besançon,Doubs,France; Tel:+33(0)3 81 51 26 47

Clinique Vétérinaire du Docteur Loulier,24 avenue Montjoux,25000 Besançon,Doubs,France; Tel:+33(0)3 81 50 46 97

Megasport,18 rue Pasteur,25000 Besançon,Doubs,France; Tel:+33(0)3 81 83 57 42

Cycles Pardon,14 rue Dole,25000 Besançon,Doubs,France; Tel:+33(0)3 81 81 08 79

Lerelaisvelo,36 rue 7Eme Armée Américaine,25000 Besançon,Doubs,France; Tel:+33(0)6 31 37 58 42

Maréchal Ferrant Méot e,21 rue Clos Dessus,25380 Belleherbe,Doubs,France; Tel:+33(0)3 81 44 31 20

Gauthe Eddy Paul Francois,24 rue Clair Logis,39600 Arbois,Jura,France; Tel:+33(0)6 30 87 55 62

Marechal Ferrant Joseph Scordo,7 rue de l Étang,39260 Crenans,Jura,France; Tel:+33(0)6 33 50 52 50

Bougnon Vitte Corinne,24 Chemin des Justices,25000 Besançon,Doubs,France; Tel:+33(0)3 81 58 88 79

Books published by LightFoot Guides

All LightFoot Publications are also available in ebook and kindle and can be ordered directly from www.pilgrimagepublications.com

The complete 2014 LightFoot Guide to the via Francigena consists of 4 books: Canterbury to Besançon, Besançon to Vercelli, Vercelli to Rome, Companion to the Via Francigena

LightFoot Guide to the via Domitia - Arles to Vercelli

Even with the wealth of historical data available to us today, we can only offer an approximate version of yesterday's reality and we claim to do nothing more in this book. The route described runs roughly parallel with a section of the via Domitia between Arles and Montgenévre (a large portion of the original route having been subsumed by the A51), continues along a variety of roads and tracks that together form a modern-day branch of the via Francigena and rejoins the official main route (to Rome) in Vercelli.

The LightFoot Companion to the via Domitia

An optional partner to the guide, providing the additional historical and cultural information that will enhance your experience of the via Domitia and via Francigena

The LightFoot Guide to the Three Saints' Way

The name, Three Saint's Way, has been created by the authors of the LightFoot guide, but is based on the three saints associated with this pilgrimage: St Swithin, St Michael and St James. Far from being a single route, it is in fact a collection of intersecting routes: The Millenium Footpath Trail starting in Winchester and ending in Portsmouth, England. The Chemin Anglais to Mont St Michel and the Plantagenet Way to St Jean d'Angely, where it intersects with the St James Way (starting from Paris).

LightFoot Guide to Foraging
Heiko Vermeulen
"Nowadays if I look at a meadow I think lunch."

A guide to over 130 of the most common edible and medicinal plants in Western Europe, aimed at the long-distance or casual hiker along the main pilgrim routes through Western Europe. The author has had some 40 years of experience in foraging and though a Dutchman by birth, has been at home all over Europe including Germany, Ireland, England and for the last 8 years in Italy along the Via Francigena pilgrim route, where he feeds his family as a subsistence farmer, cultivating a small piece of Ligurian hillside along permaculture principles, and by gathering food from the wild.

Sylvia Nilsen is a South African freelance writer who has been published in numerous local and international publications. She worked as a research agent and editor for a UK-based travel guide publisher and produced several African city and country guides. Sylvia has walked over 5 000 km of Camino trails in France and Spain, as well as from Switzerland to Rome on the Via Francigena pilgrimage. She has served as a volunteer hospitalero in Spain and is a Spanish accredited hospitalero volunteer trainer in South Africa having trained 42 new volunteers. With amaWalkers Camino (Pty) Ltd she leads small groups of pilgrims on slackpacking trails on the Camino Frances.

YOUR CAMINO on foot, bicycle or horseback in France and Spain
A comprehensive Camino planning guide offering advice to pilgrims on choosing a route, how to get to the start, info for people with disabilities, cyclists, walking with children, with a dog, a donkey or doing the Camino on horseback, with 300 pages of advice and information.

CAMINO LINGO
English-Spanish Words and Phrases for Pilgrims on el Camino de Santiago. Compiled by Sylvia Nilsen and her Spanish teacher Reinette Novóa, this is a cheat's guide to speaking Spanish on the Camino. No complicated verb conjugations or rules on grammar, this book offers over 650 words and phrases just for pilgrims.

SLACKPACKING the Camino Frances
When and where to start walking and how to get there. Three suggested itineraries for hiking daily stages of 10km to 15km: 15km to 20km and 20km to 25km. A 17-day, 5km to 8km per day itinerary for the not-so-able pilgrim wanting to walk the last 100km to Santiago in order to earn a Compostela. A list of Camino Tour Companies and Luggage Transfer services. Contact details for buses, trains and taxis along the route.

Riding the Milky Way

The story of Babette and Paul's journey, but it is not about hardships and heroes. In fact it was a motley and uninspiring crew that left Le Puy en Velay, France, in July 2005. The humans, broke, burnt-out and vaguely hoping that early retirement would save their health and sanity. The horses, plucked off the equine scrapheap in France and still grappling with their new roles as something between mount and mountain goat. The dog, doing his best to understand why he was there. But 75 days later they reached their destination, overcoming the challenges, and most importantly, finding that they had become an inseparable team. Packed with sketches and photographs, this book will inspire even the most timid traveller, while also giving practical guidelines for someone wanting to do the same or a similar journey. And finally, it is quite simply an excellent, sometimes irreverent, guide to the St James Way. Much more than just a good read.

Riding the Roman Way

"We have good equipment, our horses are fit and we are fully prepared, so why this feeling of dread? Perhaps it has something to do with knowing what to expect." Babette and Paul have come a long way since their first horseback pilgrimage and not just in kilometres. They have learnt a great deal about themselves, their animals and some of the practicalities of long distance riding, but they continue to regard themselves as incompetent amateurs and are still in search of a rationale for their insatiable wanderlust. Common sense and the deteriorating east-west political situation put an end to their original plan, riding on from Santiago de Compostela to Jerusalem in 2006, but Paul has found an equally exciting alternative: the via Francigena pilgrimage to Rome. The good news is that there will be no war zones to contend with, but the bad news is that they will be travelling 2000 kilometres along a relatively unknown route, with a 2,469 metre climb over the Swiss Alps, often under snow, even in August. Riding the Roman Way takes you alongside this intrepid team every step of the way and shares the highs and lows with disarming honesty. It also provides a detailed account of the via Francigena and offers practical guidance for someone wanting to embark on a similar journey. But be warned, this book book will inspire even the most timid traveller and you read it at your own risk.

CPSIA information can be obtained
at www.ICGtesting.com
Printed in the USA
BVOW10s0842301017

499041BV00009B/310/P

9 782917 183250